THE ULTIMATE GUIDE TO
HORSE BREEDS

THE ULTIMATE GUIDE TO
HORSE BREEDS

An illustrated encyclopedia with over 600 photographs

ANDREA FITZPATRICK

HERMES
HOUSE

This edition published in 2011 by Hermes House, an imprint of Anness Publishing Ltd, Hermes House, 88–89 Blackfriars Road, London SE1 8HA, UK; tel. 020 7401 2077; fax 020 7633 9499

www.hermeshouse.com;
www.annesspublishing.com

For all editorial enquiries, please contact
Regency House Publishing at
www.regencyhousepublishing.com

ETHICAL TRADING POLICY
Because of Anness Publishing's ongoing ecological investment programme, you, as our customer, can have the pleasure and reassurance of knowing that a tree is being cultivated on your behalf to naturally replace the materials used to make the book you are holding. For further information about this scheme, go to www.annesspublishing.com/trees

PUBLISHER'S NOTE
Although the information in this book is believed to be accurate , neither the authors nor the publisher can accept any legal responsibility or liability for any errors or omissions that may have been made.

Contents

THE EVOLUTION OF THE HORSE

A cave painting at Lascaux in the Dordogne, France, clearly shows a horse-like creature. It was painted around 15000 BC.

THE EARLIEST HORSES

It has taken nearly 60 million years for the horse to evolve from its earliest form, *Hyrocotherium* or *Eohippus*, to *Equus caballus* of the family *Equidae*, the modern horse as we know it today.

Eohippus (Dawnhorse) can be traced back to the Eocene period, between 56 and 34 million years ago, and is thought to have originated in Africa or Asia. Fossils indicate that it was the size of a small dog and weighed about 12 pounds (5.5 kilograms); instead of having one toe protected by a hoof, as in the modern horse, it had paw pads, with four toes on the front feet and three on the back.

Eohippus was a forest dweller, where it browsed among low-growing shrubs and tender leaves, perfectly suited to its environment, its light-brown dappled coat providing excellent camouflage and making it almost invisible to predators.

During the Oligocene period, which began 34 million years ago, *Eohippus* evolved into *Mesohippus* and *Miohippus*. While still forest browsers, these were larger, taller and heavier animals. Their teeth had changed from small and sharp to larger and blunter and therefore their diet. The feet had also changed: there were now three toes on the front feet, the middle one bearing most of the body's weight.

The major evolutionary leap came in the Miocene period, 24 million years ago, when climatic change transformed once swampy forests into great plains. *Parahippus* and eventually *Merychippus* now stood firmly on a single toe, but still retained the side toes. They were larger than the earlier animals with longer legs which, because they could no longer rely on the cover of trees, enabled them to flee from predators. Like other animals adapted to open spaces, eyes were positioned to the sides of skulls, allowing them to scan distances and spot predators more readily.

The Evolution of the Horse

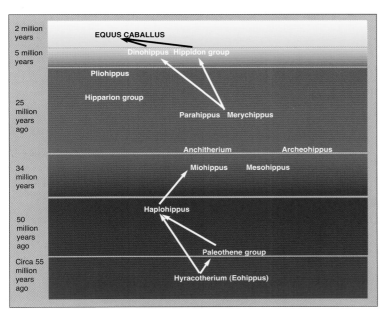

2 million years	**EQUUS CABALLUS**
5 million years	Dinohippus Hippidon group
	Pliohippus
	Hipparion group
25 million years ago	Parahippus Merychippus
	Anchitherium Archeohippus
34 million years	Miohippus Mesohippus
	Haplohippus
50 million years ago	
Circa 55 million years ago	Paleothene group
	Hyracotherium (Eohippus)

upon their habitat and the region in which they lived. The scientific classification given to these horses is *Equus caballus*, which is also the name of the modern horse.

Of the three types, the Forest Horse (*Equus caballus sylvaticus*) was the heaviest in stature and is probably the ancestor of the heavier breeds known throughout Europe. It was ideally suited to the wet marshlands of Europe, where its thick coat protected it against all weathers and particularly harsh winters.

The Asiatic Horse (*Equus caballus przewalskii*) was discovered in Mongolia by Nicolai Przewalski around 1881. It is small and tough and capable of surviving harsh conditions. While it is considered

The Ardennais is one of many heavy coldblooded European horses, probably descended from Equus caballus sylvaticus, *or the Forest Horse.*

The next significant development came around 10 million years ago, when the first horses appeared standing firmly on one toe. By now, the side toes had atrophied to what are known as splint bones, situated further up the leg. Now known as *Pliohippus*, this was very much more like *Equus* as we know it today, adapted for cropping grass and for running fast, though still rather more smaller and lighter.

The horse made its final leap to *Equus*

during the Pleistocene period, about 2 million years ago. By now it was perfectly adapted to life on the plains. It was strong, fast and well-muscled and so successful that it quickly spread throughout Asia and Europe and across the Bering Straits into America.

PRIMITIVE HORSES: THE THREE BASIC TYPES

It is thought that the primitive horses of Eurasia formed three types, depending

an important ancestor of the modern horse, it is distinguished by a slightly different genetic make-up. Although no longer found in the wild, it is still bred in zoos and safari parks.

The third type, the Tarpan (*Equus caballus gomelini*), evolved on the steppes of eastern Europe and western Asia. Well- suited to life on open plains, the Tarpan had a lighter build and was faster than the other two types, but like them was capable of withstanding extreme climatic conditions.

DOMESTICATION
The first horses were domesticated in eastern Europe and the Near East about 5,000 years ago. At that time, other

animals, such as goats, sheep, cows and dogs had been already successfully domesticated, but it was the need for a larger beast of burden, and one that would produce milk and meat, which led to the domestication of the horse. It was not until later that horses would be used for riding. By 1000 BC, domesticated horses could be found all over Europe, Asia and North Africa. From the original three types of primeval horse, four types of domesticated horses emerged, two of which could be classified as ponies and two horse types.

Pony Type 1 stood around 12hh tall and inhabited north-western Europe. It would have looked very similar to the Shetland Pony we know today, with a small sturdy body and thick coat. It would also have been perfectly acclimatized to the conditions of its habitat. Also known as the Celtic or Plateau Pony, breeds such as the Exmoor and Icelandic descended from it, producing the relatively small, chunky breeds we know today.

Pony Type 2 was somewhat larger, standing about 14.1hh. It evolved in Eurasia and as a result became extremely hardy and resistant to the cold climatic conditions of the region. It was usually dun in colour and had a dorsal stripe along its back and stripes on the legs. Prezewalski, Norwegian and Fjord ponies are all descendants of Pony Type 2.

Horse Type 1 was larger than the first two,

OPPOSITE
LEFT
The Asiatic Horse (Equus caballus Przewalskii) *was discovered in Mongolia by the explorer Nicolai Przewalski in the late 19th century.*

RIGHT
The Tarpan (Equus caballus gomelini) *evolved on the steppes of south-eastern Europe and southern Russia. Sadly it is now extinct; however, the Konik, pictured here, is thought to be a distant relative.*

LEFT
The Exmoor is descended from the Celtic or Plateau pony.

ABOVE: The Fjord is a Type 2 pony.

ABOVE CENTRE
The Barb, a Type 1 horse, is
accustomed to desert conditions.

ABOVE RIGHT
The Arab is descended from Horse
Type 2.

RIGHT
The Somalian Wild Ass has the dorsal
stripe and zebra markings of primitive
species.

OPPOSITE
Early domestication of the horse in a
wall painting from the Tomb of
Nebamum, Thebes.
The British Museum, London.

standing at 14.3hh, and had become
adapted to the deserts and steppes of
Europe and central Asia. It could
withstand long periods of drought and
heat and as a result had a fine coat and a
relatively thin skin. It had a longish head,
long neck and sparse tail and mane. It is
a close relative of the old Turkmene
horse and also of today's Akhal-Teke. Its
bloodline has also found its way into the
modern Andalusian and Barb.

Horse Type 2, like the latter type, was
predominantly a desert horse, but rather
smaller at 12hh. Its home was western Asia
and it was hardy and could withstand
extreme weather. A horse of great beauty
with a fine head and body, this was the
forefather of today's Arabian.

BELOW

Amazons driving a chariot. (Detail from the side of the sarcophagus of the Amazons, Tarquinia, 4th century BC.) Museo Archeologico, Florence.

OPPOSITE

A Roman mosaic from the 3rd century AD, showing Christ Helios, from the pre-Constantinian necropolis below St. Peter's, Vatican, Rome.

The earliest records describing horses used for riding originated in Persia (Iran) and date from the third millennium BC. By 1580 BC, horses were also ridden in Egypt, and later in Greece. This was a departure as horses had previously been regarded as beasts of burden, riding them being of secondary importance.

Throughout the centuries, moreover, horse riding began almost to assume the status of an art form, when Xenophon (c.435–354 BC), an historian and military leader famous for leading the retreat of 10,000 mercenaries for 900 miles (1500km), founded equestrianism in Athens: his definitive book on the subject is still highly regarded today.

Increasingly, riding horses came to be used for other purposes, as warhorses or for pulling chariots, tasks for which they had no rivals for centuries. Horses also played an important part in agriculture until they were replaced by steam traction and the internal combustion engine.

BREEDS, TYPES AND COLOURS

RIGHT
Warmbloods are the product of regional coldblooded horses, bred with hotbloods such as Arabs and Thoroughbreds.

BELOW
Hotblooded horses are bred for their stamina and speed.

Horses and ponies belong to one of two specific groups: breeds and types. A **breed** consists of horses and ponies which are genetically similar and which have been selectively bred to produce consistent characteristics, while reinforcing their best features; they are recognized as such in official stud books. They fall into four distinct categories:

hotbloods, warmbloods, coldbloods and ponies.

Hotbloods are highly strung and include Thoroughbreds and Arabs. They have been bred for their enormous stamina and speed, evident when racing, in which they excel.

Warmbloods are calmer creatures, having a heavier build than hotbloods. They have been bred for their extravagant paces and biddable natures, making them excellent performers at jumping and dressage. They are the

LEFT
The Hunter is classified as a type in that it has been bred for a specific purpose.

BELOW
The Clydesdale is a coldblood and most are working horses, which means that they are not as universally popular as the other two categories.

Colour is determined by genetic inheritance and is often a feature of specific breeds. These wild horses carry a variety of colours in their gene pool.

result of interbreeding with heavier coldbloods such as Shires and Cleveland Bays and were originally bred as warhorses and for lighter work on farms, mainly in northern Europe. Examples are the Hanoverian, Dutch Warmblood and Holstein.

Coldbloods, as mentioned above, are heavier types of horses such as Irish Drafts and Percherons. They are less common nowadays, heavy horses on farms being a thing of the past, and are now more often seen in the showring.

Finally, there is the pony, which

covers all the native breeds measuring less than 14.2hh.

A **type**, however, is the result of crossing breeds to produce a specific kind of horse intended for a specific purpose, such as the cob and the hunter.

COLOURS

The wild horses that originally roamed the world would have been a dull muddy colour, allowing them to blend in with their surroundings. Nowadays, through selective breeding, horses come in a variety of colours and markings.

Breeding horses to produce certain colours is a complicated business and is achieved by mixing various genetic material. This is a tricky process as some colour genes also have an effect on temperament and performance. For example, the old saying that chestnuts have a fiery temperament often seems correct. Racehorse breeders tend to favour horses carrying the black gene, present in the bay, and they do seem predominant among the winners.

In the United States and Australia, particularly, selective breeding to produce unusual colours has become commonplace, and horses now come in a striking variety of colours and markings. However, most horses fit into the basic categories listed in this section.

Bay
This is probably the most common colour, the coat varying from a light reddish-brown to deep black-brown with

black on the lower legs, muzzle and the tips of the ears, the mane and tail being also black. Bays are a genetically modified form of black. Despite its popularity, only one actual breed has emerged: the Cleveland Bay.

Brown

The coat consists of shades of nearly black or brown, which are spread evenly over the body except for the areas around the eyes, the girth, muzzle and flanks, which have a lighter 'mealy' appearance. The mane and tail may be liver, reddish-brown or nearly-black.

Chestnut

This is a red coat of any shade, ranging from a light to a dark reddish-brown which is known as liver chestnut. The

LEFT
The bay is probably the most common colour, the coat ranging from bright red to almost black.

BELOW FAR LEFT
A brown Barb horse.

BELOW LEFT
Chestnuts also come in a large range of colours – from deep liver chestnut to almost golden.

RIGHT
Dun is one of the oldest colours, and was probably a feature of prehistoric breeds.

FAR RIGHT
Grey can range from pure white, as in the Lipizzaner, to a deep almost black colour. This Lusitano is an attractive dappled grey.

mane and tail are usually of a similar colour or may be flaxen (these are called sorrels). Non-chestnut parents may have chestnut foals; if both parents are chestnut they will always have progeny that are this colour.

Dun
There are four variations on the colour known as dun, which can have red, yellow, mouse and blue tinges. Dun horses have darker markings on the muzzle and legs with the addition of a dorsal stripe which may be black or brown. Several breeds of this colour type have been developed, the most common being the Fjord.

Grey
Technically, this is not a colour but a pattern superimposed over other colours. Greys are born with dark skin which progressively lightens with age, leading to most of them eventually turning white in varying degrees. This is not necessarily a sign of old age and is known as greying out. They come with two different coat patterns, the favourite being dappled grey, which is usually the result of the lightening of the coat of a

horse which was born dark grey, known as iron or blue-grey. As the horse's colour fades, the dappling remains mainly on the legs. The other type is known as flea-bitten; these greys never turn completely white, but seem to revert instead to the base colour they had at birth: for example, some may develop blue, black or red speckles; moreover, injuries such as bites and cuts will also grow over in that colour.

Black

There are two types: non-fading black, which only fades under extreme conditions, the overall effect being a coat of a metallic, iridescent or bluish shine. When combined with white markings, such as stars or socks, it is particularly striking. Fading black is probably a more common variation: the black colour will only be retained if the horse is kept stabled or rugged when exposed to the elements. There may also be fading through sweating, when lighter patches occur under the saddle and girth areas. When the summer coat comes through, the coat will have a black sheen, but never the blue metallic effect of the non-fading type, and during the season will become a reddish-brown in appearance. Black horses aren't popular where the

climate is hot, such as the Australian outback, as black absorbs heat, leading to skin irritation. Breeds selectively bred for their black colour tend to appear in colder climates, for example, in the Fell and Friesian.

Spotted

Spotting can occur in many breeds but is most common in the Appaloosa; in fact, the breed has given its name to the

ABOVE
The spotted gene present in this Appaloosa is a throwback to prehistoric horses depicted in cave paintings.

LEFT
The Friesian is exclusively black.

spotted pattern. Markings vary from coloured spots on white, white spots on a base colour, or a scattering of small white or coloured spots.

Palomino

Much prized, these horses have beautiful golden coats ranging from pale to dusky tan; they are usually the result of a cremello crossed with a chestnut. However, the breeding of palominos is a complicated business and is more common in the United States where the colour originated. Ideally, the mane and tail should be pure white.

Cremello

Sometimes known as pseudo-albinos, these horses have cream-coloured coats which are slightly darker then any white markings present. The eyes are pale blue and glassy in appearance. This colour is not popular, particularly in hot climates, where strong sunlight can irritate light-coloured eyes. Such horses are also more prone to skin cancers and chafing. However, in cooler climates they can do rather better and their striking appearance is certainly unusual.

Roan This comes in a variety of colours and is composed of a pattern of white hairs over a base colour which is only confined to the body, the head and legs remaining in the base colour. Unlike greys, the colour does not fade, but any nicks or scratches will grow back covered in the base colour. They come in three

OPPOSITE
With its golden coat and pure white mane and tail, the palomino is highly prized: this one is a Quarter Horse.

LEFT
This Saddlebred cremello is more than striking.

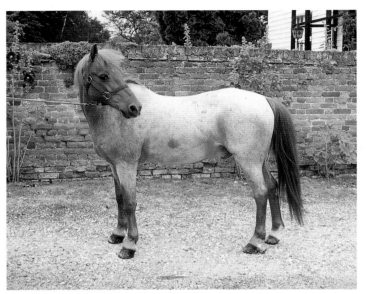

ABOVE
A strawberry roan.

RIGHT
This piebald is a striking
American Warmblood.

and tend to be predominately ponies: however, horses of the type are now becoming more common. Varieties are skewbald, which are coats with any colour patches with white, and piebald, which is black-and-white.

basic types: strawberry roan, which has a chestnut base coat, blue roan which has black, and red roan which has bay. The mane, tail, legs and muzzle markings will be the same colour as the base coat.

Coloured The definition of a coloured horse is any colour combined with white. In the United States, these are known as pintos; however, there is a huge variety of colours and markings with varying degrees of white and colour which have different names. They are highly prized and their appearance is extremely striking. In Britain, coloured types are less popular

POINTS OF THE HORSE

KEY

1 Poll
2 Forehead
3 Nostril
4 Muzzle
5 Chin groove
6 Jowl
7 Angle of jaw
8 Windpipe
9 Jugular groove
10 Point of shoulder
11 Shoulder
12 Breast
13 Forearm
14 Knee
15 Cannon bone
16 Fetlock
17 Coronet
18 Hoof
19 Pastern
20 Bulb of heel
21 Ergot
22 Point of elbow
23 Ribs
24 Belly
25 Sheath (male)
26 Stifle
27 Hock
28 Gaskin
29 Thigh
30 Flank
31 Hindquarters
32 Dock
33 Croup
34 Loins
35 Back
36 Withers
37 Crest
38 Neck

CONFORMATION

A horse's ability largely depends on its conformation. This dressage horse it bred for optimum performance and is therefore near-perfect.

When considering the kind of horse you would like, be it Shetland Pony or a Thoroughbred, it is important to understand the rules of conformation which apply to all breeds, as a horse that is well made will perform well and is far less likely to become unsound.

Study the horse from a distance and from all angles. It should stand square and the overall impression should be of balance, harmony and symmetry. The head should not be too large and should sit neatly on the neck, which should be gently arched, neither too long nor too short, tapering gradually to slightly sloping shoulders. The legs should be straight and clean with a generous amount of bone below the knee and well-developed joints. Looking at the horse from behind, make sure that the hindlegs are level with the forelegs and that the quarters are even. The buttocks should be well-developed and the tail set high, which is important for impulsion and speed. The chest should be broad and deep to facilitate good heart and lung function.

TAKING A CLOSER LOOK

Now approach the horse. Examine each leg in turn, checking that they are perfectly straight and that the hooves are symmetrical with plenty of heel. Make sure they match the size of the horse. (A large horse with small feet will have problems with weight distribution, when undue pressure will be put on the delicate bones of the foot which could, in turn, lead to foot disease and lameness.) Likewise, a small horse with proportionately large feet is likely to be clumsy and therefore prone to injury.

The coat should be bright and glossy and should lie flat; it is a good indication of a horse's general health. Look carefully at the head. This should give an indication of the horse's character. The expression should be alert, kind and intelligent, with ears pricked forward and the eyes clear and bright. A rolling eye could be an indication of bad temper as well as pain. A 'pig eye', one in which there is a lot of white

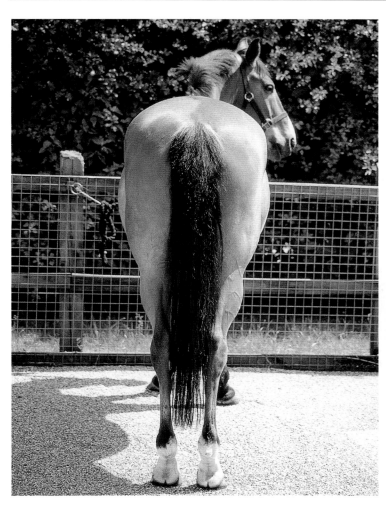

showing, is said to indicate obstinacy or wilfulness.

Remember, however, that there are exceptions to every rule: often the most unpromising turn out to be amazingly talented, proving that first impressions are not necessarily always correct.

COMMON DEFECTS

Legs These, along with the feet, take enormous amounts of punishment during a horse's lifetime. The legs need to be correctly shaped if they are to maintain good action and not to succumb to lameness. The knees of the forelegs are responsible for good balance: if, for example, the horse is 'over at the knee' or 'back at the knee', the weight will be

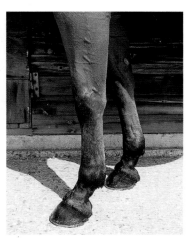

FAR LEFT
From behind, the horse should appear perfectly symetrical; any crookedness could be an indication of an old injury or congenital deformity.

BELOW LEFT
A horse's legs take a huge amount of punishment and are where good comformation is vital. The joints should be large and the bones straight with strong, hard tendons. The hoof and pastern should form a straight line.

horse may have difficulty keeping its head in balance, and may find it impossible to hold it in an unsupported outline. A 'ewe neck' is when the top muscle is weaker than the bottom, giving the neck the appearance of being on upside-down: horses with this defect should be avoided as it is a fault often impossible to correct. Likewise a bull neck should also be avoided as the horse will be difficult to control and it will be impossible to obtain sufficient flexion when schooling.

The Back This is subject to enormous strain because it has to carry the weight of a rider; it is vital, therefore, that it is as strong as possible. Look for well- developed muscles, which are the major support of the back. The horse's natural conformation is also an important factor: horses with long backs are more likely to suffer from strain; sway (hollow) backs, another feature of long-backed horses, is another sign of weakness. Horses with short backs have an advantage in that they are usually strong and often agile; however, they are also likely to overreach. It is also difficult to fit them with a saddle and the rider may end up sitting nearer the horse's loins, which is the weakest part of the back.

unevenly distributed, causing extra strain on localized areas such as the heel. Toes turning in or out are liable to cause strain on the pastern, fetlock and foot. The same rules apply to the hindlegs; hocks which are tucked under the buttocks or which are too far out from the body will hamper propulsion. Cow hocks and bowed hocks are also a sign of weakness and would render a horse undesirable.

The Head and Neck A large head is a disadvantage in the competition field, particularly in dressage and showing. The

The Akhal-Teke is a proud and ancient breed, once highly prized as a warhorse.

AKHAL-TEKE (Turkmenistan)
Origins The Akhal-Teke of Turkmenistan, a republic in central Asia which lies between the Caspian Sea and Afghanistan, is believed to be a descendant of the Turkoman or Turkmene, an ancient race of horse thought to have existed thousands of years ago, but now unfortunately extinct. It takes its name from a tribe called the Teke which still inhabits the Akhal oasis in the Karakum desert, close to the borders of Iran, where the horses traditionally live in herds under the watchful eyes of mounted herdsmen. This aristocrat of the desert is long, slim elegance personified, but even so has a hardy constitution and can go long periods without water. However, it is

The Akhal-Teke is independent, free-spirited and inclined to be wilful. It requires firm, but kind and tactful handling and is unsuitable for the inexperienced.

usually protected in its native environment when heavy rugs are used to cover its back during extremes of heat and cold. They were once hand-fed a high-protein diet, which surprisingly included eggs and mutton fat.

Historically, this 'heavenly' horse was prized by such warlords as Alexander the Great, Darius the Mede and Genghis Khan, while Marco Polo praised the Turkoman horse in his *Travels*. Nowadays, because of their great agility and athleticism, Akhal-Tekes are most often used for racing and endurance events.

Appearance The Akhal-Teke appears to break almost every rule of good conformation. Its head is carried high on a long, thin neck set at an angle of 45 degrees to the body, giving it a proud, slightly haughty appearance. It has a fine, elegant head with wide cheeks and a straight or slightly dished nose; the large eyes are bold and expressive. The nostrils are dry and flared and the ears shapely and alert. Although the shoulders are broad and sloping, the chest is quite narrow. The body is fairly short, rounded and shallow, and the long loins have little definition. The girth is quite narrow, and the very long legs appear disproportionately long to the body, and taper to small hooves.

The Akhal-Teke has an unusually smoothly-flowing and powerful action. The shape of the pasterns is unique to the breed, possibly developed from negotiating sandy desert terrain.

Characteristics The Akhal-Teke is not known for its sunny nature, in fact, quite the reverse. It is wilful and rebellious and will benefit from one firm handler which it can learn to trust. It is an intelligent animal which requires careful and sympathetic training; it does not respond well to punishment and may well try to retaliate. Due to its genetic inheritance it is unlikely to flourish cooped up in a stable and must be allowed a predominantly outdoor life, with plenty of space to wander.

Colours Chestnut, bay, grey, palomino, black, dun. All the colours, apart from raven black, are iridescent, which is extremely striking,

Height Approximately 15.2hh, though with its pronounced withers and high head-carriage the horse appears taller.

The Akhal-Teke has a rather unconventional comformation; however, the overall effect is extremely striking.

ALTÉR REAL (Portugal)

Origins Portugal has two breeds of
horses which are used in the bullring and
in *haute école* classical riding – the
famous Lusitano (page 192) and the
lesser known, but no less noble, Altér
Real. The breed had its beginnings in the
18th century when 300 Andalusian
mares, intended for the specific
requirements of the Portuguese court in
Lisbon, were brought from Jerez in Spain
to the royal house of Braganza's stud at
Vila de Portel in Portugal. After eight
years the stud moved to Altér do Chao
which gave the horse the first part of its
name, the second, *real*, meaning royal.
For many years the breed excelled not
only at classical disciplines but also as a
quality carriage horse.

The Altér Real breed came into
jeopardy during the Napoleonic invasion
of 1809–10 when troops stole the best
horses from the stud, drastically reducing
their numbers. Then in 1832 King Miguel
abdicated and much of the stud's land
was confiscated.

In later years, measures were taken to
improve the existing stock by breeding it
with Thoroughbreds, Normans and
Arabs; this, however, only served to
weaken the breed with great loss of its
original character. In the late 19th
century, however, the Spanish Zapata
family introduced more Andalusian
and Carthusian blood which reversed
much of the damage caused by the
earlier bad judgement.

The breed finally obtained the
protection it deserved in the early 20th
century when steps were taken to restore
the Altér Real to its former glory. This
was achieved with the help of Dr. Ruy
d'Andrade who with two stallions and a
handful of mares founded a top-quality
Altér Real stud which he eventually
handed over to the Portuguese Ministry
of Agriculture which administers the
breeding programme today. The Altér
Real is still used in *haute école* and
general riding.

Appearance The head has all the
distinctive Iberian qualities of the
Lusitano and Andalusian, having a fine
head with a slightly dished nose, medium-
length shapely ears, and a lively,
intelligent eye. The neck is short but well-
positioned with a pronounced arched
crest. The shoulders are sloping and the
chest is well- developed. The back is short

The Altér Real is still much in demand as a classical riding horse and many are still bred in studs all over Portugal.

and strong with large quarters. The legs are hard and very tough, the upper parts well muscled with large joints, ending in small but well-shaped hooves.

Characteristics The Altér Real has a high-stepping action which is most attractive:

this, coupled with its strength and power, makes it appear much larger than it actually is. Unlike its Iberian brothers, the Altér Real is not suitable for beginners as it has inherited a fiery and lively temperament from non-Iberian blood added in the early 19th century. It is

responsive and learns quickly but needs a competent and experienced rider in order to excel.

Colours Usually bay.

Height 15–16hh.

The American Miniature Horse, originally from Europe, should not be regarded as a pony. It is a true horse in miniature, with all the temperament and appearance of the larger animal.

AMERICAN MINIATURE HORSE (U.S.A.)

Origins This is not a pony but a scaled-down version of a horse; consequently it has all the characteristics of the larger animal. The first true miniature horses appeared in Europe in the 1600s where they were bred as pampered pets for the nobility. Unfortunately, not all miniatures had such a good life and many were used as pit ponies in the coal mines of northern Europe, including the English Midlands. In the 1900s Lady Estella Hope continued the breeding programme, and these are the lines that probably

made their way to the United States.

Today the American Miniature Horse is stylish, well-proportioned and the product of nearly 400 years of selective breeding. They make excellent all-rounders, especially in children's ridden classes such as showjumping and showing, and are also used for driving. The breed now has a closed stud book managed by the American Miniature Horse Association.

Appearance The American Miniature Horse should not exceed 34 inches (86 centimetres) or 9hh. It should have similar conformation to a large, fine-boned horse such as a Thoroughbred or Warmblood. The overall impression should be of well-balanced symmetry, accompanied by

strength, agility and alertness; essentially, it should have all the appearance of the perfect horse in miniature.

Characteristics The horse has a kind and affectionate nature. It is also gentle and placid, making it an ideal companion animal. It is excellent for children, and inspires confidence because it is easy to mount and willing to be ridden; its small stature also makes it suitable for the less able. The foals are particularly attractive, ranging from 16–21in (41–53cm) in height.

Colours All colours.

Height Up to 9hh.

The American Saddlebred has the inherited ability to move its front and back legs together on each side (known as racking). It is most elegant in motion and comfortable to ride.

AMERICAN SADDLEBRED
(U.S.A.)

Origins The American Saddlebred was developed from breeds used for trotting and pacing which were shipped over from Europe, particularly Eire and the British Isles, in the 1600s. Due to their hardy constitutions they thrived in their new home and their extravagant paces proved most popular. It was through these imports that the Narragansett Pacer was developed, named for the bay of the same name in Rhode Island; the popularity of the breed soon spread along the East Coast.

The Pacer is most unusual in that the feet of one side move one after the other, a trait noticeable in many old breeds originating in Asia and Europe. Moreover, the gait proved far more comfortable than the jolt of the four-time trot. Though now extinct, Narragansett mares were bred with Thoroughbred stallions to produce what was known as the American Horse – an excellent all-rounder – which also retained the ability to learn the pacing gait. These, used in the various breeding programmes combining Morgan, Standardbred and Thoroughbred blood, eventually produced today's Saddlebred.

Today they are highly prized in the showring, equally useful in harness and ridden classes, in which they are mainly used; but they are capable of competing in other events and make excellent showjumpers and dressage horses.

The Saddlebred is born with a traditional walk, trot and canter but has

also inherited the ability to learn the slow-stepping gait and also the rack. However, its high-stepping carriage can be falsely encouraged by keeping the feet long and sometimes by building the feet up; in some cases the muscles under the dock are nicked to produce an unnaturally stiff and high tail carriage (this is illegal in most countries). In other cases it can be fitted with a tail brace when stabled to preserve the high tail-carriage, thus depriving the horse of any comfort when at rest: these practices require extreme modification or preferably banishment if this beautiful horse is to achieve recognition in the broader equestrian world.

Gaits The Saddlebred's gaits place it apart from other breeds and include the slow gait or running walk, the stepping pace, and the slow rack. The rack is performed when both hooves on either side in turn are lifted almost similtaneous, and all four hooves are off the ground together at certain moments; it is quite spectacular when combined with the horse's high-stepping action.

Appearance The Saddlebred has a commanding presence and subtle expression of movement. The head is small and narrow, carried high, and it has an alert and intelligent expression accentuated by its fine pricked ears. The eyes are gentle but intelligent and the nose is straight with slightly flared nostrils. The neck is long and elegant and is carried high. The withers are also high

This beautiful palomino Saddlebred is being ridden in Western-style saddlery.

and run neatly into the back which is fairly long, as is the barrel-shaped body. The shoulders are narrower at the top than the bottom and sloping to create the trademark fluid action. The tail-carriage is naturally high, joined to flat quarters which flow into strong powerful loins.

Characteristics The Saddlebred is biddable and easy to train. It is gentle and affectionate, loves people, and enjoys being handled. It is also spirited and proud with a keen intelligence and an alert demeanour. Under saddle, however, it can become excitable.

Colours All the usual solid colours, including palomino and roan. There is often a good deal of white on the head and legs. The coat, mane and tail are fine and silky in texture.

Height 15–16.1hh.

The Saddlebred has a fine, well-porportioned head with an intelligent expression.

The American Shetland bears little resemblance to its shaggy Scottish ancestor; infusions of Hackney and Thoroughbred blood have made it more like a horse than pony.

AMERICAN SHETLAND (U.S.A.)

Origins As the name suggests, the American Shetland's ancestors were the native ponies of the Shetland Islands, situated off the north coast of Scotland. In 1885, 75 of these ponies were imported to America by Eli Elliot and thrived in spite of the warm humid conditions of the south-eastern states where they were raised, and which led to the formation of the American Shetland Pony Club in 1888.

Today, the American Shetland is nothing like its Scottish ancestor, being lighter in stature with longer, finer legs. This is because the original American Shetlands were bred with small Arab, Thoroughbred and Hackney breeds, resulting in a small horse rather than a stock pony.

Nowadays the breed excels in various driven classes, such as the two-wheeled roadster, four-wheeled buggy, and light sulky. It is also good with children and will happily complete in pony as well as breed classes and hunter-pony events. It is ridden in either English or Western tack.

Appearance The American Shetland possesses all the showy attributes of its small horse ancestors, combined with the strength and workmanlike character of the Shetland Pony. The head is quite long and is more horse- than pony-like; the nose is straight, the ears longish, and the eyes horse-shaped. However it has retained many of the Shetland characteristics: the mane and high-set tail are furnished with thick, strong hair. The

neck is quite short but the legs could be considered overlong, though they remain strong. The hooves retain the strength and shape of the Shetland Pony's.

Characteristics Having inherited many of the attributes of the horse, the American Shetland has an equable temperament which, combined with its small size, makes it ideal for children to ride. It is reasonably hardy and therefore easy to maintain.

Colours All the usual solid colours, including roan, dun and cream.

Height Up to 11.2hh.

Despite its fine appearance the American Shetland is relatively hardy and makes an excellent children's pony. Its strength and stamina also makes it suitable for driving, for which it is often used.

The Andalusian was originally a prized warhorse, said to have been used by El Cid as well as Napoleon's armies. The Andalusian excels in all the difficult manoeuvres of haute école, *for which it remains famous today.*

ANDALUSIAN (Spain)

Origins This is one of the oldest breeds to have been handled and ridden by man: there is further evidence of this fact in cave paintings, which confirm that horses of this kind were present in the Iberian Peninsular around 5,000 BC.

The Andalusian's lineage stems from the Sorraia Pony, which still exists in Iberia, and the Barb which originated in North Africa, with Arab and Oriental strains. It evolved in the peninsular, most of which was then known as Andalusia, at around the time of the Moorish occupation of 711. The result was a horse with a proud, high, head-carriage, and highly-placed extravagant paces.

It was particularly valued as a warhorse, possessing all the necessary qualities to enable it to perform well in battle. (It is interesting to note that El Cid's mount, *Babieca*, was an Andalusian.) Later, in the 16th century, the *conquistadores* brought the horses with them to the Americas where it became the basis of all American breeds.

The Andalusian bloodline is evident in around 80 per cent of modern breeds and has had particular influence on the Connemara, native to Ireland, the Lipizzaner of the Balkans, and the Cleveland Bay and Welsh Cob of the British Isles. This also applies to the American breeds which share direct lineage with the Lusitano, Carthusian, and Altér Real.

But this popularity didn't last for ever, and in around 1700 the Andalusian's

heavy, robust conformation fell out of favour, when lighter, sleeker animals, used for hunting and racing, became more fashionable. The breed suffered even more when a plague and famine almost wiped them out, a few surviving in the Carthusian monasteries of Castello, Jerez and Seville, where breeding continued from the best of the animals.

Today's horse can still be traced back to these lines, the purest and most beautiful of which are still referred to as *caballos Cartujanos*. The extreme rarity of these animals forced the Spanish government to ban their export for over 100 years, but the embargo was lifted in the 1960s, and Andalusians now enjoy popularity around the world.

Today the Andalusian is used for bullfighting and display riding, where its power and agility make it eminently suited to intricate movements. They excel at advanced classical dressage and also at showjumping and are also used for general riding and driving. They are often to be seen in hand in the showring.

Appearance These muscular horses have great presence and beauty. The neck is heavy with a well-developed crest. The mane is abundant and should be kept long. The head-carriage is noble and high, the forehead wide with expressive, medium-length ears. The eyes are dark-brown and gentle, the nostrils flared, and the jaw is large and well-muscled. The withers are well-rounded and the shoulder long and sloping. The chest is broad, the croup rounded, and the low-set tail is thick and long. The body is rounded and short-coupled, adding to the overall strength. The legs are strong with large joints and the hooves are round and compact.

The Andalusian is famous for its extravagant paces. Movement is elevated and extended, making the horse look as if it were floating. All paces are smooth, showy and spectacular.

Characteristics Andalusians are proud and courageous, spirited to ride but with amiable temperaments. They have soft mouths, making them extremely obedient when ridden properly.

Colours Grey and bay coats are most in evidence, but others are accepted by the Andalusian Horse Association. In Spain, according to the studbook, only grey, bay and black are acceptable.

Height 15–16.2hh.

ANGLO-ARAB (U.K.)

Origins The Anglo-Arab derives its name from two of the world's greatest breeds, the Thoroughbred, which is of English (Anglo) origin, and the Arab. In the United Kingdom Anglo-Arab breeding rules are very strict, and only these two breeds can be present. Other countries have their own rules, with some adding elements of their own native breeds, the French Anglo-Arab being one of them. There are other stipulations, however, and at least 25 per cent Arab is the norm.

Because the Anglo-Arab is a mixture of two breeds it is not actually recognized as such, with one exception: the fore-mentioned French Anglo-Arab. There are other variations which appear all over Europe, the Gidrán or Hungarian Anglo-Arab, the Shagya Arab, also from Hungary, the Russian Strelets-Arab and Spain's Hispano-Arab.

Anglo-Arabs make superb riding horses and excel in most disciplines, including showjumping, eventing and dressage. They also do well in riding-horse showing classes where their manes and tails can be plaited, unlike the pure Arab which must be left as it is. The combination of the Thoroughbred's complaisant nature and the strength, stamina and intelligence of the Arab

make an ideal combination. The interesting thing about breeding Anglo-Arabs is that you never know how they are going to turn out: they can be predominantly Arab or Thoroughbred, or a combination of both; either way they are ideal all-rounders and extremely rewarding to ride.

Appearance Ideally, the Anglo-Arab should have the body of a Thoroughbred and the tail and head-carriage of the Arab, though this can vary; some are also lighter boned than others. The head should have the unmistakable Arab traits with a dished or straight profile, though not as extreme as that of the Arab. The eyes show that it can be spirited on occasions; the nostrils are large and flared. The ears are medium-sized, fine, pointed and expressive. The head-carriage is fairly high with a well-developed crest. The Anglo-Arab should have the good sloping shoulders, deep chest and powerful hindquarters of the Thoroughbred. The tail-carriage can be either high like the Arab or lower as in the Thoroughbred.

Characteristics Anglo-Arabs are usually affectionate and intelligent. They are also brave and spirited and will always give of their very best.

Colours Most usual is brown, bay, chestnut and grey, while black is rare. There is often white on the face and legs but never on the rest of the body.

Height 14.2–16.1hh.

Anglo-Arabs make excellent all-rounders and excel at showjumping, eventing and dressage. Featured left and opposite left is Crocus Jacob *with rider Jean-Luc Force of France at the 2000 Olympics.*

51

The Appaloosa has long been the popular choice of Native Americans though today it is enjoying worldwide popularity.

APPALOOSA (U.S.A.)

Origins The gene which produces the spotted permutation in horses is an ancient one, as indicated by the Cro-Magnon depictions of such horses in caves. For many centuries horses such as these were highly prized in Europe and Asia and are often featured in 17th-century Chinese art.

The *conquistadores* introduced the spotted gene to the Americas with stock which they bought with them, then generations of these horses eventually passed to the Nez Percé Native Americans, who inhabited north-east Oregon along the Palouse river. They were probably the first tribe to have selective breeding programmes, and adhered to strict guidelines to produce the best stock. It was therefore the Nez Percé who first developed the Appaloosa, said to be America's oldest breed.

Settlers eventually wiped out the Nez Percé, however, and the Appaloosa dispersed throughout the country with strains made weaker through random breeding.

Nowadays the Appaloosa is enjoying renewed popularity: the horse does not have to be spotted but there are three requirements: sclera around the eyeball, striped hooves, and the skin beneath the hair must be mottled.

The Appaloosa is an excellent all-rounder, commonly used in Western events such as roping, cow pony and barrel racing and looks well in Western tack. They also appear in showing classes, particularly in Britain, such as riding horse and coloured horse, and are also good at cross-country and showjumping.

There are some obvious differences between American and European Appaloosas. The U.S. types have been crossed with Quarter Horses and have developed the size and conformation of this breed. In Europe, Appaloosas are larger and more like warmbloods, making them ideal for jumping and dressage. These are also becoming popular in the United States.

Appearance This is a workmanlike horse, the head fairly plain with short, tapered ears, the eyes alert and inquisitive with the mandatory white rings or sclera around the edges of the eyeball. The neck and body are compact and well-muscled and the quarters are powerful with well-developed limbs. The tail and mane hair is usually quite sparse. The hooves should be striped.

Characteristics Appaloosas are great all-rounders: they are good-natured and hardy with plenty of stamina, speed and agility.

Colours/patterns There are various colour permutations, including white with chestnut, bay and black. They can also be one overall colour or roan.
Blanket White over the quarters and loins with a contrasting base colour.
Spots White or dark spots appearing over all or on a portion of the body.
Blanket with spots A combination of the above.
Roan Blanket Partially roan, usually patterned over the quarters and loins.
Roan Blanket with Spots A roan blanket which has spots within it.
Leopard White with dark spots.
Snowflake Dominant spotting over the quarters and loins.
Frost White specks with a dark background.

Height 14.2–15.2hh.

The Arab is an ancient breed whose hot blood has been used to improve many other breeds. It was of primary importance in the development of the Thoroughbred.

ARABIAN (Middle East)

Origins The Arab, or Arabian, is one of the oldest of the hotblooded breeds, and its bloodlines are present in many modern breeds of today which extend throughout Europe and the United States. The name is not strictly accurate as the original 'Arab' could have been a small Oriental-type wild horse which lived in Eastern Europe, the Near and the Middle East. The Arab was further developed as Islam assimilated the breed and Muslim invaders used it as cavalry. Today's modern Arabians can date their descent from five foundation mares known as Al-Khamesh (The Five), said to have been selected by Mohammed for their obedience.

The Arab was also of great importance to the Bedouin, the nomadic Arabs of the desert, who can trace their association with the breed back to 3000 BC to a mare called Baz and a stallion called Hoshaba. Arab blood is therefore highly effective when mixed with other breeds, and usually brings great improvements to the resulting offspring.

Arab horses were so-named when they were imported from the Arabian peninsular to Britain in the 19th century. The Arab is also the foundation horse for the Thoroughbred.

Arabs are extremely beautiful, with a delicacy that belies their strength and stamina. They shine in riding events such as dressage, riding horse, and in-hand showing. They also excel in disciplines that rely on strength, such as endurance

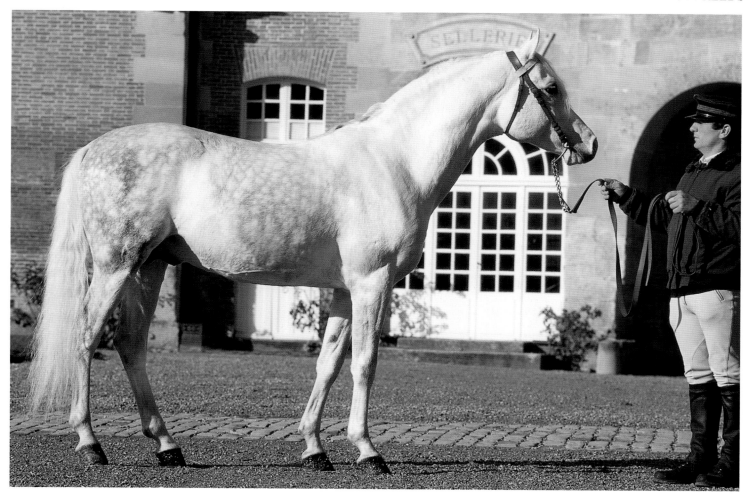

riding and racing. Arabs have the reputation of not being able to jump, which is untrue; they are keen jumpers but lack the ability to compete at high level.

Appearance The head is short and refined, with a dish-shaped profile and a tapered muzzle with large nostrils. The eyes are large, wide-spaced and low-set, and the ears small, shapely and set well apart. The jaw is rounded and forms a curved arch where head and neck meet, known as the *mitbah*.

The back is slightly concave with sloping shoulders and well-defined withers. The croup is level and the girth deep. The tail is set high. The legs are strong, hard and clean with flat knees, short cannons, and well-defined tendons; the hooves are hard and tough. The Arab also has a distinctive skeletal feature in that it has less vertebrae, i.e. 5 lumbar, 17 rib, and 16 tail, compared with 6-18-18 in other breeds, giving it a short-coupled appearance. The horse's action is as if it were floating on air. Due to their desert origins they have a fine coat and skin which is designed to

release heat. Consequently, they require special care in winter, though they are tougher than Thoroughbreds.

Characteristics Arabs are famous for their intelligence and responsiveness. They are also affectionate and respectful of other animals and human beings, being especially good with children. The reverse side of their character is fiery and courageous; they can also be stubborn if asked to do something against their will.

Colours All solid colours are possible, but chestnut and grey are most common.

Height 14–15.2hh.

OPPOSITE
LEFT and RIGHT
Arabians, apart from their obvious beauty, are prized for their agility and stamina; for this reason they are predominately used for endurance riding.

LEFT
An Arabian and rider in traditional Arab costume.

BELOW
This youngster is already showing the characteristics of a hotblooded horse.

The Ardennais is one of the heavier of the draft breeds. Today, it can still be seen at work in France and Belgium.

ARDENNAIS (France)

Origins This ancient breed originated in the border country between France and Belgium, though it is regarded as French. A heavy draft horse, it is thought to be descended from the prehistoric Diluvial Horse of Solutré and was highly prized by the Romans, probably evolving into the great warhorse of the Middle Ages. In later centuries it continued to be used as a cavalry horse and was part of Napoleon's invasion of Russia in 1812, its hardiness enabling it to cope with the harsh Russian winters.

The original Ardennais was fairly small, but by breeding it with the much larger Belgian Brabant it increased in size and shape to the horse it is today, one of enormous strength and stamina. By the 19th century, further breeds where added, such as Arab, Thoroughbred, French Boulonnais and Percheron. This resulted in three distinctive types: the old original type which is around 15hh; the Trait du Nord, which is much larger and heavier; and the Auxois, which is very heavy, and is by far the most removed from the original. The Ardennais is still used as a heavy draft horse today.

Appearance The Ardennais is one of the heaviest of the heavy draft type. Unusually, the head is quite fine, the ears are small and wide apart, the eyes are prominent and friendly, and the nose is straight. The neck is quite short, broad and very strong, as is the back. The legs are short and thick-set.

Characteristics The Ardennais has been bred to do heavy work, which is evident in all aspects of its conformation. It is good-natured and obedient.

Colours The most common colour is strawberry roan, with distinctive black points, though any other solid colour is acceptable apart from black.

Height 15–16hh.

The Australian has many of the characteristics of its Arab ancestry, including strength and stamina. They are excellent all-rounders and are also used for pony-trekking, where their sure-footedness is a great asset.

AUSTRALIAN PONY (Australia)

Origins During the colonization of Australia many horses were imported and became an important part of Australian life. Ponies were also imported but were not paid any particular attention until the late 19th century when a breed type began to emerge. By the 1920s this was starting to be recognized, and a stud book was started a little later on.

The Australian Pony is a combination of many breeds – Welsh, Arab, Thoroughbred, Shetland and Exmoor, to name but a few. These are now so intermingled that no single characteristic is uppermost, apart, perhaps, from the Welsh and Arab influences which can be seen in a fine head and neat legs. The result is an excellent all-rounder – good at jumping and agile enough for children's riding events; it is also perfect for trail-riding and endurance events.

Appearance The head is the pony's most striking feature and is evidence of its Arab ancestry. The ears are spaced well apart, short and well-shaped; the forehead is broad and the eyes are large and kindly; the nose is slightly concave with slightly flared nostrils, leading down to a fine muzzle. The neck is well-developed with a silky, flowing mane; the withers are fairly pronounced and flow into a longish back with well-developed quarters; the legs are fine and tapered with strong tendons and short cannons and the hooves are hard and shapely.

Characteristics The Australian Pony is fairly lightweight and its hotblood ancestry is immediately obvious. It is, however, extremely hardy and has great stamina. It is known for its sound constitution and is therefore easy to care for and ideal for children, being good-natured and obedient. Its most striking attribute is its free-flowing action.

Colours All colours are acceptable, with white on the head and legs but not on the body. The most common colour is grey.

Height 12–14hh.

AUSTRALIAN STOCK HORSE
(Australia)

Origins The Australian Stock Horse, otherwise known as the Waler, has a history that began in the 18th century, when horses were imported into Australia from South Africa and Chile. These tended to have excellent constitutions, being descended not only from Iberian, Arab, Barb, Criollo and Basuto stock, but also from Indonesian ponies. However, the quality of the first horses was said to be not good enough, though later infusions of Arab and Thoroughbred greatly improved the stock.

The Australian Stock Horse was predominantly used by stockmen, where its hardiness and stamina were assets on the enormous sheep and cattle stations of the country.

The breed, also known as the New South Wales Horse, or Waler, was once important as a cavalry horse, used by the British in India from about 1850, but soon became popular with stockmen where its soundness and endurance were assets in the huge expanses of the Australian outback; it was also used in harness.

By the 1940s the Waler, as it was now mainly known, had become a quality horse, but after the Second World War the population was allowed to dwindle. It was bred with other horses which subsequently weakened the breed until it became rather inferior. Today, steps are being taken to improve it by using Quarter Horse, Arab and Thoroughbred, but, as yet, the Waler is not a consistent breed.

Appearance The ideal Waler has a fine head with a broad forehead, straight nose, and medium-length alert ears. The eyes are kind, inquisitive and intelligent. The neck is long and elegant with a slight crest, and the shoulders are sloping. The chest is broad with a deep girth, while the body is of medium length with strong loins and well-developed quarters. The legs are strong with shapely hooves.

Characteristics The Waler has excellent stamina and endurance. It is obedient and willing to work and is kind and intelligent.

Colours Most often bay, though all solid colours are possible.

Height 15–16.2hh.

In recent years the Australian Stock Horse has been improved using Throughbred, Arab and Quarter Horse blood. It is now regarded as a quality horse, though not yet a consistent breed.

The Auxois is a good all-round draft horse, used particularly for forestry work. Despite its bulk it is surprisingly agile.

AUXOIS (France)

Origins The Auxois is closely related to French Ardennais stallions that were bred with Bourguignon mares, but infusions of Percheron and Boulonnais were added in the 19th century to further enhance the breed and to differentiate it from the Ardennais. The horse is still used for farming as well as forestry where its immense strength is harnessed for clearing trees. It has another role in the tourist industry, where it is used to draw gypsy caravans.

Appearance Similar to the Ardennais, the Auxois has a rather short, broad head with small alert ears and a kindly expression. The neck is set well on the shoulders and is short and muscular. The withers are well defined with a broad chest, strong sloping and muscular shoulders, and a short back and strong loins; the quarters are wide and well developed with a low tail-carriage. The legs are short with large joints and a small amount of feathering. Despite its bulky appearance, the Auxois has a light and supple gait.

Characteristics Strong and sturdy with plenty of stamina. It is a willing worker and has an equable temperament.

Colours Bay, chestnut and either bay or red roan.

Height 15–16hh.

AZTECA (Mexico)

Origins The Azteca has now replaced the virtually extinct Mexican strain of Criollo horse and is one of the world's newest breeds. Work on the breed began in 1972, its foundation consisting of Andalusian stallions which were bred with expertly selected South American Criollo and Quarter Horse mares. The advantages of using these three breeds was to give the Azteca fine qualities of breeding coupled

with the hardiness and huge stamina of the Criollo. It also ensured that a link was maintained with Mexican horse-breeding traditions. The intention to avoid Thoroughbred or European warmblood types was deliberate. The Azteca was bred to be an elegant riding horse with a definite Spanish/Latin stamp. It is used for leisure as well as competition.

Appearance The Azteca has many of the characteristics of its Spanish ancestry. The head is medium to small, with small alert ears and beautiful eyes with a touch of hauteur. The nose is either straight or slightly dished with large flaring nostrils. The neck is well set, with plenty of muscle and an elegant arch; the shoulders are sloping with a medium-length body, strong, large quarters, and a slightly low-set tail. The legs are substantial with plenty of muscle and bone.

Characteristics The Azteca has the noble mien of the Andalusian, the hardiness of the Criollo, and the speed, agility and amiability of the Quarter Horse.

Colours All colours except piebald and skewbald.

Height 14.3–15hh.

BARB (North Africa)
Origins The Barb has had an enormous influence on many breeds. It is of ancient origin, taking its name from the Barbary Coast of North Africa, which is now Morocco, Algeria, Tunisia and Libya,

The Barb, though rather plain in appearance, has been most influential in the development of other breeds. It is much prized for its stamina.

Sadly there are few pure-bred Barbs left, as many are now crossed with Arabs to produce general riding horses.

where the Carthaginians bred cavalry horses 2,000 years ago. The breed was probably influenced at an early stage by Arab blood brought to North Africa by the Muslims and also hotblooded Oriental types. A great many were imported to Europe, particularly England, where there are many references to 'Barbary' horses, the most famous being Richard II's 'Roan Barbary'. Here they were also bred for the cavalry and were prized for their speed and stamina.

Nowadays, pure-bred Barbs are a rarity as the cross-breeding of Arabs and Barbs to produce a good general riding horse is practised throughout North Africa. The Barb is not a handsome horse and is inclined to be bad-tempered, but it has had a tremendous influence on other breeds, particularly in Europe and the Americas. The Andalusian of Spain, the Connemara Pony of Ireland, the Thoroughbred, and even the Criollo of South America are all believed to contain Barb blood.

Today the Barb is used for general riding, racing and display purposes. It remains very popular in its native land but receives little recognition elsewhere.

Appearance The Barb is fairly lightweight and bred for life in the desert. The head is long and narrow with a slightly dished face with medium well-shaped pointed ears; the eyes are kind and intelligent. The neck is of medium length with a pronounced crest. The withers are prominent and the shoulders flat. The

legs are fine, but strong, and the hooves are hard and well shaped, a feature of all desert horses. The mane and tail are full with the tail set low on flat quarters.

Characteristics The Barb is quite stand-offish and inclined to be bad-tempered. However, it has a reputation for extreme toughness, speed and stamina – qualities which have made it popular for improving other breeds.

Colours Most common is black, bay and dark brown, though Barbs with Arab blood can have other colours such as grey.

Height 14.2–15.2hh.

BASHKIR (Russia)

Origins The Bashkir was once bred by the Bashkiri people of the lower slopes of the Urals to pull their troikas, while the mares' milk was used to make a fermented alcoholic drink called *kumiss*. The breed is very old and has evolved in an extraordinary fashion: it has the stocky body, large head and small nostrils common to horses raised in very cold climates; but the strangest feature is its winter coat which grows to about 6in (15cm) in length and falls in tight ringlets.

In the United States, where there are approximately 1,500, they are known as Bashkir Curlies, some of which have recently been imported to the United Kingdom. Here they are mainly used for showing and endurance riding, but in

their native land they are used in harness and their long hair is spun into fabric; moreover, they are used for meat and their milk is still used. Another strange factor is the Bashkir's blood, which differs in composition from that of other horses; they also have a higher respiratory and heart rate.

Appearance The original Bashkir has a large head with small ears. The eyes have an intelligent expression, the nose is straight, and the nostrils are small. The U.S. version has been bred with a smaller head which appears to balance more neatly on the body. It has a well-developed neck, longish body, and short stocky legs typical of horses from cold climates, where in winter they develop a layer of fat to keep themselves extra warm. In summer the coat is like that of any other horse, apart from the fact that the mane and tail remain curly.

Characteristics These hardy animals are good-natured, affectionate and willing workers.

Colours Most common colours are chestnut, palomino and bay.

Height Approximately 14hh.

The Bashkir is a very old breed, well adapted to cold conditions. It grows a long, thick, curly coat to help it through winter.

BASUTO

The Basuto possesses Arab and Barb bloodlines introduced by Dutch settlers in the 19th century. Over the years the breed has been allowed to deteriorate, though efforts have recently been made to improve matters.

BASUTO (Lesotho)

Origins The Basuto, or Basotho from Lesotho, previously Basutoland, which is an enclave of South Africa, had its beginnings in the early 19th century and is derived from Arabs and Barbs which were brought to South Africa by Dutch settlers. Over the years they were allowed to became rather thin and scraggy in appearance and due to bad breeding their conformation deteriorated.

The breed virtually disappeared in the early 20th century when animals were exported and crossed with Thoroughbreds and Arabs to give them more substance. The Basuto was eventually saved by a society established in the later 20th century to improve and revive the breed. As well as the usual paces, the Basuto has two extra gaits, called the triple and the pace.

Appearance The head is rather large with an underdeveloped, shortish neck. The body and legs are strong and wiry with hard hooves.

Chacteristics The Basuto is tough and can survive adverse conditions on very little food and water. They are only used for riding as all draft work in done by cattle.

Colours All solid colours as well as grey.

Height Up to 14.1hh.

BAVARIAN WARMBLOOD

Bavarians have been bred with Rottaler, Hanoverian, Westphalian, Trakehner and Thoroughbred to create the perfect all-round sports horse. They are large and well-developed and excel at dressage, eventing and showjumping.

BAVARIAN WARMBLOOD
(Germany)

Origins The original Bavarian Warmblood was the Rottaler, a heavy horse bred from Norman and Oldenburg stallions. It was used for pulling carriages and for field work during the Second World War, when it was in great demand.

Today, the Bavarian Warmblood is something of an innovation, composed of Rottaler mixed with Hanoverian, Westphalian, Trakehner and Thoroughbred bloodlines to produce a much lighter, more elegant warmblood sports horse capable of all disciplines. It was recognized as a breed in 1963.

Appearance This large elegant horse is similar in stature to the Hanoverian, though of a slightly lesser weight. It has a neat head, thick well-set neck, a heavy chest with a long sloping shoulder, and high withers. The back is fairly long and well-muscled with strong legs and large hocks.

Characteristics The Bavarian is a good-natured and willing worker. It has been bred to excel in all disciplines, which includes dressage, showjumping and eventing.

Colours Usually chestnut in various shades.

Height 16.2hh.

The Belgian Warmblood was created as a sports horse, and can regularly be seen in top competitions, particularly dressage and showjumping. Those that don't quite make the grade, however, make fine riding horses.

BELGIAN WARMBLOOD (Belgium)

Origins This is a relatively new breed, having been developed in the last century. It is the product of the selective breeding of Belgium's finest cavalry horses, as well as heavier breeds used in agriculture. They have been improved with Thoroughbreds and Anglo-Arabs as well as with other already established European warmbloods, such as the Hanoverian, Holstein, Selle Français and Dutch Warmblood. The result is a quality riding and competition horse which excels in international competition, particularly showjumping, eventing and dressage.

Appearance The Belgian Warmblood is near perfect in conformation and has many of the Thoroughbred characteristics. The head is of medium size with a straight nose and kind, alert eyes. The neck forms a graceful arch and is long and well-developed. The chest is substantial with a deep girth and sloping shoulder. The back is of medium length with muscular loins and powerful quarters. The legs are strong with large joints and the hooves are well shaped.

Characteristics Belgian Warmbloods are much admired for their fluid paces, supple action, and jumping ability. They are spirited and courageous as well as kind and willing.

Colours All solid colours.

Height Never deviates between 16.1 and 16.2hh.

The Black Forest has much in common with the Noriker. Besides being a riding horse, it is not uncommon to see it working on farms and engaged in forestry work.

BLACK FOREST (Germany)

Origins The Black Forest is based on the ancient Noriker breed, a horse that was selected because of its capabilities in mountain regions. These were mated with other local breeds to produce the Black Forest and in 1896 an association and stud book were established to protect the breed. This stipulated that only Belgian Heavy Draft (Brabant) stallions could be bred with Black Forest mares, thus improving and enlarging the breed to make it a strong draft horse. However, many farmers who did not approve of introducing Belgian Heavy Draft horses carried on using local native stallions and even forged their foals' identity papers. By the early 1900s, however, the authorities finally recognized the Schwartzwald farmers' needs and they were allowed to carry on as they had before.

Today the breed has been standardized with around 700 mares and 45 stallions at the Marbach/Weil stud, state-owned by Baden-Württemburg, and which always has about 16 stallion standing at stud. The breed is still used not only for farming and forestry work, but also as a carriage horse and, because of its nimble and lively gait, often for riding.

Appearance In appearance, the Black Forest lies somewhere between a Haflinger and a Noriker. The head is medium-sized and fairly plain with a straight or slightly Roman nose and soft eyes. The neck is short, well-developed and strong, with a straight shoulder. The body is sturdy with sloping quarters and a low-set tail. The legs are short with plenty of bone and hard hooves that have a little feathering.

Characteristics Lively, agile and willing.

Colours Most commonly chestnut, with a pale mane and tail; also a dark silver dapple, which is most popular.

Height 15–16hh.

The Boerperd took its name from the Boer Wars in which it was widely used.

BOERPERD (South Africa)

Origins The Boerperd, or Boer Horse, has a history that runs side by side with the white settlers of South Africa and the arrival of the Dutch in Cape Town in 1652. The first horses seen in the region were of Oriental blood and were imported from Java, which in turn were sold by the Dutch East India Company to the Free Burghers in 1665. Over the years, however, significant inbreeding had taken place so measures were taken to improve the breed by introducing Arab blood to the stock.

This practice continued for 150 years until a definite type emerged known as the Cape Horse. Meanwhile, some Iberian breeds arrived in the Cape in 1793 which may or may not have had an effect on the native horses. In the late 18th and early 19th centuries Cape Horses remained very popular and were prized for their endurance, stamina, speed and intelligence, which made them useful military horses.

Over the years there were various other influences on the breed, such as Flemish horses, and Hackneys, Norfolk Trotters and Cleveland Bays further enhanced the breed, which continued to survive despite disease and the Boer Wars in which it proved its worth, and which finally gave the Boerperd its name.

Appearance The Boerperd owes much of its appearance to its Arab and Oriental forebears. The head is small and wedge-shaped with a slightly dished or straight nose and a small, neat muzzle with flared

nostrils. The eyes are bright and intelligent and the ears are medium-sized and alert. The body is short and compact with a neatly sloping shoulder, deep girth, and well-proportioned muscular legs with good bone. The hooves are tough and shapely.

Characteristics The Boerperd is spirited, courageous and intelligent, with plenty of stamina and agility.

Colours Most solid colours and grey.

Height 14.2–15.2hh.

RIGHT and OPPOSITE
It may be large but the
Boulonnais has a surprising turn
of speed.

BOULONNAIS (France)

Origins The ancient Boulonnais may have been bred from Numidian horses imported by Julius Caesar's army around 54 BC, which were in evidence along the coast of the Pas-de-Calais prior to the invasion of the British Isles. Then came the Crusades and the Spanish occupation of Flanders when other breeds with Oriental bloodlines, such as the Arab, Barb and Andalusian, were introduced to the region and bred with the Roman-type horses to produce the original Boulonnais; Mecklenburg blood would later further shape the breed.

The Boulonnais is known as the 'thoroughbred' of draft horses because of its elegance, agility and turn of speed. It is well known for its spectacular gait which made it popular as a carriage horse; it was also a willing worker in the fields and was even used as a riding horse. It was most famous for a race called *La route du poisson* (The Fish Route) which occurred every two years. It commemorated a time during the 17th century when it was used for the rapid transport of freshly caught fish from the English Channel to Paris in less than 24 hours.

The popularity of the breed has made it a valuable improvement to other heavy breeds as well as providing the foundation blood for many competition horses.

Appearance There are two types of Boulonnais: the smaller 'fish-cart' horse which was used for the fish transportation and is now very rare and no larger than 15.3hh. Seen today is the large type, with its large elegant head with wide forehead and slightly Roman nose, inquisitive eyes, wide nostrils and small pricked ears. The neck is thick and muscular with a well-defined crest and a thick mane. The chest is wide with a deep, rounded rib cage. The withers sit deeply into the muscles of the shoulders and back. The back is straight and the legs are solid and strong; unlike many heavy breeds the legs have little hair.

Characteristics The Boulonnais is energetic, lively and enjoys work.

Colours The most usual colour is grey, with the occasional chestnut. There is currently a breeding programme to produce other colours – particularly black.

Height Around 16.3.

BRABANT (Belgium)

Origins The Brabant, or Belgian Heavy Draft Horse, comes from the area of Belgium that has Brussels as its capital. It is of ancient origin, only slightly more recent than the Ardennais to which it owes part of its lineage: the other part of its inheritance is thought to have stemmed from the Flanders Horse of the 11th to 16th centuries, which in turn is believed to be descended from the ancient horses of the Quaternary period. For centuries Belgian breeders produced their stock by selective breeding, which also included inbreeding.

The Brabant's very existence is a direct result of the geology of the area;

the rich heavy soil required a horse with great pulling power and big strong joints to enable it to lift its huge feet out of the thick clods of mud. As a result, three distinct bloodlines emerged 100 years ago which intermingled to create the modern Brabant: the *Gros de la Dendre*, which was muscular and strong with huge legs; the *Gris de Nivelles*, with good conformation and a certain elegance; and the *Colosse de la Mehaigne*, which was large and had a lively temperament.

Over the centuries, the Brabant has had enormous influence on today's modern breeds, much in the same way as the Arab bloodline has been added to improve existing stock. In the Middle Ages the horse was imported all over Europe and its bloodlines are present in the German warmbloods. The Russians introduced native breeds to it to produce working horses and its influence is also present in the Shire, Irish Draft and Clydesdale, to name but a few. Today, Brabants are still part of the foundation stock for the breeding of warmbloods.

The Brabant is an ancient draft horse, bred for working the heavy soil of its native land. It is still used today for farm and forestry work.

They now appear throughout the world where they are still used in agricultural work, logging and as dray horses. They can also be seen in the showring.

Appearance The head is fairly square with a straight profile, small pricked ears, and deep-set eyes with a kindly expression. The neck is short and very strong and set high with a large crest. The shoulders are sloping and the chest is wide and deep.

The body is short with a well-muscled back and strong quarters. The legs are fairly long and muscular and the hooves are large, rounded and tough; there is not much feathering present.

Characteristics The Brabant is an extremely docile animal, to the point that it could almost be described as sluggish. However, it has an equable nature, is obedient, and possesses pulling power

equal only to the Shire's, for which it is highly prized. It is a hard worker with plenty of stamina and a strong constitution, requiring relatively little food for its size.

Colours Most common is light chestnut with a flaxen mane; also acceptable is red roan, bay, dun and grey.

Height 16.1–17hh.

The Brandenburg was originally bred to work as a carriage horse and on farms. Today, however, it is exclusively used as a riding and sports horse.

BRANDENBURG (Germany)

Origins In the late 18th century a stud at Neustadt was founded and it was here that the Brandenburg was developed. The breeding programme resulted in a warmblooded horse that was heavy enough for use on farms but sufficiently elegant to pull carriages.

By the end of the Second World War the breed was reassessed and using Hanoverian and Trakehner stallions the Brandenburg was remodelled into the lighter warmblood sports horse much in demand today. The Brandenburg excels at dressage, showjumping, eventing and driving.

Appearance The attractive head is fine and medium-sized, set neatly onto a medium-length, well-formed neck. The back is straight and strong with rather a long croup. The legs are strong, straight and of medium length.

Characteristics The Brandenburg is kind and even-tempered; it is also obedient and a willing worker.

Colours Predominantly bay.

Height 16.2hh.

BRETON

The Breton is probably France's most popular heavy horse, and although the breed standard is relatively new, its history dates back many thousands of years.

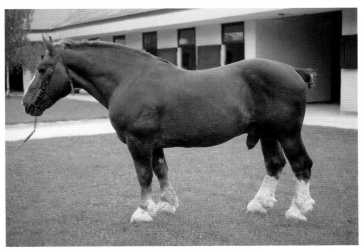

BRETON (France)

Origins The Breton originated in a department of north-west France called Bretagne (Brittany). The breed standard was formed quite recently, but the history of its development goes back 4,000 years when the Aryans introduced Asian stock to Europe. In Brittany, the demanding climate and poor-quality land caused local horses to adapt to their environment, resulting in a horse that possessed great strength and durability. The Breton is therefore the result of evolution over hundreds of years and long periods of selection carried out by breeders from old varieties of native horses.

Brittany has a long history of breeding distinguished horses which stretches back to the Middle Ages; in fact, the Breton horse was much prized by military leaders around the time of the Crusades, even though the breed was small at just 14hh. The Crusaders' Oriental horses, which they brought back with them from the East, were then bred with the Brittany horses to produce two separate strains: the *Sommier*, a slow packhorse, and the *Roussin*, used for riding and as a warhorse. The two types remained popular for centuries, and by the 18th century had been crossed with Ardennais, Boulonnais and Percheron to produce a much larger, stronger animal, which was known as the Grand Breton.

By the 19th century infusions of Norfolk Trotter had been introduced along with Hackney to produce a lighter but still substantial animal useful for light draft and military work; when used as a carriage horse it was known as the Postier-Breton. As well as the Grand Breton and the Postier Breton there is another type, the Corlay Breton, developed from crosses with Arab and Thoroughbred and is probably the nearest to the original horse of Brittany, being no bigger than 15hh.

Appearance The head is square with a heavy jaw. The ears are small and expressive and the eyes bright and kind. The nose is straight, though slightly dished in the Corlay Breton, and the nostrils are large. The neck is short with a well-developed crest and the short-coupled body is wide and muscular, as is the croup. The shoulders are long and the legs are short and muscular with strong cannon bones.

Characteristics All three Breton types have an equable nature and are willing workers. They are extremely hardy and have plenty of stamina, making them easy to maintain.

Colours Most common are chestnuts, but roans, bays and greys are also acceptable.

Height There is a range of sizes from 14.3hh (Corlay) to 16hh (Grand Breton).

The British Warmblood was created to compete with the other warmblooded sports horses of Europe.

BRITISH WARMBLOOD (U.K.)

Origins The Warmblood has been of particular importance to British competition for a very long time and is the result of Thoroughbred crossed with Irish Draft. These make excellent eventers and showjumpers and have been proving their worth since the middle of the 20th century when equestrian sports began to take off in earnest.

One aspect of equestrianism in which the United Kingdom did not excel was dressage. The sport had long been popular in Europe, where European warmbloods were especially bred for the purpose. However, over the last 30 years or so the discipline had been gaining popularity in the United Kingdom as British riders have become more interested in dressage as a sport. It was

necessary for them to continue to use European warmbloods, but it was eventually felt that Britain should have a warmblood of her own, which led to the formation of the British Warmblood Society in 1977.

The term 'warmblood' loosely describes a wide range of breeds from all over Europe, each with its own specific set of criteria. It is generally understood that true warmbloods are of European stock and not the Thoroughbred-Irish cross which is technically a warmblood but not recognized as such.

The British Warmblood is based on various European bloodlines, but so far the breed is not consistent, even though registration of these animals is strictly controlled with only the very best being recognized. The British Warmblood continues to enjoy great success in dressage and jumping.

Appearance Because the British Warmblood breeding programme is still in its infancy there is no consistent type. But generally speaking their appearance fits the standards of most European warmbloods.

Characteristics Kind and intelligent. Like most warmbloods they are obedient and enjoyable to ride.

Colours All solid colours, with white on the face and legs acceptable.

Height Approximately 15–16.3hh.

Australia had no native breeds of her own; the Brumby was introduced by settlers who turned the horses loose and let them run wild.

BRUMBY (Australia)

Origins Australia had no native horses of her own until they were introduced during the country's gradual colonization, and in particular by settlers who arrived during the 19th-century gold rush. There was not only an influx of people, therefore, but of animals, and this included the horses which they brought with them. During the First World War many of the horses escaped or were turned loose to run wild: these were the forefathers of the modern-day Brumby, a name said to be derived from the aboriginal word for wild (*baroomby*).

Appearance Because of the variety of animals which reverted to a wild state, there is no specific breed type; consequently Brumbies come in all shapes, sizes and colours.

Characteristics The horses are now almost totally feral, making them difficult to catch and almost impossible to train. They are prolific breeders and for this reason have come to be regarded as pests. This has led to such extensive culling that they are now quite rare.

Colours All solid colours, dun, roan and coloured.

Height Up to 15hh.

The Buddenny was originally used as a cavalry horse, but today is used as a general riding and sports horse.

BUDENNY (Russia)

Origins The Budenny, or Budyonny, is a relatively young breed, created by the Russians to fit the basic criteria of a Perfect Russian Horse, a standard which is centuries old. A Russian horse should be an excellent all-rounder, equally at home ridden as pulling a carriage. Development of the breed began in 1921 when the devastation of the First World War and the Revolution made it clear that a good cavalry horse was required. The horse was named after Marshal Budenny (1883–1973), who was responsible for the breed's development.

As a cavalry horse it was obliged to satisfy a number of requirements: it needed enormous stamina, a good turn of speed, and the ability to jump; obedience and an equable nature were also needed, as well as great courage. The breeding programme took place at Rostov where there was a military stud. The breed is based on Don and Chernomor mares crossed with Thoroughbred stallions; Chernomors are similar to Dons, though rather lighter. They also introduced

Kazakh and Kirgiz blood, though this was not as successful. The breed was eventually recognized and was registered in 1949.

Today the Budenny is used as a performance horse and in all disciplines including racing, endurance, and showjumping. It is also used in harness.

Appearance The Budenny bears a close resemblance to the Thoroughbred, being tall and powerful with good bone and muscle. The head is medium-sized and sits well on the neck. The nose is straight or slightly concave and the nostrils are wide. The ears are of medium size and the eyes are bold. The neck is long and set high and the withers are also high. The back is fairly short and is inclined to flatten towards the withers. The loins are wide, medium-length and muscular. The croup is usually long. The shoulder is of medium length and sloping. The legs are clean and strong and the hooves well shaped and hard.

Characteristics Due to its military breeding, the Budenny has plenty of courage and spirit. It is also obedient and has a good disposition.

Colours Budennys are nearly always chestnut, with an iridescent sheen inherited from the Don. Bays and browns occasionally appear.

Height Approximately 16hh.

CAMARGUE (France)

Origins The horses that inhabit the salt marshes and lagoons of the Rhône delta in south-east France are semi-wild and spend much of their time grazing the sparse vegetation. They are very ancient and are probably descended from the Diluvial Horse. They also bear a striking resemblance to the primitive horses painted in the caves at Lascaux in prehistoric times; it is also likely that Oriental and Barb blood runs in their veins because of their facial shape.

The breed was further enhanced in the 19th century by the introduction of Postier Breton, Arab, Anglo-Arab and Thoroughbred, though these additions seem to have had little bearing on the

horses' overall appearance.

There is an annual round-up in the Camargue when suitable horses are selected for riding purposes while the weaker and substandard colts and stallions are culled: this may seem ruthless but there is no doubt that it has led to improvements in the breed.

Camargue horses are traditionally ridden by the *gardiens* who use them for herding the famous black bulls of the region and for festivals in which their dazzling horsemanship is displayed. The horses are also used for trekking the region, now a popular tourist attraction.

Appearance The head is rather square, with a broad forehead, short, broad ears, and expressive eyes. The neck is short and well-developed, the shoulder is upright, and the back is short with a low-set tail. The legs are strong and the hooves well shaped and tough. The mane and tail are abundant.

Characteristics Camargues make obedient and willing riding horses; they are extremely agile and have the ability to turn sharply at full gallop. As trekking ponies they are sure-footed and have plenty of stamina. However, they never quite lose their independent spirit and retain something of their wild inheritance.

Colours Usually grey, though bay and brown sometimes appear. Foals are born dark but become grey as they mature.

Height 13.1–14.2hh.

The Carthusian is lesser known than the Andalusian, though no less important.

CARTHUSIAN (Spain)

Origins The Carthusian shares much of its history with the Andalusian. In the mid-15th century the Carthusian monks of Jerez de la Frontera were bequeathed 10,000 acres (4,000 hectares) of grazing land, which they used for the selective breeding of the highly revered Iberian horses, being determined to preserve the pure Iberian blood. When the monarch insisted on Neopolitan being added to the stock they flatly refused and continued to breed their fine Spanish horses. In 1808–14 Napoleon invaded the peninsular and stole many of the best of the stock. The monks, in an attempt to preserve the breed, rescued the remaining horses and from these few the modern Andalusian emerged, which was fairly heavy, and the Carthusian, which was Iberian mixed with Arab and Barb to produce a lighter breed.

Appearance The Carthusian is slightly smaller than the Andalusian and not as heavy. The head is broad with a straight, proud profile and widely-spaced alert ears. It has large intelligent eyes.

Characteristics Intelligent and good-natured as well as spirited and courageous. Carthusians are easy to handle, complaisant and obedient.

Colours Usually grey, but occasionally chestnut and black.

Height Up to 15.2hh.

CASPIAN (Iran)

Origins The Caspian is claimed to be the oldest breed of all and its history would seem to bear this out. Although domesticated, its bloodline is remarkably pure, with descent that appears to have been traced from a prehistoric Oriental horse. Fossils of a horse of this type were found in Iran which are almost an exact match of the bone structure of today's Caspian. A likeness of the horse can also be seen on a seal belonging to Darius the Great who ruled Persia (Iran) around 500 BC. The Caspian is probably the prototype of the Arab; consequently Caspian blood is in many of today's breeds.

It was thought that this small horse became extinct around the 10th century, so it was all the more amazing to discover a herd of 40 of them roaming a

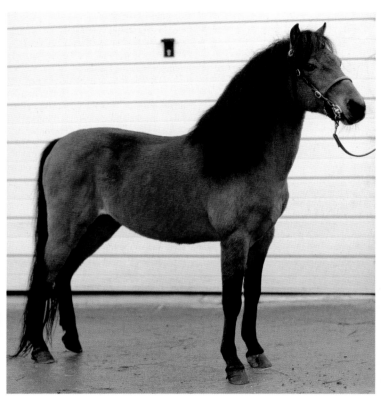

with large nostrils. The eyes are large and intelligent. The neck is set quite high and is strong and elegant; the shoulders are sloping and the body is of medium proportions though quite narrow.

Characteristics The Caspian, though pony-like in size, has the heart of a horse. It also has all the qualities needed to make it excellent for riding, being affectionate, intelligent and obedient. It is far from dull and has plenty of spirit. It would also makes a good driving pony.

Colours Usually bay, chestnut and grey.

Height 10–12hh.

The Caspian claims to be the oldest breed in the world and was thought to have become extinct in the 10th century. Amazingly, however, a small herd of them were discovered in the 1960s, wandering free in an isolated valley in Iran.

remote region of the Elburz mountains in 1965. These were shipped to England were a breed society was established to preserve this rare and ancient breed, and was the start of studs being formed all over the world.

Nowadays, its small stature makes it an ideal horse for children and its even temperament makes it suitable for beginners.

Appearance The Caspian is typical of the Oriental type. The head is small and fine with small, alert ears and a straight nose

The Cayuse was the favourite of Native Americans who improved the breed through selective breeding. Today, however, it is very rare, with only a few small herds existing in California.

CAYUSE (U.S.A.)

Origins The Cayuse is very different from other American breeds which more often than not are descended from Spanish and Arab horses brought over by the conquistadors in the 16th century. The Cayuse's ancestry is practically unknown, but it is generally thought to be descended from French horses, probably Percherons, which were imported to Canada in the 1600s; Percherons were popular with the Canadians who used them to improve their own workhorses.

It was the French Canadians who introduced their horses to America where there are records that they bartered them with Pawnee Indians in St. Louis. Consequently, it was the Native Americans who bred these heavy horses with Spanish and Oriental blood to produce a horse capable of speed, strength and endurance.

In the 1800s the Cayuse was established as a separate breed and it was again the Native Americans, who were superb horsemen, who continued to refine the breed through selective breeding. Strangely, it is the Percheron throwback which produces the spots and marking which often appear on the Cayuse; in turn, the Cayuse has influenced both the Paint and Appaloosa.

Today the Cayuse is rare and only exists in California. Great efforts are being made to preserve the breed.

Appearance The Cayuse has many of the attributes of its Spanish inheritance, having a fine head with straight nose, small ears, and kind eyes. The neck is medium-length and well-developed with rather high withers and a good sloping shoulder. The body is strong and sturdy with short but strong legs, probably inherited from its Percheron forebears. The sloping pasterns make it capable of a broken walk which is most comfortable for the rider over long distances.

Characteristics The pony is small, stocky and very strong, but with all the nobility and bearing of its Spanish forebears.

Colours All, including coloureds and spotteds.

Height Around 14hh.

CLEVELAND BAY (U.K.)

Origins The excellent Cleveland Bay is Britain's oldest breed and dates back to medieval times. Gradually, however, it became rarer, and numbers dipped to a critical level in the last century. Thankfully, it is once more gaining in popularity and numbers have begun to increase.

The breed is related to the Chapman Horse which lived in north-east Yorkshire in the Middle Ages and which received Iberian and Barb bloodlines. Clevelands were then used mainly as packhorses and for agricultural work where they were greatly admired for their strength and ability to carry heavy loads for long distances. The name comes from the area (Cleveland) where they were bred and the fact that their colour is bay.

Later the breed was crossed with Thoroughbred to produce a lighter, elegant carriage horse which is a feature

of the Cleveland Bay today. Sadly the previous type is now extinct.

In a previous age the Cleveland Bay was very popular, but the development of motorized transport saw its demise and by the 1970s the breed had been reduced to an all-time low. In some respects, however, they are still very much in evidence; Cleveland Bays have been kept at the royal mews since King George V introduced them, and the Hampton Court Stud still actively breeds them for state and ceremonial occasions.

Today Cleveland Bays and part-breds can be seen in showjumping, dressage, eventing, driving and hunting, where they are admired for their sure-footedness and great stamina.

Appearance The horse possesses a large noble head on a long muscular neck attached to a sloping shoulder and long, deep body. The strong, shortish legs have plenty of bone and no feathers.

Characteristics Clevelands are calm and intelligent and seemingly possess the ability to think for themselves. They are honest, strong and confident with enormous powers of endurance.

Colours Exclusively bay, with a rich black mane and tail and black-stockinged legs with no white.

Height 16–17hh.

A couple of hundred years ago it was a common sight for Clydesdales to be working farms and hauling loads over great distances. Sadly their numbers have dwindled, placing them in danger of extinction. Fortunately, they are now on the increase and can be seen in the showring or used for ceremonial purposes, such as pulling wedding carriages.

CLYDESDALE (U.K.)

Origins The establishment of the Clydesdale began in the late-17th century when Lanarkshire farmers and various dukes of Hamilton supposedly imported Flemish stallions, ancestors of the Brabant, to Scotland. The farmers were skilful breeders and mated them with native heavy draft mares already in existence; over the next 100 years or so, English Shire, Friesian and Cleveland Bay blood was also added. The result was known as the Clydesdale and it was highly prized as a draft horse. The Clydesdale Horse Society was established in 1877, almost a century and a half after the breed first began to evolve.

The breed soon became popular as a general farm horse and also for haulage over long and short distances; Clydesdales could be found in most major cities of Scotland, the North of England and Northern Ireland, as well as in agricultural areas. In fact, the horse became popular the world over, when considerable numbers were imported to North America, Canada and Australia.

The Clydesdale differs from most heavy draft horses, which tend to be squat and plain-looking; in fact, with its short-coupled body, long legs, and high head-carriage it looks positively refined.

As with all heavy horses the Clydesdale breed began to decline with the development of motorized transport and reached an even lower ebb in the 1960s and 70s. However, a few families kept the breed going and today numbers have increased though the horse is still

classified as 'at risk' by the Rare Breeds
Society. Today they are highly valued in
the showring as well as in harness and as
dray horses, where they take part in
displays and are even used to pull
wedding carriages.

Appearance The head is proudly held with
medium, well-shaped ears which are
pricked and alert; the eyes are kind and
intelligent. The nose is slightly Roman
and the nostrils large. The neck is long
and well-set, with a high crest leading to
high withers. The back is slightly concave
and short and the quarters are well-
developed and powerful. The legs are
straight and long with plenty of
feathering. The feet are large and require
careful shoeing as contracted heels have a
tendency to develop.

Characteristics These charming horses are
energetic with an alert, cheerful air. They
are even-tempered and enjoy the
company of other horses and human
beings. They are extremely strong with a
lively action and a slight tendency to dish.

Colours Clydesdales can be bay, brown
and black and usually have white patches
all the way up the legs and under the
belly, which can turn roan in places.

Height 16.2hh, but some males may reach
17hh or more.

The Comtois has plenty of stamina, its sure-footed confidence making it an asset in mountain regions.

COMTOIS (France)

Origins The Comtois is an ancient coldblooded breed which is thought to have been brought to France by the Burgundians, a Germanic people who invaded Gaul in the 5th century and established their kingdom in east-central France, centred on Dijon.

The Comtois originated in the Franche-Comté and Jura mountains on the borders of France and Switzerland. By the 16th century the breed was used to improve Burgundian horses, which gained a good reputation as warhorses in the cavalry of Louis XIV and were also used by Napoleon in his invasion of Russia. In the 19th century it was bred with other draft breeds, such as the Boulonnais and Percheron, to produce a heavier horse; by the early 20th century it was further improved using Ardennais stallions.

Nowadays the Comtois is also bred in the Massif Central, the Pyrenees, and the Alps, where its stamina and sure-footedness makes it perfectly suited to these mountainous regions. However, it is mainly used for hauling logs and for work in vineyards. It is the second most popular draft breed in France after the Breton.

Appearance The Comtois is lightly built for a draft horse. The head is large, the eyes alert and intelligent, and the ears small and neat. The neck is short and well-developed and the body is stocky and powerful with a deep girth. The back is long and straight with muscular hindquarters. The legs are short and strong with a small amount of feathering. The mane and tail are full.

Characteristics The Comtois is very hardy and lives to a ripe old age. It is good-natured, obedient and hard-working.

Colours Various shades of chestnut with a flaxen mane and tail, also brown or bay.

Height 14.1–15.1hh.

CONNEMARA (Ireland)

Origins The Connemara is Ireland's only native breed, although it is not indigenous to the country. It is thought that it was brought to Ireland 2,500 years ago when the Celts settled in Ireland and brought their ponies with them. The Celts were traders and travelled to and from Mediterranean ports, which makes it likely that their ponies were of Oriental descent, probably Barb. In medieval times these were bred with the Irish Hobeye, which was a much coveted riding horse, famous for its speed, agility and endurance.

Legend has it that further blood was added to the breed when the Spanish Armada sunk off the coast of Ireland and Iberian horses swam ashore and mated with native breeds. Later the breed was further improved with infusions of Hackney, Welsh Cob, Irish Draft, Clydesdale and Thoroughbred.

The Connemara derives its name from the region of that name which a few hundred years ago included Connaught and Galway. The terrain is rocky and mountainous with very little vegetation. The weather can be atrocious with piercing winds and driving rain coming in from the Atlantic. Consequently, the Connemara has evolved into an extremely hardy specimen, which is sure-footed and agile and has extraordinary jumping abilities.

Historically, it was used as a draft animal, transporting peat and seaweed as well as taking potatoes and corn to

The Connemara makes an excellent child's competition pony, particularly as it is a naturally good jumper.

market. Nowadays it is used for hunting, eventing, showjumping and driving; it is often crossed with the Thoroughbred to produce an excellent jumping horse.

Appearance The Connemara is a riding pony of excellent quality. The head is fine and set quite high, with small pricked ears, clever eyes, and a straight nose with fairly large nostrils. The neck is of medium length and well-muscled and the shoulders are sloping, with a deep girth, a straight back, and well-developed quarters. The legs are short but elegant and strong with very hard hooves.

Characteristics The Connemara is intelligent with a calm and kindly disposition. It is an excellent all-rounder and being hardy is easy to maintain.

Colours Most commonly grey, but also bay, black, dun and brown.

Height 13–14.2hh.

Connemaras are often bred with Thoroughbreds to produce jumping horses.

OPPOSITE
Connemaras are often seen in the showring. This dun stallion is a champion, ready to compete at a Dublin Show.

BELOW and RIGHT
These young Criollo horses are
allowed to run wild in the foothills
of Mount Lanin in Patagonia
until they are old enough for
breaking in.

CRIOLLO (Argentina)

Origins The Spanish *conquistadores* were responsible for the existence of the horse in the Americas and what better stock to introduce than the Arab, Barb and excellent Iberian. It is these three bloodlines which make up the Criollo, the native horse of Argentina. For many hundreds of years it roamed the plains (*pampas*) of Argentina, where extreme conditions of heat and cold resulted in the natural selection of horses that are among the toughest in the world.

The Criollo became the horse of the *gaucho*, or South American cowboy, who quickly recognized its excellent qualities of hardiness, stamina, speed and resilience (they were also used as packhorses).

They are now the subject of a selective breeding programme designed to preserve the horse's special features. In Argentina this entails an annual breeders' test in which Criollos travel for 750 miles (1200km) for 15 days carrying 242lb (110kg), their only food and drink being what they can forage for themselves *en route*.

Today, herds live in a semi-wild condition on the enormous ranches of South America, where they are caught and broken in as required. They are still used as stock and riding horses and when crossed with Thoroughbreds make excellent Polo Ponies.

Appearance The horse's toughness is apparent from its stocky exterior. The head is broad with wide-set eyes and a slightly dished nose; it has fairly large ears. The neck is well-developed with a wide back and chest and strong quarters. The back is short with sloping shoulders and the short, sturdy legs have plenty of bone.

Characteristics The Criollo is tough, can survive on next to nothing, and is an obedient worker. It is able to withstand some of the harshest conditions in the world.

Colours Most commonly dun with a black mane and tail, an eel stripe down the centre of the back, and zebra markings on the legs. Other colours are chestnut, bay, black, roan, grey, piebald, skewbald and palomino.

Height 14–15hh.

The Dales is strong and hardy, making it an excellent riding and driving pony for adults and children alike.

DALES (U.K.)

Origins The Dales pony is the only British native breed which has never been completely wild. Its earliest descendant is the Celtic Pony, though it was elements of

the sure-footed Scottish Galloway, used as a pack pony and which worked in the lead mines situated high on the moors, which truly gave birth to the breed. Further improvements came with infusions of Friesian, Welsh Cob and Clydesdale.

The Dales pony is a native of the upper dales of the eastern slopes of the Pennine range, from the High Peak in Derbyshire to the Cheviot Hills near to the Scottish Border, and is often confused with the similar Fell pony from the western side of the Pennines; before the breeds were split they were collectively known as Pennine ponies.

The Dales pony proved popular and comfortable to ride and was strong enough for draft work. It had excellent stamina and was able to thrive on the bleak uplands of the dales. They were the versatile workhorses of the hill farmers, perfect for small farms and capable of pulling cartloads of a ton or more. They were also used as shepherds' ponies and could cover great distances with burdens of 170lb (77kg), often with a rider as well, and in deep snow. When not working around the farm they were also used for days out hunting where they proved their jumping skills.

Today, Dales ponies feature in showing classes and also in trekking and harnessed driving competitions.

Appearance A neat head which is broad between the eyes, which are bright and alert. The ears are small and curve slightly inwards. The Dales's trademark is a long forlock which hangs down the centre of the face. The neck is fairly long and well- developed with a long thick mane. The body is short with a deep girth, sloping shoulders and well-developed hindquarters. The legs are sturdy with feathers around the fetlocks.

Characteristics The Dales pony is extremely tough, its strong legs and feet and sturdy body allowing it to cope with heavy loads. It is hardy and undeterred by adverse weather conditions. It is alert with a quiet intelligence and is a willing worker.

Colours Dales ponies are usually black, with some bays, browns and greys and very occasionally roans. White should be confined to a star or snip on the face, with only a little on the fetlocks of the hindlegs.

Height Up to 14.2hh.

*The Danish Warmblood was
established in the 20th century
and is a superb quality horse.*

*OPPOSITE
The Danish Warmblood excels as
a sports horse, as can be seen here
at the 2000 Olympic Games. The
horse's name is* Canute, *and it is
ridden by Thomas Velin, of
Denmark, naturally enough!*

DANISH WARMBLOOD (Denmark)

Origins The story of the Danish
Warmblood begins in Holstein which
until the mid-19th century was Danish
territory and allowed the Danes easy
access to German warmblood stock
through the Cistercian monasteries of
Holstein. For centuries the monks had
been breeding the old-style heavy
Holstein with highly- bred Iberian
stallions to produce useful multi-purpose
horses; these practices were therefore far
from new.

The Royal Frederiksborg Stud, which
was founded in 1562 near Copenhagen,
was already breeding Andalusians and
Neopolitans, and this stock was interbred
with a small Danish breed and the larger

Jutland Heavy Draft (both coldbloods),
with infusions of Turkish and Dutch
breeds and later English Thoroughbred
added. This created the excellent all-
rounder known as the Frederiksborg for
which the monks of Holstein had been
striving (page 136). The stud closed in
1862, but some of the stock survived in
the hands of private breeders.

By the middle of the 20th century the

Danes realized that they needed to create
a competition sports horse of superb
quality to rival other European breeds.
Subsequently, they decided to breed the
Frederiksborg-Thoroughbred mares with
Thoroughbred, Anglo-Norman,
Trakehner, Wielkopolski and Malopolski
stallions to create the truly superb Danish
Warmblood. It is interesting to note that
Hanoverian was not used, which is
unusual, as it is present in most other
European warmblood breeds.

These horses are the supreme masters
of high-level competition, though the less
talented still make wonderful all-purpose
riding horses. They particularly excel at
dressage and showjumping.

Appearance The conformation of the
Danish Warmblood is near-perfect: it has
a noble head with large, intelligent eyes
and fairly long, tapered ears. All elements
of the body are in perfect proportion,
from the long, well-developed neck to the
straight well-boned legs and shapely feet.

Characteristics Admired for its fluid paces
and supple action which makes it so
popular as a dressage horse, the Danish
Warmblood is spirited and courageous
but at the same time kind and willing.

Colours Bay is most common but all solid
colours are acceptable. A little white is
allowed on the head and legs.

Height 16.1–16.2hh.

RIGHT
This Dartmoor stallion is of show quality, and others like it are regularly to be seen in mountain and moorland classes in the showring.

OPPOSITE
LEFT
These are Dartmoor ponies living in their wild state, though they are closely monitored to ensure the survival of the breed.

RIGHT
The Dartmoor is an excellent child's pony as its small size makes it easily manageable. It is also popular for driving.

DANUBIAN (Bulgaria)

Origins The Danubian is a relatively new breed which was established in the early 20th century. The aim of the Bulgarian breeders was to produce a sensible light draft and riding horse by mating the larger, heavier type of Nonius stallions with the higher-quality Gidrán mares, which produced offspring that were strong and sturdy with excellent stamina and endurance. But the Nonius genes are rather dominant, and despite various other breedings with Arabs and Thoroughbreds the Danubian still displays the rather mundane attributes of the original stallions, even though the Nonius is renowned for its even temperament, strength and ability.

Today the Danubian is still used as a riding and light draft horse and is often crossed with Thoroughbreds to produce performance horses.

Appearance The head is rather plain but with good proportions. The ears are of medium length and the eyes smallish. The body is chunky and sturdy, rather cobby, with a shortish well-developed neck, strong shoulders and a deep girth. The legs are well-muscled at the tops and have plenty of bone.

Characteristics The Danubian is a sensible, willing worker, with good stamina and endurance. It is kind and easy to handle.

Colours Usually dark chestnut or black.

Height 15.2hh.

DARTMOOR (U.K.)

Origins There is evidence that ponies inhabited Dartmoor as early as 2000 BC, a fact confirmed by remains excavated on Shaugh Moor. The earliest written reference to the Dartmoor is in the will of Awifold of Crediton who died in 1012. The breed stems from the Celtic Pony which then bred with other British natives; later there were additions of Roadster, Welsh Pony, Cob, Arab and in recent times Thoroughbred.

The Dartmoor pony comes from the county of Devon in the south-west of England and gets its name from the area of wild moorland where it still roams.

Standing over 1,000ft (305m) above sea level, with wind and rain driving off the sea, it can be an inhospitable place with rocky outcrops and sparse vegetation. Consequently, the pony is extremely hardy and sure-footed and has plenty of stamina.

However, Dartmoors fail to thrive if left solely to their own devices and require hay in the winter, which farmers put out for them. This was confirmed during the Second World War when Dartmoor was completely out of bounds. As a result, the population dwindled to only two stallions and 12 mares because of harsh winters without supplementary feeding. Nowadays the breed has been greatly improved and with careful monitoring is now flourishing. Children like to ride Dartmoors and they are also used for showing and driving.

Appearance The Dartmoor has a small, neat head, nicely set, with small, alert ears and an intelligent and kindly eye. The neck is of medium length and fairly well- developed, as are the back, loins and quarters. The tail is high-set, the legs are shapely but sturdy, and the hooves are well formed and hard.

Characteristics Dartmoors make excellent children's ponies, and their small size makes them easily manageable. They also have kind and docile natures.

The Dartmoor's most striking feature is that it moves with almost no knee flexion, which produces a long, free-flowing stride similar to that of a horse's and very comfortable for the rider.

Colours Mainly bay and brown with only a little white on the legs and face.

Height Up to 12.2hh.

The Don, the favourite mount of the Cossacks, originated in the harsh conditions of the Russian steppes; it is consequently hardy and able to withstand extremes of temperature.

DØLE GUDBRANDSDAL (Norway)

Origins The Døle-Gudbrandsdal originated in the Gudbrandsdal valley, which is situated between the city of Oslo and the North Sea coast. Though much bigger, they are not dissimilar to the Dales and Fell ponies of Great Britain and it is thought that they share much of the same ancestry, namely the prehistoric Celtic Pony and the Friesian. This is feasible as the Friesian people are reputed to have traded all over Europe as well as the British Isles and Scandinavia.

Over the centuries the Døle was crossed with other breeds, including Heavy Draft, Norfolk Trotter, Arab and Thoroughbred. The result was a horse that was strong and heavy enough for haulage as well as riding.

Today there is another Døle type: the original horse was extensively bred with Thoroughbreds to produce the Døle Trotter which is still used for trotting races in Norway.

The Second World War saw a depletion in numbers but since 1962 efforts have been made to improve the quality of these horses by a breed society that will only register stallions with sound conformation and a good racetrack record. Døle's are still used on farms and are particularly useful for forestry work.

Appearance The Døle is the smallest of the draft horses and resembles a large pony. The head is small and neat with a broad forehead, straight or slightly Roman nose, and a square muzzle. The ears are small and alert and the eyes kind but inquisitive. The neck is short and well- developed with a slight crest. The chest and shoulders are very strong, the girth is deep, and the back is long with powerful, well-muscled hindquarters. The legs are short with good bone and feathering around the heels, and the hooves hard.

Characteristics The Døle is a hardy breed, well able to withstand harsh winter conditions. It requires a modicum of care but can survive on little food. It is even-tempered and a willing worker.

Colours Usually bay, brown, chestnut or black, but occasionally grey and dun. The Trotter types often have white on their legs and faces.

Height 14.2–15.1hh.

DON (Russia)

Origins The Don is Russia's most famous breed. It originated in the harsh Russian steppes, where it once roamed in herds, surviving the freezing winters and torrid summers with nothing but sparse vegetation for food.

The original steppes breed, known as the Old Don, was bred with various Orientals, such as the Arab, Karabakh and Turkmene, and Orlov and

Thoroughbred were added to improve the Don's conformation and give it incredible stamina.

The horse was the preferred mount of the Don Cossacks, it was also used by the Russian army, and its extreme toughness made it an excellent hunter, particularly in pursuit of wolves. Today, the Don's hardy constitution makes it an excellent endurance horse. It is also used to improve other breeds.

Appearance The overall picture of the Don is one of strength and robustness. The head is fairly small and neat with a slightly dished or straight nose which clearly indicates its Arab heritage. Ears are small and shapely and the eyes are large and intelligent. The neck is set high and should be arched; however, many have ewe necks. The back is fairly long, straight and wide with sloping quarters and a straight shoulder. The legs are clean but in some cases can be sickle-hocked. Moreover, the placement of the pelvis restricts movement and causes a stilted action (this fault had largely been bred out). The hooves are well-shaped and hard.

Characteristics Tough and sturdy with an independent nature, qualities which have found their way into other breeds.

Colours The most striking feature of the Don's coat is its iridescent sheen. It is most commonly chestnut but can also be bay, brown, black and grey.

Height Approximately 15.2hh.

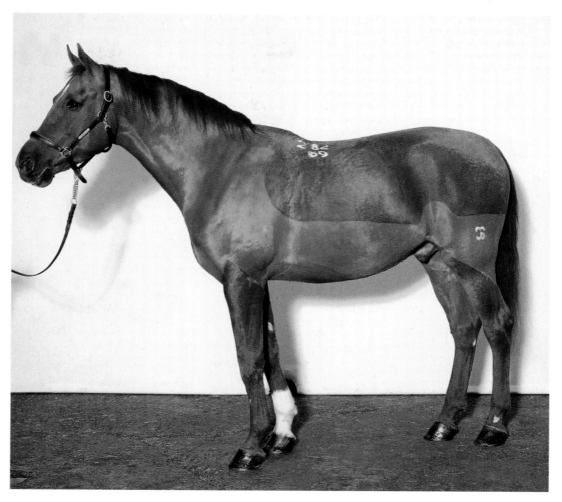

Because of its size and strength, the Dutch Heavy Draft was popular with farmers, who used it for hauling heavy loads.

DUTCH HEAVY DRAFT
(Netherlands)

Origins The modern Dutch Draft is a relatively new breed, registered in the early 20th century when the Royal Association of the Netherlands Draft Horse was formed. However, documentation of a heavy draft horse has existed since around 1850, while Holland and Belgium have had heavy horses for centuries, most notably the

Colours Predominantly chestnut and bay, less commonly grey and black.

Height Up to 17hh.

Although a few Dutch Heavy Drafts are still bred for farming, the majority are now to be seen in the showring.

Brabant and Ardennais, whose history is very ancient.

These horses were crucial to the prosperity of the farming community where their strength and massive feet made them capable of working heavy soil. It was these two breeds, along with native Zeeland-type mares, that created the Dutch Draft, the purity of which has long been protected with only registered parents allowed entry to the stud book.

The Dutch Draft is an enormous horse for its height and is still used for heavy work on farms and for pulling brewers' drays. It can also be seen in the showring.

Appearance The head is large and square but also quite attractive with a flat forehead and small but gentle eyes. The ears are small and straight, the nose is straight, and the nostrils are large and flaring. The neck is short and well-developed, while the body is short and deep and massively strong. The legs resemble tree trunks with abundant feathering present on the legs.

Characteristics The Dutch Draft is agile for its size, with a lively gait. It has a long working life and is tough, intelligent, kind, willing and immensely strong.

*The Dutch Warmblood is
probably the most celebrated of
the warmblood sports horses,
excelling in competition year
after year.*

DUTCH WARMBLOOD
(Netherlands)

Origins The Dutch Warmblood is a
relatively new breed, its stud book having
been opened in the Netherlands in 1958.
It is enjoying huge success in
showjumping and dressage and is in
demand worldwide as a top-class
competition horse.

The Dutch Warmblood differs from
most European warmbloods in that it is
not based on any breed which existed in

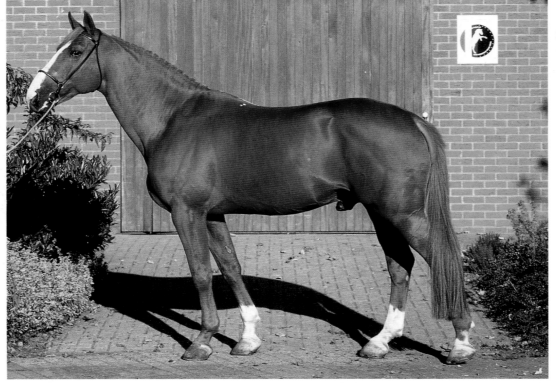

slightly different form in previous
centuries and which has been improved
upon. It contains breeds from all over
Europe. The bases of the Dutch
Warmblood are the Gelderlander and the
heavier Groningen, which have been in
existence in the Netherlands since the
Middle Ages. The breeds themselves
consist of many European strains, the
Gelderlander being a combination of
Andalusian, Norman, Oldenburg,
Hackney and Thoroughbred, to name but
a few. The Groningen was created from
Friesian and Oldenburg stock, which was
chosen to produce correct conformation,
good paces and a strong presence. A kind
and willing nature and a certain amount

of hardiness were also valuable traits.

Initially, the Dutch Warmblood was created by mating these two, with Thoroughbred added later to correct remaining conformation faults. The result was a little temperamental in character; to improve this, Hanoverian and Selle Français were added for level-headedness and acquiescence.

Appearance The Dutch Warmblood is lighter than many warmbloods. The head is attractive, with an intelligent, alert expression in the large, lively eyes and medium-sized pricked ears. The neck is well-set, long and muscular. The withers are prominent and the back is short and straight with powerful, slightly sloping quarters and a high-set tail. The shoulders are sloping and the legs are long and well-developed with strong, shapely hooves.

Characteristics The horse is renowned for its extravagant and elastic paces which make it such a competent performer at dressage and showjumping. It also has a sensible attitude to work with enough spark to perform the actions required of it. Its equable nature makes it amenable, a boon for the less experienced, and its flowing action makes it comfortable to ride.

Colours Most commonly bay, but chestnut, grey and back are also possible.

Height 16hh plus.

EAST BULGARIAN (Bulgaria)

Origins The East Bulgarian is unusual in that is contains no native Bulgarian foundation stock, unlike most European warmbloods and other performance horses which have combinations of native and Thoroughbred stock. It was the Bulgarians' intention to create a horse which had excellent conformation, stamina and endurance, and could be used as a riding and light draft horse as well as in competition and performance work.

The breed came into existence at the end of the 19th century when the Kaiuk and Vassil Kolarov studs began a breeding programme, using Thoroughbreds and Thoroughbred crosses from Britain as well as Arabs and Anglo-Arabs. The established breed was similar to a middleweight Thoroughbred, which was further improved with more Thoroughbred blood. Now that the breed is truly established, mating occurs largely within the breed.

The East Bulgarian is a fine horse and its quality is immediately apparent. Today, it is used for general riding and competition, either ridden or in harness.

Appearance The head is fine, proud and noble, with a straight nose tapering to a neat muzzle with large, flared nostrils. The ears are medium-length and alert, the eyes expressive and lively, and the neck long and well-set. The body is similar to the Thoroughbred's with sloping shoulders and a broad and deep chest and girth. It has well-developed hindquarters and loins, with well-muscled upper legs which are fine and long. The hooves are strong and well-shaped.

Characteristics The East Bulgarian is beautifully made – proud, poised and elegant. Its stride is long and supple with all the speed, stamina and endurance of the pure-bred Thoroughbred and Arab. Although spirited and keen, it is also good-natured and eager to work.

Colours Mostly commonly chestnut or black, but occasionally bay and brown and very rarely grey.

Height Around 15.2hh.

EAST FRIESIAN (Germany)

Origins For 300 years the East Friesian and the Oldenburg were regarded as the same breed, both having sprung from the same foundation stock. The two finally split with the division of Germany into East and West (the Oldenburg in the West) after the Second World War. Both the Oldenburg and the East Friesian are composed of Friesian, English half-bred, Oriental, Thoroughbred, Cleveland Bay and Yorkshire Coach Horse, after which the breeds began to differ.

The breeders of Eastern Europe favoured lighter horses that were more Oriental in appearance, so as well as adding horses from Poland and France, they also turned to Arabs. They consulted the Babolna Stud in Hungary, which is the oldest and most respected in Europe, from whence they took Arab stallions and in particular the famous stallion Gazal, which played an important part in the improvement of the breed. The East Friesian had by now changed so much that it bore little resemblance to its brother, the Oldenburg. In latter years, lighter Hanoverians have also been added to make the horse more suitable for performance and competition.

Appearance The East Friesian's head is fine and wedge-shaped and similar to that of the Arab; it has medium-length pointed ears, kind and intelligent eyes, and a straight nose. The neck is long and elegant, set on nicely sloping shoulders. The chest and girth are deep. The body is medium-length with strong loins and well-developed hindquarters. The legs are long and strong.

Characteristics The East Friesian is a quality sports horse with boundless energy, stamina and endurance. It has a spirited but kindly nature and is always eager to work. It requires the same care an any fine quality horse in the form of winter shelter and a regimen of feeding and exercise.

Colours Most solid colours and grey, but there can be white on the face and lower legs.

Height 15.2–16.1hh.

OPPOSITE
LEFT
Dutch Warmbloods are particularly good at dressage. Here is Ferro, ridden by Corby van Baalen of the Netherlands, executing a piaffe *at the 2000 Olympics.*

RIGHT
A Dutch Warmblood mare and foal at stud in the Netherlands.

The Eriskay is Britain's rarest breed and is the subject of a programme to preserve it and keep it pure. Small herds of Eriskays can still be seen on the small island between South Uist and Barra.

ERISKAY (U.K.)

Origins The history of the Eriskay is an ancient one, it being a true native breed with Celtic and Norse connections. The ponies once roamed all over the Western Isles of Scotland, where they were caught and used as work ponies to carry seaweed and peat in panniers laid across their backs, and also in harness. They were not only strong but also hardy, and were able to survive on the sparse vegetation that was the only food available.

The menfolk were fishermen and spent most of their time at sea, leaving the ponies mainly in the care of the women and children. By the 19th century, however, mechanization was causing a dramatic depletion in numbers with only

a few ponies remaining. By the 1970s only a handful were left living on the isle of Eriskay, situated between South Uist and Barra. This is how the pony got its name and where it remained undisturbed, with no other stock to dilute the bloodline, thus keeping the Eriskay pure. The breed is still counted a Category 1 pony on the rare breed list and is in fact still the rarest breed in Britain.

Today, with the introduction of breeding programmes, numbers are on the increase and Eriskays are proving popular for many children's riding activities, including pony club events, showjumping and eventing. They are also successful as driving ponies, with harnessed pairs excelling at high levels of competition.

Appearance The head is fairly plain and workmanlike, with bold eyes spaced well apart in a wide forehead. The ears are small and the nose straight with a tapering muzzle, and the expression is inquisitive. The neck is set high and proud with sloping shoulders and a deep chest. The body is short and strong with well-developed quarters and a low-set tail. The legs are fine, with a little feathering on the fetlocks, and small hard hooves. The coat is very dense, but not particularly long, and is waterproof to protect it from the harsh environment.

Characteristics The Eriskay makes an excellent family pony. It is good-natured, easy to handle, and needs little looking after; indeed, it will happily live out all year round. Eriskays thrive on human companionship and seem to like children in particular. Nevertheless, they are very strong and despite their small size will carry an adult with ease.

Colours Ponies are usually grey but foals are born black or bay and lighten as they mature. No other colours are possible.

Height 12–13.2hh.

Eriskays are always grey, but foals are often born dark and lighten as they mature.

EXMOOR (U.K.)

Origins The Exmoor is truly ancient, said to have existed before the Ice Age when similar ponies migrated south from Alaska, and where bones that match the modern pony have been found. Exmoor's isolated position, covering remote areas of the counties of Devon and Somerset, has ensured that very little cross-breeding has occurred, which has maintained the purity of the breed; indeed, the Exmoor pony is one of the purest breeds in the world, unlike its cousin, the Dartmoor, which is more accessible and has consequently gone through many changes.

Exmoors are truly wild ponies and still live up on the moors, though today they are closely monitored, being regarded as a rare breed with only 1,000 ponies worldwide. In the United Kingdom there are aproximately 300 breeding mares which produce around 130 foals a year. Half of these mares still live on Exmoor and to protect the purity of the breed each foal is inspected, numbered and branded on its flank, with the society's mark and herd number on the shoulder.

There are also various farms in the area which are involved with the breeding of Exmoors, with the result that its future is now looking much brighter. Nowadays Exmoors are also being bred in other parts of Britain, but all still use the moor ponies as their foundation stock to ensure the purity of the breed. Ponies which have been broken are used for children's riding events as well as for driving classes.

Appearance The head is large with a broad forehead and hooded eyes to protect the pony from the elements: this is known as 'toad-eyed'. The ears are thick and short and the nose straight. The neck is thick and well developed with a deep chest; the short, fine legs are nevertheless muscular and strong, with a little feathering around the fetlocks. The hooves are small and hard. The coat is dense with a thick, wiry mane and tail.

Characteristics Exmoors are extremely tough and can live out all year round. If they are to be domesticated, they must be caught and broken in while young. They are good-natured, willing and obedient and make good children's ponies.

Colours Bay, brown or dun with black points. There should be the distinctive mealy markings around the eyes, muzzle and flanks, but with no white whatsoever.

Height Mares should not exceed 12.2hh or stallions 12.3hh.

The ancient Exmoor breed is now rare, with only 1,000 ponies existing worldwide. There are still herds living wild up on the moors which are closely monitored to keep the breed pure and ensure its survival.

Falabellas are regarded as small horses rather than ponies. They make affectionate pets, even though they are too small and weak to ride, except by the smallest of children. However, they are capable of pulling very small carts.

FALABELLA (Argentina)

Origins The Falabella was created a century ago by the Falabella family at their ranch near Buenos Aires in Argentina. The breed was established by crossing small Thoroughbred and Arab stallions with Shetland Pony mares; then, using selective inbreeding, the Falabella became smaller and smaller to produce the breed as we know it today.

The Falabella is not a pony: it is a miniature horse with all the conformation and character of a horse. However, the conformation of some is not ideal due to too much inbreeding and they can consequently look rather odd; moreover, they are weak for their size and can only be ridden by the very smallest children. Today, breeders are attempting to rectify these faults and are generally trying to improve the breed.

Falabellas make ideal pets and are most affectionate, and because of their small size are even allowed into peoples' homes. They should receive the same level of care as a Thoroughbred.

Although they cannot be ridden, Falabellas are popular in specially allocated in-hand showing classes and are capable of pulling small carts.

Appearance A Fallabella should resemble a miniature Thoroughbred or Arab, if correctly bred, though some specimens show evidence of their Shetland ancestry. The head is refined and horse-like, with a straight nose and small, flared nostrils. The small ears are wide-apart, and the eyes kind. The body is medium-length with a slim frame and the legs are fine and resemble those of a Thoroughbred.

Characteristics This is a delightful breed and provides all the pleasures of a larger breed at a much reduced cost as far as land requirements are concerned. However, its constitution is less that robust and it requires the same care that one would give to any finely bred horse. It is amenable, docile and obedient.

Colours Falabellas come in all solid colours as well as grey and roan. Appaloosa markings are also common.

Height No taller than 30in (76cm).

The Fell looks remarkably similar to the Friesian, which was added to improve the breed, hence the predominantly black coat.

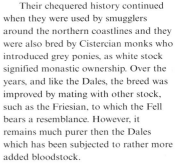

FELL (U.K.)

Origins The Fell is closely related to the Dales pony, though it originated on the western side of the Pennines. It is a descendant of the Celtic Pony which once roamed much of northern Europe, and which the Romans used as draft animals and in raids against the Picts. They were later used by reivers – cattle-raiders of the Scottish Border country – who required ponies with strength, stamina and sure-footedness.

Their chequered history continued when they were used by smugglers around the northern coastlines and they were also bred by Cistercian monks who introduced grey ponies, as white stock signified monastic ownership. Over the years, and like the Dales, the breed was improved by mating with other stock, such as the Friesian, to which the Fell bears a resemblance. However, it remains much purer then the Dales which has been subjected to rather more added bloodstock.

Like many native breeds, numbers declined during and after the two world wars, when farms switched to machinery and motorized transport as they became more readily available. However, the Fell remained popular as a riding and driving pony and its fortunes have happily been reversed. Today the Fell is an all-round family pony, strong enough to carry an adult and docile enough for children to ride. They make excellent trekking ponies and are therefore popular in the tourist industry. They are also used in harness and the occasional farmer still uses them to herd sheep.

Appearance The Fell bears a strong resemblance to the Friesian. The head is noble with a broad forehead and a straight or slightly dished, tapering nose with large flaring nostrils. The eyes are proud and intelligent and the ears small and neat. The head sits well on the neck, which is of medium length, strong but not overdeveloped. The shoulders are

well-muscled and sloping, ensuring a good smooth action. The body is sturdy with a strong back and deep chest. The legs are strong and muscular with fine feathering present on the backs of the legs; the hooves are well-shaped and are a characteristic blue colour. Mane and tail should not be trimmed but should be left to grow naturally.

Characteristics The Fell Pony has an excellent constitution and like most mountain and moorland ponies is hardy and able to live out all year round. It is easy-going and enjoys the company of humans beings; however, it is a free spirit and can be wilful at times. Fell Ponies are famous for their excellent paces, which make them comfortable to ride. They excel at endurance events and are fast into the bargain, which is an asset in harness.

Colours Pure black with no white markings is the most popular, but bay, grey and brown are also possible. A small amount of white is permissable in the form of a small star on the forehead or a little around the fetlocks.

Height Up to 14hh.

FJORD (Norway)

Origins It is likely that the Fjord is descended from the Przewalski or Asiatic Wild Horse, which in turn is descended from the horses of the Ice Age; it seems to have retained much of its ancestors' characteristics, for example, the pale coat, dorsal stripe down the back, and occasional zebra stripes on the legs, typical of the ancient breed. The primitive breed was improved over many hundreds of years by breeding with the Celtic Pony and Tarpan. The result has been used for thousands of years, and there is evidence that it was used in raids and battles, as evidenced by Viking artifacts. The Vikings had a particularly bloodthirsty approach to selection in which they allowed stallions to fight to the death, when the victor became the breeding stallion.

The breed still has its mane clipped in the fashion to be seen on Viking rune stones; the mane is unusual in that it is cream on the outer edges and black in the centre, being part of the dorsal stripe. The mane is therefore clipped so that the black part is prominent.

The Fjord has been used to improve many other northern European breeds, including Icelandic and Highland. Today it can be seen over most of Scandinavia, mainly used as children's riding ponies. It is sure-footed and excellent at trekking and long-distance endurance events. It is also popular in harness, where it has been successful in competition. Some are still used around the farm for light ploughing and as packhorses.

Appearance The head is attractive, being short and wide with short, neat ears, a slightly dished face and large nostrils. The eyes are large and kind. The neck is short and thick, accentuated by the clipped mane, a tradition which has survived since ancient times. The body is sturdy with sloping quarters and a low-set tail. The legs are strong with good bone and the feet are tough and hard.

Characteristics The Fjord's most striking features are its dorsal stripe and primitive appearance.

Colours Usually a pale gold or dun colour, with a black dorsal stripe running from the poll to the tail; this also runs through the centre of the mane, the outer sections of which are white. Some also have zebra stripes on the legs.

Height 13.2–14.2hh.

The Fjord is most likely the descendant of the Przewalski or Asiatic Wild Horse on account of the characteristic dorsal stripe running from poll to tail. The pony's mane is often clipped short to reveal the black stripe running down the centre, with white hairs at the outer edges.

*The Frederiksborg was bred
mainly for the cavalry and also as
a carriage horse, though today it
is used for general riding.
Frederiksborg stock was also used
to produce the excellent Danish
Warmblood.*

FREDERIKSBORG (Denmark)

Origins The Frederiksborg's history is
long, stretching back to the mid-1500s
when the Royal Frederiksborg Stud was
founded. The aim of the stud was to
breed a horse for the classical *haute école*
method of training which reached its
peak of popularity in the 19th century.

The breed is based on a small native
Danish breed and Jutland Draft mares
which were bred with Andalusian and
Neopolitan stallions. These were then
mixed with Turkish and Dutch breeds as
well as Thoroughbreds.

The Frederiksborg made its name as
a warhorse and also as a carriage horse.

However, because it was in such demand,
many were sold abroad which
dramatically depleted the stock; this was
further aggravated by the closure of the
stud in 1862. Some stock survived in the
hands of private breeders and the
Frederiksborg was then further improved
to bring it up to modern competition
horse standards by breeding it with
Oldenburg, Friesian, Arab and
Thoroughbred. Today it is mainly used as
a general riding horse and also in harness,
though it can still be seen around farms.
It is interesting to note that
Frederiksborg-Thoroughbred stock was
the basis of the much more popular
Danish Warmblood.

Appearance The Frederiksborg has all the
characteristics of a warmblood. The head
is fairly broad with a straight nose,
intelligent eyes, and alert medium-length
ears. The neck is thick but carried high
and proud. The body is of medium length
with a good strong shoulder and deep
chest. The legs are long and well-
developed.

Characteristics An excellent all-rounder,
possessing strength, stamina and an
equable disposition. The Frederiksborg is
particularly well known for its trot, which
is high-stepping and floating.

Colours Usually chestnut.

Height 15.1–16.1hh.

FRENCH ANGLO-ARAB (France)

Origins The Anglo-Arab derives its name from two of the world's greatest breeds, the Thoroughbred, which is of English (Anglo) origin and the Arab. The rule for Anglo-Arab breeding is very strict in the United Kingdom, and only these two breeds can be present. However, as this is not a standardized breed the resulting progeny can either resemble the Thoroughbred, the Arab or a little of both.

The French Anglo-Arab is different in that it is a composite breed, originated in the 1830s by a veterinary surgeon called Gayot. It was later developed with the bloodlines of two stallions, an Arab called Massoud and a Turk called Aslan, together with three Thoroughbred mares.

Today the breeding of a French Anglo-Arab consists of pure-bred Arab, Anglo-Arab and Thoroughbred. To register a French Anglo-Arab in the stud book the horse must have at least 25 per cent Arab and no other blood other then Arab and Thoroughbred going back six generations. The French Anglo-Arab excels in all disciplines, including racing and endurance.

Appearance This horse exudes quality. The head is small and fine with either a straight or sightly dished nose and a tapering muzzle with fine expressive nostrils. The eyes are kind and intelligent and the ears medium-length, well-shaped and alert. The head is carried high and sits well on a long shapely neck; the body is medium-length and sinewy with a deep girth and sloping shoulders. The legs are long, fine but strong.

Characteristics This horse combines the Arab's intelligence and beauty with the Thoroughbred's size and speed.

Colours Chestnut is the most common; however, all solid colours are acceptable with white allowed on the legs and face.

Height 15.2–16.3hh.

The French Anglo-Arab exudes quality and combines all the excellent traits of the Arab and Thoroughbred.

The French Trotter has all the fine characteristics of the Thoroughbred, with the noble head and beautiful conformation that exudes quality.

FRENCH TROTTER (France)

Origins The first trotting racetrack in France opened in 1839 at Cherbourg and since that date the sport has not looked back. The first races were a means of selecting suitable stallions and became quite an event. The most popular trotters at that time were Norman and Anglo-Norman breeds; later, these were crossed with Norfolk Roadsters from Britain and by the end of the 19th century the breed was further enhanced by infusions of British Hackney, Orlov Trotter from Russia, and Thoroughbred. These breeds did much to create a popular and much respected trotter and with the later addition of American Standardbred, which greatly improved it, the breed was considered complete.

In 1906 a stud book was created for French Trotters, though the breed itself wasn't recognized as such until 1922. To be acceptable for registration it was necessary that the horse be able to trot .62 mile (1 km) in 1 minute 42 seconds. This was later extended to include only horses whose parents had both been registered, thus ensuring the purity of the breed. Recently, however, further infusions of Standardbreds have been made to improve the breed and its paces; the result is a world-class trotting horse which even surpasses the Standardbred itself.

Today it is predominantly used for the sport for which it was bred, both under saddle and in harness; however, French Trotters also make good riding horses and even good jumpers. The horses which have been bred for riding have also been used to sire competition horses, particularly the Selle Français.

Appearance In appearance, the French Trotter's Thoroughbred ancestry is much in evidence, with a noble head, broad forehead, medium-sized far-apart ears, and kind, intelligent eyes. The nostrils are large and flaring. The neck is long and well-developed with a straight shoulder, deep chest, and well-formed, powerful quarters. The legs are muscular with plenty of bone and well-shaped hooves.

Characteristics The French Trotter has all the fine characteristics of the Thoroughbred. It has a good turn of speed, plenty of stamina, and a kind and even temperament, though it is not without spirit. The harness horses are usually a little smaller and lighter then the ridden types.

Colours Like the Thoroughbred, all solid colours are available, with the occasional roan. Greys are quite rare.

Height Approximately 16.2hh.

The Friesian is an ancient breed, dating back 3,000 years, which has been gradually improved to produce a stunning horse capable of performing classical dressage.

FRIESIAN (Netherlands)

Origins The Friesian is the Netherland's only surviving indigenous breed and is descended from a native breed which roamed Friesland, the western part of the ancient region of Frisia, 3,000 years ago, and where the remains of a similar coldblooded horse have been found. As riding horses, the Friesian's history is an ancient one, with evidence that they were used by Roman soldiers when they were building Hadrian's Wall around 150 AD; this is also supported by the fact that Fell and Dales breeds native to the Pennines are also descended from Friesians. Friesian blood is also present in the Orlov Trotter as well as most American trotters.

Over the years the original breed, which was rather heavy and plain, was infused with Oriental and Andalusian blood which improved it to such as extent that during the 17th century Friesians were seen along with Spanish horses performing *haute école* and were in demand as elegant carriage horses. During the 19th century, however, the Friesian became a rarity, the breed almost exclusively restricted to Friesland, where it was used as a general riding horse and trotter. By the end of the First World War the Friesian was in dire peril of extinction, with only three stallions and a few mares still in existence. Thankfully, with careful breeding and an infusion of Oldenburg blood, the Friesian is once again flourishing; today, it is in evidence all over the world, much admired for its noble presence and expressive trot, which is particularly striking in harness. It is still used in *haute école* disciplines.

Appearance The head is proud and of medium size with small, alert ears which point sightly inwards. The eyes are kindly and expressive. The head-carriage is high and elegant, and the neck of medium length with a high crest. The withers are well-developed, tapering into the back muscles, and the shoulders sloping. The back is of medium length,

RIGHT
Traditionally the Friesian is quite a small horse, usually standing at about 15.2hh; however, with its popularity as a dressage horse increasing, it is now being bred larger, and can attain 16hh.

OPPOSITE
Harrods, the famous London Knightsbridge store, runs a coach and four drawn by four Friesians; one can only admire their choice.

strong and straight, leading to well-developed loins and quarters. The legs are clean and strong with slight feathering, and the mane and tail long and luxuriant; when showing, mane and tail should be left untrimmed.

Characteristics The Friesian has a proud bearing but is nevertheless gentle and amenable if rather energetic.

Colours Black, with only the smallest of white stars permitted on the face.

Height 15–15.2hh. However, some Friesians have been bred larger, some over 16hh.

OPPOSITE
The Furioso is a fine quality horse with many of the attributes of its Thoroughbred forebears.

BELOW
A herd of Furioso horses at stud in Hungary.

FURIOSO (Hungary)

Origins As a breed, the Furioso has only existed for about 150 years. It was developed by Hungary's famous Mezöhegyes Stud, which was founded by the Habsburg Emperor Joseph II in 1785, and where the Nonius was also bred.

In 1840 the stud imported an English Thoroughbred called Furioso, and in 1843 another, North Star, which was a Norfolk Roadster. They mated these two with Nonius and Arab mares, the result being two very distinctive breeds, the Furioso and the North Star. By 1885, however, the two breeds had merged to such an extent that only one breed remained, with Furioso traits predominating.

Today the Furioso is used as an all-round riding horse and is an excellent jumper. It has plenty of stamina which also makes it a competent steeplechaser.

Appearance The Furioso is a quality horse possessing all the attributes of its Thoroughbred forebears. The head is fine with a straight nose leading to a squarish muzzle. The ears are medium-length and shapely. The eyes are inquisitive and bold. The neck is long and elegant with fine sloping shoulders; the girth is deep and the legs are long and strong. The quarters are well-developed with a high tail-carriage.

Characteristics Most noticeable is the action of the high-stepping knee, which is inherited from the Nonius. The Furioso makes an elegant carriage horse as well as a riding horse; it has the amenability of the Thoroughbred, together with its spirit and courage.

Colours Usually brown, black or bay with only minimal white markings.

Height Approximately 16.1hh.

The Galiceño, of Iberian origin, is strong and hardy. It is able to carry a man all day over large distances without tiring. It has an unusual gait, known as a 'running walk'.

GALICEÑO (Mexico)

Origins The first horses to arrive in the Americas came with the Spanish *conquistadores* in the 16th century. Many either escaped or became the property of the native population, eventually becoming almost indigenous to the continent. The Galiceño is descended from the Garrano mountain ponies of Portugal and Galician horses from north-west Spain, said to have come to Mexico with Cortez. Though used by the Mexicans, they were also allowed to roam in a semi-wild state, where the breed developed through natural selection.

The Galiceño has much Arab blood in its make-up and has inherited many of the characteristics of the breed, in looks as well as stamina. Galiceños are popular in North America as children's riding

ponies and do well in children's competitions. In Latin America they are still used for work on ranches, where strength and stamina is important; in fact, the Galiceño is capable of carrying a man over rugged terrain all day without tiring. It has an ususual gait, known as a 'running walk', which enables it to cover ground quickly, efficiently and smoothly, making it ideal for riding and in harness.

Appearance The Galiceño is small and compact, its Arab ancestry apparent in the head, which is fine and narrow, with thin pointed ears, a small muzzle, and large, flaring nostrils. The eyes are large and intelligent. The neck is long and well-developed with a long, full mane. The withers are prominent with a good sloping shoulder and a deep girth. The body is quite stocky, but the back is unusually narrow. Unlike the Arab, the tail is set low and, like the mane, is allowed to grow long. The legs are fine but very strong, with well-shaped hard hooves.

Characteristics The Galiceño is well-known for its toughness, stamina and ability to travel long distances without tiring. It is comfortable to ride because of its long, smooth gait. Its intelligence and quick reactions make it an excellent competitor.

Colours All the usual solid colours, including palomino, dun and grey. Part-coloureds or albinos are not permitted.

Height 12–13.2hh.

GARRANO (Portugal)

Origins The Garrano, the 'little horse' of Portugal, is an ancient breed, its origins dating to prehistoric times. It comes from the Minho and Tras-os-Montes areas of northern Portugal, and was probably bred with Oriental horses, such as Barbs and Arabs, which were brought to the Iberian peninsular during the Moorish occupation of the 8th century. These greatly improved conformation and the Garrano's ability to work and be ridden. The pony is used for a wide range of tasks, for haulage, in the army, for general agriculture, forestry and trekking, and as a packhorse.

Appearance This lightweight pony owes much of its appearance to its Oriental ancestors, though the conformation of the primitive pony is still in evidence. The head is small and fine with a slightly dished face. The back is short and the hindquarters underdeveloped. The shoulders are rather straight, but the legs are fine and well- muscled, ending in strong, neat hooves. There is a shaggy mane and tail.

Characteristics Tough and hardy, Garranos require little care. They have great strength and stamina with plenty of energy and are good-natured and amenable.

Colours Bay or dark chestnut.

Height Up to 14hh.

The Garrano is Portugal's oldest breed dating back to prehistoric times. It is used for general riding and farm work.

This team of Gelderlanders is taking part in a coaching marathon.

GELDERLANDER (Netherlands)

Origins The Gelderlander, or Gelderland, is a warmblood which originated in the province of Gelder in the Netherlands. The breed was created by Dutch farmers who required an all-round workhorse for their own use, as well as an animal they could sell on as a good-quality riding and carriage horse. In fact, the Gelderlander has been used by many royal houses throughout Europe to draw carriages on state ceremonial occasions.

Native heavy mares from the Gelder were bred with Andalusian, Neopolitan, Norman, Norfolk Roadster and Holstein stallions to produce a well-built horse. In the 19th century the breed was further improved when East Friesian, Oldenburg, Hackney and Thoroughbred were introduced. Today the horse is an excellent

all-rounder, with a talent for showjumping; its high-stepping action is presumably inherited from its trotter forebears. The Gelderland appears in the 0

Appearance A plain but well-porportioned head with a straight or slightly Roman nose. The ears are fine, shapely and expressive, and the eyes are kind. The neck is fairly long and muscular with a slightly pronounced crest. The withers are prominent and the back is long and straight with a short croup and high-set tail. The girth is deep with a long sloping shoulder, strong, muscular legs and large, tough hooves.

Characteristics The Gelderlander has a charming, easy-going disposition and is a willing worker. It is a good all-rounder, equally at home jumping or as part of a team pulling a carriage.

Colours Most common is chestnut; however, black, bay or grey is often seen. There is a good deal of white on the head and legs.

Height 15.2–16.2hh.

The Gelderlander was bred as an all-rounder, to work on farms and as a carriage horse. Today the breed has lost much of its popularity to the Dutch Warmblood; fortunately, there are still breeders around who ensure that the breed continues.

GIDRÁN (Hungary)

Origins The Gidrán was developed at the the Mezőhegyes State Stud, which was founded by the Habsburg Emperor Joseph II in 1785. This important breeding establishment in Hungary was also responsible for the development of the Nonius in the early 19th century and the Furioso from 1885. But in about 1816 it had developed another breed, the Hungarian Anglo-Arab or Gidrán. The Hungarians required a cavalry horse with the stamina, strength and courage of the Arab though rather larger.

The creation of the Gidrán was complicated as there is far more varied blood in its composition than the traditional Anglo-Arab with its varying amounts of Arab and Thoroughbred. The stud imported an Arab stallion said to have originated from the Siglavy (Seglawi) strain which was called Gidrán Senior. He was mated with various breeds of mare, such as Arab, Turkish and Spanish-Naples. From these unions seven colts were born which became Mezőhegyes's premier stallions.

In 1820 the Spanish-Naples mare, Arrogante, gave birth to a colt which was named Gidrán II and became the foundation stallion of the breed; today all Gidráns can be traced to this one stallion. The breed was developed using Arab, Transylvanian, Spanish, Nonius and native Hungarian and by 1893 Thoroughbred blood was added to further improve the breed as well as Shagya Arabs Gazal III and Siglavy II,

which added more Arab attributes to the breed. The end result was a horse that was very fast, was a good jumper, and had excellent stamina.

Nowadays the Gidrán is used for competition riding and driving, and its excellent breeding makes it suitable for improving other breeds. However, it is now extremely rare with less than 200 Gidráns left in the world, placing it in very real danger of extinction.

Appearance The Gidrán has all the excellent qualities of the Anglo-Arab. It has a fine intelligent head with a straight or slightly dished face, fine alert ears, and an inquisitive look. The neck is long and beautifully shaped. The body is strong, sturdy and muscular with long, straight legs. The quarters are powerful, as with all horses capable of great speed.

Characteristics All the qualities of its noble ancestry are immediately apparent, as well as an impression of strength, power and vigour. The Gidrán has great courage and will power which, coupled with agility and intelligence, makes it an excellent competition horse.

Colours Usually chestnut.

Height 16.1–17hh.

The superb Gidrán has all the attributes of the Anglo-Arab, with enormous presence and elegance. This horse is shown at the famous Mezőhegyes State Stud in Hungary, where the breed was developed.

GOTLAND (Sweden)

Origins The Gotland, or Skogruss, the 'little horse of the woods', is an ancient breed, said to be directly descended from the wild Tarpan, and has lived on the island of Gotland in the Baltic Sea for 4–5,000 years, and probably much longer. Because of its isolation, and the commitment of the local inhabitants to keep the breed intact, there has been little or no cross-breeding, and the Gotland has remained largely true to type. The Russ, as some of the locals call it, still lives on the wooded wild moors of the island to this day.

Gotlands were also kept on the mainland, where in 1886 the breed was improved with a Syrian stallion; consequently, their blood is not as pure as their island cousins. For centuries they worked on local farms and also became popular in other European countries, where they were exported for use in light haulage and also in mines. Like many native breeds, numbers declined rapidly with the onset of mechanization in the early 1900s. In the 1950s, however, the continuity of the breed was assured when the Swedish Pony Association was formed, set up by the government to protect this unusual and attractive breed, which was further improved with two Welsh stallions. Today the breed is flourishing and is used in trotting races and as a general children's riding pony, at which it excels.

Wild Gotlands still roam the moors and forest of Lojsta under the watchful eye of local farmers, breeders and a caretaker who visits them daily.

Appearance The head is medium-sized with a broad forehead, small pricked ears, a straight nose, and large, clever eyes. The neck is medium-length and well-developed with prominent withers; the back is straight with sloping hindquarters. The full tail is low-set, and the legs are fine but very strong, with small, well-shaped hard feet.

Characteristics The Gotland is robust and long-lived, with many surviving into their 30s; they are energetic, intelligent and friendly, and make excellent first mounts.

Colours Usually black, bay, dun or chestnut. Some have a dorsal stripe, indicative of their primitive origins.

Height 11.2–13.2hh.

GRONINGEN (Netherlands)

Origins The Groningen's bloodline has been of vital importance in the breeding of modern warmbloods in the Netherlands, the prototype being an old Dutch breed which originated in the north-eastern province of Groningen; it was bred for use as a heavyweight riding horse as well as for general farm use.

The breed was established by crossing

East Friesian and German Oldenburg with the native stock of the area. A heavier horse was needed to farm the heavy soil of the region, so Suffolk Punch and Norfolk Roadster stallions were also introduced to make the Groningen a more substantial animal than its near neighbour, the Gelderlander, which came from a region of lighter soil. Both horses are the foundation of the now internationally famous Dutch Warmblood, and the powerful well-developed quarters of the Groningen can clearly be seen in the new breed, which is an excellent showjumper. Nowadays, however, the Groningen, along with the Gelderlander, is a rare breed.

Appearance The Groningen has a long, rather plain head with long ears and a docile expression. The neck is medium-length and well-developed, with prominent withers; the back is long, the croup flattened, and the tail high-set, with very muscular quarters. The girth has plenty of depth and the legs are short and strong with plenty of bone. The hooves are well-shaped.

Characteristics Good-natured and amenable, the Groningen has great strength, stamina and power – attributes which it has passed to the Dutch Warmblood.

Colours Mainly black, brown and bay.

Height 15.3–16.1hh.

The Hackney was bred in the 18th century as a carriage and riding horse. It is distinguished by its high-stepping gait, displayed to the full in the showring.

OPPOSITE
Hackneys come in both horse and pony sizes. While moving at a substantial speed, this Hackney pony is showing off its amazing high-stepping paces.

HACKNEY (U.K.)

Origins The Hackney breed first emerged in the 18th and 19th centuries in Norfolk and Yorkshire, where it was used by farmers who prized it for its stamina. A little later it came to be used for sport, particularly for trotting both in harness and under saddle, and was capable of amazing speeds: one mare, Nonpareil, was said to have trotted 100 miles (160km) in just under ten hours. But it was as a high-stepping carriage horse that it was principally known, making it indispensable until the 1920s when it was gradually replaced by the motor car.

The Hackney owes its trotting ability to its breeding: its probable foundation stock consisted of Norfolk and Yorkshire trotter which was bred with Arab and Thoroughbred blood for heightened performance. Hackney ponies are also

derived from English trotters with additions of Fell and Welsh Pony. Both Hackney horses and ponies have a registered stud book which was established in 1883.

Today the Hackney is underutilized, usually seen in the showring, where its extravagant paces are demonstrated, harnessed to smart renovated carriages. But they are beginning to be seen in driving competitions and even dressage, showjumping and eventing. They are also mated with other breeds to enhance the modern sports horse.

Appearance The head-carriage is high and proud, with fine, alert ears and intelligent eyes. The nose is straight or slightly Roman. The neck is long and well-developed, with a high crest leading to good sloping shoulders and a short-coupled body. The quarters are strong and powerful and the legs sturdy with plenty of bone.

Characteristics The Hackney is a lively, fiery animal and most definitely not for the novice. It has enormous stamina and the ability to trot for many miles without tiring. It is best known for its extravagant action, where the front legs are brought up very high before being flung straight out from the shoulder.

Colours Mostly bay, brown and black; less commonly chestnut and roan. There is usually white on the head and face.

Height Pony 12–14hh: horse 14.2–15.2hh.

HAFLINGER (Austria)

Origins The history of the Haflinger is obscure and there are various opinions as to its true origins. It is thought to be from the South Tyrol on the Austrian side of the border with Italy, though borders have changed many times throughout history, making the exact location impossible to pinpoint. However, the Haflinger is not unlike the slightly larger Avelignese from the Italian side.

The Haflinger may have been the result of native stock breeding with Oriental horses which were left behind when the Ostrogoths were driven north by the Byzantine forces in the 6th century. Another story is that King Louis IV of Germany gave a Burgundian stallion to his son as a wedding gift, which was mated with local mares of Oriental origin to produce the Haflinger breed; either way there is little doubt that Oriental blood is present.

But it is a definite fact that the modern Haflinger breed was improved in 1868 when the Arab stallion El Bedavi XXII was imported to the region and bred with Haflinger mares; today, all Haflingers are related to this one stallion.

The Arab blood can clearly be seen in the fine head which is in sharp contrast to the stocky body. Nowadays, the Haflinger is still to be found in Austria, where it is closely monitored in government-organized breeding programmes as well as by private individuals. The breed is also popular the world over, particularly in Europe, where it is used in the forests

RIGHT
A Haflinger foal.

BELOW
The Haflinger's Arab breeding is noticeable in the head, though not the body, which is rather stocky.

and farms of the Tyrol. It is useful in harness, and as a children's riding pony and family pet.

Appearance The Haflinger has a noble Arab head with a slightly dished nose, large, attentive eyes, small alert ears and neat nostrils and muzzle. The neck is well- proportioned with fine sloping shoulders, good withers and a deep girth. The body is broad and strong with muscular quarters and a high-set tail. The legs are of medium length with very strong, tough hooves.

Characteristics The Haflinger is a sociable animal and enjoys the company

of people. It is intelligent, trustworthy and docile, making it an excellent work pony as well as children's pet. Haflingers are hardy and require only moderate feeding; however, they do require shelter from cold winds and wet weather. Their most striking feature is their flaxen mane and tail.

Colours Various shades of chestnut, liver or red, sometimes with a little dappling over paler areas. White patches are undesirable. The distinctive flaxen mane and tail are usually left long.

Height Up to 14hh.

HANOVERIAN (Germany)

Origins The Hanoverian has a long history, the earliest reference to it being in the 8th century when it was used at the Battle of Poitiers, in which Charles Martel stemmed the advance of the Saracens. These were heavy warhorses, probably a mixture of native, Spanish and Oriental influences.

The horses owe their evolution to warfare, and by the Middle Ages developed to be large, cob-like and capable of carrying a knight together with his heavy armour. The type was favoured for many centuries, but changes in warfare techniques meant that a lighter horse was eventually required. At this time the Hanoverian was still a heavy breed, even though it was taller and more agile than the cob type; by the 17th century there were three distinctive types of horse bred

for military purposes: the Hanoverian, Mecklenburg and Danish.

But it was in the 18th century that the Hanoverian truly came into its own, when a member of the House of Hanover in the person of George I ascended the British throne in 1714, but spent much of his reign in Hanover; for the next 100 years or so the Hanoverian was nurtured and improved. English Thoroughbred stallions were bred with Hanoverian mares, and Cleveland Bay was also added to produce a horse that was still quite heavy and which was used for farm and coach work.

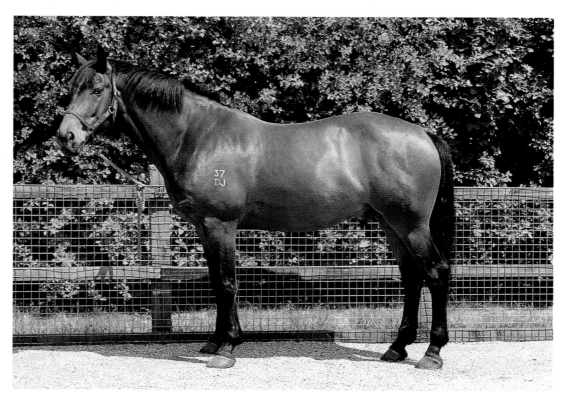

There are several lines of Hanoverian: this one is of a slightly chunkier type than some of the others.

HANOVERIAN

RIGHT

The Hanoverian was once a highly-revered warhorse, when it was a lot heavier in stature. Nowadays, because of Thoroughbred influence, it is much more elegant and suitable for competing in dressage, showjumping and eventing.

OPPOSITE

For Pleasure, *ridden by Marcus Ehning of Germany in the 2000 Olympics.*

It was George II who established the state stud at Celle in 1735, where horses for agriculture, riding and driving were bred. Here the Hanoverian breed was improved still further with the addition of Thoroughbred and Trakehner blood; the

Hanoverian breed registry was founded in 1888. The end result was a horse which is similar to the fabulous competition horse of today – probably

the best known of all warmbloods – which excels the world over in top dressage and showjumping. Nowadays, the Society of Breeders of the Hanoverian Warmblood Horse is responsible for the purity of the breed. Approximately 150–160, most of them stallions, are kept by the state and are based at Celle, where they are required to undergo tests for soundness, conformation and character for several months before they are allowed to mate.

The Hanoverian has played a large part in the improvement and formation of other warmblood breeds, such as the Westphalian, Mecklenburg and Brandenburg. Hanoverians now come in

two types: the heavier ones are used for showjumping, while the lighter ones, which have more Thoroughbred blood, are used for dressage.

Appearance The Hanoverian is near-perfect in conformation and its Thoroughbred characteristics are immediately discernible. The head is of medium size with a straight nose and keen, alert eyes and pricked ears. The neck has a graceful arch and is long and muscular, while the chest is well-developed with a deep girth and sloping shoulder. The back is of medium length with muscular loins and powerful quarters. The legs are strong with large joints and the hooves are well-shaped.

Characteristics The most important feature of the Hanoverian and one of the important tests that stallions have to undergo at Celle is one of character: only horses with an even temperament and a willing nature are allowed to breed. Hanoverians are noble and proud with an excellent free-flowing action which allows them to excel at advanced dressage.

Colours All solid colours, often with white on the face and legs.

Height 15.2–17hh.

OPPOSITE
The Hanoverian's Thoroughbred breeding is clearly evident in its fine features and noble countenance.

LEFT
Gigolo, *ridden by Isabel Werth of Germany, executing a flying change at the 2000 Oympics.*

HIGHLAND (U.K.)

Origins Like all Scottish native breeds, the Highland has an ancient history, as the often-present distinctive dorsal stripe indicates. The foundation breed is Celtic Pony, mixed over the centuries with Galloway, which is now sadly extinct, plus various European breeds such as Percheron, Spanish, Barb and Clydesdale. In the 19th century Arab was also added to bring the pony up to today's exacting standard.

The pony is not only native to the Highlands, there is also a smaller variety which inhabits most of the Western Isles. It has always lived and worked with the Scottish crofters and was used in farming, forestry, haulage and general riding where its equable temperament and sure-footedness were valuable assets. It was also taken to war, used in both the Boer and First World Wars.

Even though there has been a stud book for the Highland since the 1880s, there is no set breed standard; consequently, there is quite a diversity of types and bloodlines. However, white marks are frowned upon and stallions with anything other than small stars on their foreheads cannot be registered. The Highland has proved equally popular in other countries, and there are studs in Europe, Australia, the United States and Canada.

By the mid-1950s the Highland achieved yet more popularity with the advent of pony trekking, where once again its temperament, sturdiness and agility make it suitable for both adults and children. In fact, the pony can carry up to 210lb (95kg) with ease. Today the Highland is used in a number of children's events, including jumping, cross-country and pony club games, as well as in long-distance endurance events, showing and driving.

Appearance The Highland is a stocky, well-built pony. It has a small pretty head with a straight nose, small, often pricked ears, and large kind eyes. It has a strong body with a fairly long, well-developed neck, a neat shoulder, deep girth, and a well-muscled back. The legs are well-boned and sturdy, with hard well-shaped hooves and feathering around the fetlocks. The mane and tail are thick and silky and are left long.

Characteristics Friendly, with an even temperament and a willingness to work. Highlands make excellent children's ponies, are hardy, require a little extra feeding, and will live out in all weathers. Their agility, intelligence and endurance makes them ideal for all pony events.

Colours All solid colours including grey and a variety of shades of fox, cream, gold, yellow and mouse.

Height Up to 14.2hh.

courage, stamina, and ability. It also earned favour as a coach horse. After the Reformation, the monastery land was returned to the landowners who continued the horse-breeding tradition.

By 1686 the Holstein was so respected that strict guidelines were introduced to protect and improve the breed which had by now become popular throughout Europe. By the 18th century the Holstein's reputation was so great that vast numbers of horses were exported. Unfortunately, not all horses were bred to the exacting standards which had once prevailed and the breed began to deteriorate.

By the 19th century the decline was halted, and measures were taken to save and improve the breed. As the demand for warhorses grew less, the Holstein was needed as a quality carriage horse; for this purpose, Yorkshire Coach Horses and Cleveland Bay stallions were mated with Holstein mares, which was a great success, and the breed received a new lease of life.

After the Second World War, Thoroughbred was also added to refine the breed, which also improved the Holstein's jumping ability and general character. Today, it is a supreme sports horse which excels at showjumping, dressage and eventing. It has also been bred to good effect with other warmblood breeds, most effectively with the Hanoverian.

Appearance The Holstein is quite different

RIGHT and OPPOSITE
The Holstein is greatly respected as a competition horse, excelling at dressage, showjumping and eventing.

HOLSTEIN (Germany)

Origins The Holstein is probably descended from a native breed called the Marsh Horse, which once roamed the wetlands of the Elbe estuary in what is now called Schleswig-Holstein. The breed Holstein dates back to the 13th century when Gerhard I, Count of Holstein and Storman, allowed the monks of the monastery at Uetersen grazing rights for the quality horses they bred. These were native stock mixed with Andalusian, Neopolitan and Oriental blood to produce a heavy, useful horse which was valued by farmers for its strength and reliability and as a military horse for its from other warmbloods in that it has a large, rangy build with a huge stride. The head is long and straight with large, flaring nostrils. The ears are expressive and the eyes are large and gentle. The long neck is elegant and well-developed, with high withers; the back is long and straight. The shoulders are shapely and sloping, contributing to the huge stride. The chest is broad and the girth is deep, while the quarters are slightly sloping, muscular and powerful. The legs are long and muscular.

Characteristics The Holstein is a beautiful, well-balanced horse with an amazing ground-covering, elastic stride. The overall effect is of a horse that is elegant and which carries itself lightly. It is good-natured, obedient and eager to work. Its large size and scope means that it is much in demand as a top-flight competition horse.

Colours Most commonly bay, though all solid colours, together with grey, are permitted.

Height 16–17hh.

HUÇAL (Poland)

Origins Poland's Huçal or Huzal is a direct decendant of the now-extinct Tarpan which once ran wild in Eastern Europe. It is also closely related to the Konik, which shares similar breeding. However, the Huçal not only has native pony blood, it also has large amounts of

BELOW RIGHT
Icelandics are ideal for children,
being hardy, agile and with plenty
of stamina.

OPPOSITE
The Icelandic evolved from ponies
brought to the island by Celts and
Vikings in the 9th century. They
are referred to as horses as there
is no word for pony in the
Icelandic language.

Arab in its ancestry, when in the 19th century it was purposely bred for use in harness as well as a general farm pony. This Arab blood, however, means that most of its primitive origins have become masked; however, throwbacks appear from time to time which betray its Tarpan ancestry.

Because it originated in the Carpathian mountains of southern Poland, it is often referred to as the Carpathian. It is still bred today at a stud near Gorlice, where its role has changed very little. However, it does make a good children's pony.

Apearance A strong head with great character indicating its Oriental origins. The neck is of medium length and quite thick but with a good carriage. The body is stout and sturdy with medium-length legs with good bone and very tough hooves.

Characteristics The Huçal is bold, tough and courageous. It has a kind and willing disposition and its good balance and compact body make it ideal for work over mountainous terrain. It can live in the harshest conditions and manages to survive on very little food.

Colours Mostly bay with a dark stripe on the back. Can also be dun, chestnut, black or dapple.

Height 12–13hh.

ICELANDIC (Iceland)

Origins Iceland does not have its own indigenous breed of horse. The Icelandic is derived from the Fjord and Døle horses of Norway, and the Celtics, Shetlands, Highlands and Connemaras of the British Isles, which were brought to Iceland by Celts and Vikings in the 9th century. Because of the limited space on board their ships, the cargo would have consisted of only the best specimens; once settled, the invaders allowed their horses to mate freely

together to produce the Icelandic breed as we know it today. This resulted in a hardy animal which lived in a semi-wild condition and was able to survive Arctic winters. It was mainly used for farming and for riding over icy terrain.

It is interesting to note that in 982, the importation of horses was banned to prevent the spread of disease, as a result of which the Icelandic was allowed to interbreed; however, later selective breeding means that conformation and health faults have been all but eradicated.

Historically, the Icelanders have been protective of their breed, wishing to preserve it in the country where it evolved. Nowadays, however, they are exported to other countries where they are popular as children's riding ponies as well as for trekking. Even though the Icelandic is a pony in stature, it is always referred to as a horse because there is no word for pony in the Icelandic language.

Appearance The Icelandic is well-constructed. The head is of medium length, having a typical pony character with small pricked ears and soft, expressive eyes. The neck is well-set, and the chest is broad with a deep girth. The body and legs are stocky and strong and the feet are extremely hard.

Characteristics The Icelandic is ideal for children, being tough and hardy and happy to live out all year round. The pony has two extra gaits: the *tolt*, which is a running walk with four beats, and is as fast as a canter and very comfortable; and the flying pace, which makes great demands on horse and rider and which has two beats and is used for racing. The pony can reach speeds of up to 30mph (48km/h) and is impressive to watch. However, it is late to mature and shouldn't be backed until the age of 4.

Icelandics live to a ripe old age, often working up until they are 30; in fact, an Icelandic in Britain is known to have died aged 42.

Colours Icelandics come in all solid colours as well as skewbald, palomino, dun and grey. One colour, silver dapple, is much prized, where the body is a rich brown and the mane and tail appear almost silver by contrast. In winter the coat is very thick with three distinct layers.

Height 12–13.2hh, and very occasionally 14.2hh.

The Irish Draft was bred as an all-rounder, equally capable of work around the farm as a day out hunting over difficult terrain.

OPPOSITE
Irish Drafts have Thoroughbred in their make-up, which is why they make such excellent showjumpers.

IRISH DRAFT (Ireland)

Origins The history of the Irish Draft can be traced back to the Celts who invaded Ireland and brought many breeds with them, most notably Oriental and Spanish horses which they mated with their Celtic Ponies. Later, in the Middle Ages, Ireland was settled by the Norman-English and their much larger, heavier horses would have been of European origin. These were bred with the Irish horse to produce a more substantial animal which was of use to farmers, being capable of ploughing, hauling, general riding, as well as hunting over Ireland's often difficult terrain.

By the 18th century the Irish Draft was improved with additions of Thoroughbred and Arab blood and possibly also Barb and Turkmene. The result is a horse of excellent conformation, still capable of heavy work, but one which excels as a riding horse. It had all the docility and common sense of a heavier, coldblooded breed, but with the sparkle and verve of a hotblooded Arab or Thoroughbred.

During the Potato Famine of 1845–46 the Irish Draft's numbers diminished; Ireland's economy was in a state of turmoil and horse breeding ceased. But by the end of the century the breed had picked up, along with a change of attitude, when it was decided to introduce heavier stock, such as Clydesdale and Shire, to make it a much bigger, heavier draft horse. In 1917 a stud book was opened, but by the end of the First World War the breed was once again in danger, as mechanized transport began to dominate farming and haulage. By now, the Irish Draft was predominantly a riding horse, particularly a hunter.

By the early 20th century, however, more Thoroughbred blood was introduced to produce the horse we know today. The breed is still predominantly a hunter, but it has been mixed with other breeds, particularly the Thoroughbred, to make it a superb competition horse which has inherited the Irish Draft's love of jumping, excelling at both cross-country and eventing. A little of the Irish Draft is also present in some steeplechasers.

Appearance The head is neat, with a straight nose, medium-length ears, and a noble mien. The neck is shortish and very strong with slightly pronounced withers and a long sloping shoulder. The chest is broad and the girth is deep. The back is medium-length and well-muscled, with strong loins and sloping, powerful quarters. The legs are sturdy and muscular with good bone, and the hooves are large and round.

Characteristics The Irish Draft has all the substance of a medium-weight draft horse, but its hotblood ancestry has also given it its refined appearance, with no excess hair on the legs as in most heavier breeds. It has great stamina, agility and courage, and is generally good-natured and willing. Irish Drafts make excellent hunters: they will happily gallop over the roughest ground and jump almost anything in sight, while using intelligence and common sense.

Colours Bay, brown, chestnut and grey.

Height 15–17hh.

The Italian Heavy Draft encompasses a variety of other breeds to make it a substantial though refined heavy horse.

ITALIAN HEAVY DRAFT (Italy)

Origins The breed was first established in 1860 at the state stud at Ferrara by breeding native stock, Lombardy stallions from the Po delta, with local mares. Arab, Hackney and Thoroughbred were also introduced to create a fairly lightweight horse which was used for light draft work.

By the 1900s, however, it was obvious that an animal with much greater strength and size was required, so existing mares were bred with Brabant, Boulonnais, Ardennais and Percheron. The result, however, was too large and cumbersome and did not appeal to Italian sensibilities, so the lighter Postier Breton was added to produce a horse that was heavyweight, but not too large, and with plenty of agility and energy.

Appearance The head is rather small and fine for a heavy breed, with a broad forehead, straight nose, neat muzzle and large nostrils. The ears are small and pricked and the eyes intelligent and eager. The neck is well-set, short and very well-developed. The large shoulders and chest are muscular and broad with a deep, short body and large muscular hindquarters and loins. The legs are shortish and sturdy, with plenty of bone and a little feathering around the fetlocks.

Characteristics Some Italian Heavy Drafts are lively and temperamental while others are quiet and docile. However, all are friendly and good-natured.

Colours Chestnut, some with a flaxen mane and tail. Also bay and red roan.

Height 14.2–16hh.

The Jutland was orginally bred as a warhorse, but was refined by mating with other breeds, most significantly the Suffolk Punch.

JUTLAND HEAVY DRAFT
(Denmark)

Origins The Jutland has an ancient and colourful history. It is descended from the coldblooded prehistoric Forest Horse, which much later mated with other indigenous stock to produce a heavy horse that was the favoured mount of armoured knights of the Middle Ages. The breed was further defined when Cleveland Bay and Yorkshire Coach Horse were added to give the horse more substance.

But it was the Suffolk Punch that really made the Jutland Heavy Draft the horse it is today. Selective breeding to improve the breed began around 1850, the aim being to produce a strong horse suitable for the heavy draft work involved in farming. The breed was developed further in 1862 with the importation of a Suffolk Punch-Shire stallion cross called Oppenheim, which is the ancestor of the greatest Jutland stallion lines, in particular Aldrup Menkedal, which is now considered the foundation stallion of the breed.

The Jutland has also been influential in the formation of other breeds, such as the Schleswig Heavy Draft and the Danish Warmblood. The breed stud book was established in 1881.

Appearance The head is a little heavy and plain, with a slightly Roman nose. The ears are medium-length and the eyes have a soft, kindly expression. The neck is set high, and is thick, arched and muscular. The withers are rather flat, merging into the broad back. The chest is broad, the girth deep, and the shoulders straight and muscular. The back is short with rounded loins and hindquarters. The legs are short, stocky and well-boned with plenty of feathering.

Characteristics Plenty of energy and a keen attitude to work, coupled with a kind and calm temperament.

Colours The Jutland often inherits the trademark chestnut of the Suffolk Punch, usually with a paler mane and tail. It also comes in other solid colours as well as grey and roan.

Height 15–16hh.

KABARDIN (Russia)

Origins The Kabardin is descended from the Tarpan – the wild horse of eastern Europe and western Asia, which sadly became extinct in captivity in 1887. The Kabardin remained unchanged in type until the Russian Revolution when, like many other Russian breeds, steps were taken to improve it. The original Kabardin was bred with Karabakh, Turkmene, Persian, and Arab blood to create a much bigger, stronger horse which could be used for riding and general farm work, also as a pack animal.

It is an excellent mountain horse, being sure-footed, agile and intelligent, with the innate ability to search out the safest route. It has great stamina, enabling it to work all day under the harshest conditions without tiring.

The breed remains popular to this day in its place of origin, the republic of Kabardino-Balkaria, where it is still used for light draft work and for riding. Elsewhere, it is used as a competition horse and also to improve other breeds.

Appearance The head is quite long, often with a slightly Roman nose. The longish ears point inwards and are set close together. The eyes are wise and intelligent and the nostrils flared. The neck is long and well-developed and the back is straight and strong; the legs are long and fine, but nevertheless very strong. The overall impression is of a horse with strong Oriental influences.

Characteristics The Kabardin is a hardy breed capable of living out all year round, given extra feeding. It has a good constitution and mostly lives to a ripe old age. It is kind, obedient, trustworthy and intelligent.

Colours Usually bay, black, brown and very occasionally grey.

Height 14.2–15.1hh.

KARACABEY (Turkey)

Origins Turkey's horse population is very large and still plays an integral part in the day-to-day lives of the Turkish people. They are used for general riding, farm work and haulage. Turkey has various

RIGHT AND OPPOSITE
The Kabardin is descended from the now-extinct Tarpan. It was infused with other breeds to produce a large sturdy animal which is sure-fooded and has great stamina.

types of horse, but the Karacabey is the only one to throw offspring which run consistently true to type.

It is known that the Karacabey is descended from native Turkish stock and is therefore considered to be the original Turkish horse. The breed itself is a relatively new one, beginning in the 1900s when native mares were bred with Nonius stallions which the Turks imported from Hungary; Arab was also added in large quantities to refine the breed and to add stamina, agility and speed. Today the Karacabey is still used for light draft work, riding, as a packhorse, and as mounts for the Turkish cavalry.

Appearance The head is proud with a straight nose. The ears are alert and of medium length, and the eyes are kind and intelligent. The neck is quite long and arched, the shoulders sloping and the girth deep, with a medium-length body, good hindquarters and fine, strong legs.

Characteristics The Karacabey is a sturdy horse with good stamina and endurance. It is good-natured and a willing and obedient worker.

Colours All solid colours, also grey and occasionally roan.

Height 15.1–16.1hh.

The Kathiawari is thought to have originated from stock brought to India by Alexander the Great. By far their most distinctive feature is their curly ears.

KATHIAWARI (India)

Origins Some are of the opinion that the original Kathiawari horses were descended from horses brought to India by Alexander the Great. Another theory is that they sprang from the wild horses of Kathiawar. However, the breed that was in evidence over 100 years ago was not a particularly attractive one, tending to be rather small and stunted as well as narrow in the body. It did, however, have assets which made it extremely useful: it was hardy, with amazing stamina and endurance, and had the ability to work all day with very little sustenance. It also had tough, hard feet which enabled it to cope with rough terrain.

This original stock was eventually enhanced by breeding with Arab, which greatly improved conformation. The breed is mainly to be found in the province of Gujarat, which comprises Rajkot, Bhavnagar, Surendranagar, Junagadh and Amreli.

Appearance The Kathiawari's most striking characteristic is its ears, which point inward almost meeting in the middle. These are also extremely mobile and can rotate 180 degrees. The head is fairly long with a slightly Roman nose, the forehead is broad, and the eyes are large, kind and intelligent. Much of its Arab inheritance is immediately obvious; it is lightweight with fine legs, but with a predisposition to sickle hocks.

Characteristics Very hardy and strong.

Colours Most commonly chestnut but other colours are possible, including bay, grey, dun, and coloured.

Height 14–15hh, depending on regional differences.

The Kladruber is impressive and proud. It is an amalgam of many breeds, including Andalusian, Neapolitan and Lipizzaner, to name but a few.

KLADRUBER (Austria)

Origins The breed was established in 1597 by the Emperor Maximilian II of Austria, where it was bred at the Kladruber Stud which is situated in the former Czechoslovakia. Today the stud still produces Kladruber horses, which are composed of many different breeds. Heavy Alpine mares were originally mated with Barb and Turkish stallions, then later with Andalusian, Neapolitan and Lipizzaner, resulting in horses that

were used exclusively to draw coaches and appear in parades of the Austrian Court in Vienna.

However, the Second World War eventually took its toll of the breed with numbers plummeting to dangerously low levels; it was therefore decided to revive and improve the breed by adding Anglo-Norman, Hanoverian and Oldenburg blood, which was mixed with the remaining stock. Today, the Kladruber is doing well and is used for general riding and for light haulage.

Appearance The Kladruber has inherited many of the attributes of the Andalusian, Neopolitan and Lipizzaner. The head is noble with a broad forehead, straight or slightly Roman nose, medium well-shaped ears, and an alert expression with large, kind and intelligent eyes. The neck is high-set and well-developed; the girth is deep and the chest broad. The body is of medium length and is sturdy with large quarters. The legs are well-muscled with good bone and well-shaped hooves.

Characteristics The Kladruber has an equable temperament and is a willing and obedient worker. It has an attractive high-stepping action.

Colours Usually grey, though blacks are also bred.

Height 16.2–17hh.

KNABSTRUP (Denmark)

Origins The Knabstrup's origins go back 200 years or so, but its ancestry is far more ancient, dating back to the prehistoric Forest Horse. The Knabstrup is unusual for a European horse in that it has a distinctive spotted coat. This is thought to be inherited from prehistoric forebears, many of which were spotted, as can be seen in ancient cave paintings.

In the 16th and 17th centuries spotted horses were very popular at European courts, but the Knabstrup was founded much later, in the early 1800s, when an Iberian mare of the Knabstrup Estate in Denmark was mated with a palomino Frederiksborg stallion. The foal was born with a spotted coat of many colours which also had an attractive sheen. This became the foundation stallion of the Knabstrup breed.

Unfortunately, because subsequent horses were bred primarily for their unusual coats, insufficient care and attention was given to their conformation, leading to gradual deterioration, when the breed lost its popularity and almost disappeared. In recent years the horse has been improved with the addition of Thoroughbred blood and is popular once again. Today it is used as a general riding horse and also features in showing classes and, because of its spots, even the circus.

Appearance The head is large with a straight or Roman nose. The ears are small and well-pricked and the eyes have a kind, gentle expression. The muzzle is square with large, open nostrils. The neck is high-set and there are well-developed shoulders and a broad chest. The back is rather long with slightly sloping quarters, and the legs are strong with good bone. The mane and tail are rather sparse.

Characteristics The Knabstrup is a good-quality riding horse with excellent natural paces. It is kind and intelligent, easy to train, and an obedient and willing worker.

Colours/patterns There are various colour permutations similar to the Appaloosa, such as white with chestnut, bay and black. One overall colour or roan is also possible.
Blanket White over the quarters and loins with a contrasting base colour.
Spots White or dark spots over all or on a portion of the body.
Blanket with spots A combination of the above.
Roan Blanket Partially roan, with patterning usually over the quarters and loins.
Roan Blanket with Spots A roan blanket which has spots within it.
Leopard White with dark spots.
Snowflake Dominant spotting over the quarters and loins.
Frost White specks with a dark background.

Height 15.2–15.3hh.

The Knabstrup's most distinctive feature is its spotted coat, which makes it popular as a circus performer. However, it is mostly used as a general riding horse.

The Konik is the closest relative to the now-extinct Tarpan and attempts are being made to preserve the Tarpan gene-pool present in the breed.

KONIK (Poland)

Origins The Konik, or 'little horse', resembles the wild Tarpan of eastern Europe and western Asia which is now extinct. The Konik itself is not a specific breed and there is no particular standard. However, there are around five types, some with native blood and others with Arab added.

The Konik, being related to the Tarpan, which was a small horse of Oriental origin, has a small, neat head, dorsal stripe and zebra markings. Sadly the last remaining Tarpan died in captivity in 1887, having been hunted to extinction some ten years earlier.

In the last century efforts were made to revive the ancient breed by preserving the Konik's Tarpan genes. These reconstituted Tarpans, as they are now known, live wild in a nature reserve where they are beginning to manifest many Tarpan characteristics. Today Koniks are mainly used for farm work and occasionally as children's ponies.

Appearance A strong head with great character that shows its Oriental origins. The neck is of medium length and quite thick but with a good carriage. The body is stout and sturdy with medium-length legs with good bone, which are slightly feathered, and tough hooves.

Characteristics The Konik is hardy and will live out all year round with little extra feeding and care. Some can be wilful and difficult – a throwback to their wild Tarpan origins.

Colours Usually light-brown or dun and sometimes bay. The mane and tail are full and the dorsal stripe and zebra markings are sometimes visible.

Height 12.2–13.3hh.

Latvians come is three distinctive types, the lightest used as a competition horse.

LATVIAN (Latvia)

Origins The Latvian is thought to have an ancient history, though no one can be certain of its origins; but the general opinion is that it is either descended from the prehistoric Forest Horse, a heavy type that once roamed over northern Europe, or that it evolved from an indigenous Lithuanian pony crossed with Tarpan and Arab blood. It is thought that the latter is more likely.

Today there are three distinctive types of Latvian, depending on the other breeds with which it has become intermingled. The heaviest is the Latvian Draft which is the original breed present in the other two and which has been infused with Finnish Draft, Oldenburg and Ardennes to make a substantial draft horse which is not so heavy that it cannot be ridden. The medium-sized version is the Latvian Harness Horse, which came into being in the 1920s when the original Latvian was bred with Hanoverian, Oldenburg and Norfolk Roadster to make a lighter and more elegant carriage horse. The final, lighter, Latvian is a more recent addition, having received infusions of Arab and Thoroughbred to make a horse which is rather more of a warmblood and does well in competition. Today all three are still used by farmers and competition riders.

Appearance The three types may vary in stature, but they are all unmistakeably Latvian. The head is longish and noble with a straight nose and large nostrils, proud eyes, and small well-shaped ears. The neck is long and nicely placed with sloping shoulders, a deep girth and a longish body with well-developed quarters. The legs are shapely though volume of bone depends on type. The mane and tail are thick and full.

Characteristics Latvians are incredibly strong with excellent stamina and an equable temperament.

Colours All solid colours and the occasional grey.

Height 15.1–16hh.

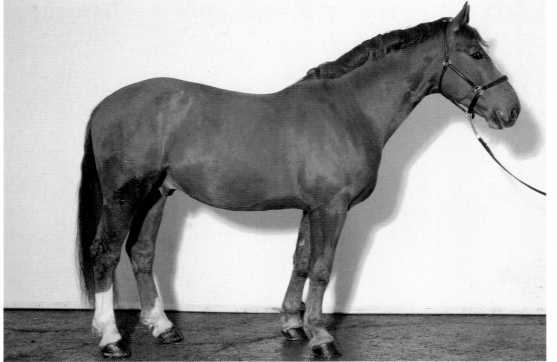

LIPIZZANER (Austria)

Origins The Lipizzaner is probably one of the world's most recognizable breeds due to its association with the Spanish Riding School of Vienna. Despite its origins in what is now Slovenia, the Lipizzaner has a much more ancient history, dating back to the 8th century and the Moorish occupation of Spain. The Moors brought with them horses of Oriental origin, such as Arabs and Barbs. These were bred with the heavier Iberian horses, which in turn produced the Andalusian which is the most important element in the Lipizzaner's breeding.

In 1580 Archduke Charles, son of the Holy Roman Emperor Ferdinand I, and who had inherited Austria-Hungary, sought to improve his horses, deciding to school them in *haute école*, a form of equitation that featured spectacular leaps into the air, which was becoming increasingly popular. To this end he founded a stud at Lipizza, which also specialized in breeding carriage horses, and filled it with quality Spanish (Iberian) horses, known to be capable of the discipline. He used these as the foundation stock of the Lipizzaner, crossing them with heavier native breeds as well as Barb, Arab, Andalusian and other European breeds such as Neopolitan and Kladruber. Thus, over a period of several hundred years, the classical riding horse was born.

The Spanish Riding School of Vienna, that most famous riding establishment, had been founded in 1572. The name was not due to its Spanish riding traditions

A Lipizzaner stallion on display at the Spanish Riding School of Vienna. The name was adopted due to the Spanish origins of the horses.

but because of the Spanish origins of the horses. The aim of the school was to teach the art of classical equestrianism to men of noble breeding. The original venue was a crude wooden structure which was replaced by the splendid building which was comissioned by Charles VI in 1735 and which is still in use today. The Spanish Riding School is stocked exclusively with Lipizzaner stallions.

When the Austrian-Hungarian Empire collapsed, the stud was moved to Piber in Austria, and during the Second World War was evacuated to Germany for its own protection. Today, the Lipizzaner is bred mainly at Piber (which supplies all the stallions for the Spanish Riding School) but also at Lipizza and Babolna in Hungary, and in the Czech Republic, Slovenia and Romania. Nowadays, as well as performing in the Spanish Riding School of Vienna, the Lipizzaner is also used as a draft horse and for carriage driving. They are also becoming popular as general riding horses.

Appearance The Lipizzaner breed was based on six foundation stallions, and their different characteristics can be seen in its descendants today. Lipizzaners can therefore vary according to which of the six bloodlines has been used, but generally speaking they are of an Iberian type, similar to the Lusitano and Andalusian. The head is large with either a straight or Roman nose. The ears are finely pointed and alert and the eyes kind and intelligent. The neck is well-set, powerful and well- muscled with a good crest. The chest is wide with a deep girth. The shoulders can be slightly straight and short. The back is long but strong and muscular with powerful quarters and a slightly low-set tail. The legs are shortish but powerful, with small, well-shaped, tough hooves.

Characteristics The noble Lipizzaner possesses all the qualities of its breeding: the agility and balance of its Iberian forebears as well as the stamina and refinement of the Oriental. They combine stamina and endurance with natural balance and agility, are kind, intelligent, willing and obedient, but with plenty of sparkle. They are late to mature, usually around the age of 7, and should not be worked too young. However, they stay sound for a long time and usually live to a good age.

Colours The Lipizzaner is famous for its grey (white) coat. Foals are born dark, but most lighten to become pure white by the age of 7. Very few remain brown or black. Traditionally, the dark Lipizzaners are kept at the Spanish Riding School as reminders of their Spanish forebears which were bay, black, brown or roan.

Height 15–15.3hh.

LUNDY (U.K.)

Origins The Lundy is not a true native breed, but was created in 1928 by crossing New Forest mares with Thoroughbred, Welsh and Connemara stallions. The resulting ponies were then turned loose on the island of Lundy in the Bristol Channel, where they bred further to produce a semi-native pony. The breeding programme was not as successful as anticipated but a few ponies still remain on the island.

Appearance Attractive and full of character. The head is fairly large with a full mane, a straight nose, neat muzzle and large kindly eyes. The ears are small and alert, the body is long, and the legs are sturdy with slight feathering.

Characteristics The Lundy lives out in harsh winter conditions, confirming that it is a hardy breed with plenty of stamina. It is also sure-footed and agile. They are kind, willing and easy to keep as they require little feeding and will live out all year round. They make good children's ponies if caught and broken in while young.

Colours All solid colours as well as grey and dun.

Height Around 13.2hh.

The Lundy is hardy, easy to care for, and full of character.

The Lusitano has a shared heritage with the Andalusian of Spain, both being descended from Iberian stock, though the Lusitano has remained slightly truer to its origins.

LUSITANO (PORTUGAL)

Origins The Lusitano shares its heritage with the Andalusian, both being descended from the Iberian riding horse. The Lusitano gets its name, which was only adopted in the early 20th century, from Lusitania, the Roman name for Portugal. The origins of the breed go back to around 25,000 BC to the ancient ancestors of the Sorraia breed which can be seen in cave paintings in the Iberian peninsula.

Unlike the Andalusian, the Lusitano's breeding has remained much truer to its Sorraia ancestry, with infusions limited to Oriental, Garrano and Spanish blood. This mix hasn't changed for centuries and today care is taken only to use horses with obvious Iberian characteristics to keep the breed true to type.

The Lusitano was mainly bred for and still used for working the farms around the fertile River Tagus and also for bullfighting, known as the *corrida*, as well as for *haute école*. In Portugal the bull is thankfully not killed and the whole event is performed with the rider on horseback. Nevertheless the Lusitano has to be incredibly agile and fast to avoid injury.

These horses are highly prized and receive *haute école* schooling to enhance their precision so that they can survive the demanding and dangerous spectacle. The Lusitano stallions are trained to these high standards before they are sent to stud, and all fighting horses are left entire; it is thought that geldings lack the

courage and intelligence to work in the bullring.

Today they are still used for farm work, bullfighting, and also for lower levels of dressage. Infusions of Lusitano are also used to improve other breeds.

Appearance The Lusitano has a noble countenance. The head is quite long with a straight or slightly Roman nose and flared nostrils. The ears are of medium length, well-shaped and alert. The eyes are keen and intelligent, the neck is set high with a well-developed muscular crest and well-defined withers. The sloping shoulders are powerful and the chest is broad with a deep girth. The back is short and strong and the loins broad, with quarters that are not too large. The Lusitano's high-stepping action is attributed to its strong, long hocks which are capable of great impulsion with deep flexion achieved by a well-developed second thigh (stifle).

Characteristics This noble and courageous horse is kind, good-natured and obedient. It is level-headed and not given to panic, important attributes in a fighting horse.

Colours All solid colours as well as grey.

Height 15–16hh.

Lusitanos were originally bred for farmwork, but are also used in the bullfight or corrida, *where the horses require lightning reflexes and the utmost agility to avoid injury. This is where their* haute école *training comes in, contributing greatly to the safety of both horse and rider.*

The Malopolski is a well-bred spirited horse which excels in competition.

MALOPOLSKI (Poland)

Origins The Malopolski, also known as the Polish Arab, was originally bred as a general riding and driving horse which could also be used on farms. It is based on native Mazuren and Posnan stock; however, these two breeds now barely exist having been incorporated not only into the Malopolski but also into its distant relative the Wielkopolski (page 292). The breed also has a good deal of Arab blood, as suggested above, and Thoroughbred, and Gidrán and Furioso from Hungary.

The Malopolski is now split into two, depending on which of these two Hungarian breeds is dominant. The Darbowski-Tarnowski has a predominance of Gidrán blood and the Sadecki Furioso, with the result that there is no definite conformity. Today the breed is mainly used as a competition and riding horse, and they are still used in harness.

Appearance The Malopolski's head is very Arab in appearance, with a wedge-shaped head and a slightly dished or straight nose depending on the strain. The ears are small and shapely and the eyes lively and intelligent. The neck is high-set, long and elegant with a slight crest; the shoulders are sloping, with a broad chest and a deep girth. The hindquarters are well-muscled with a high-set 'Arab' tail. The legs are long with good bone and well-shaped hooves.

Characteristics The Malopolski is an excellent jumper, making it a good all-round performance horse. It has a lively and spirited temperament which requires skilful handling.

Colours All solid colours as well as grey and roan.

Height 15–16.2hh.

MANGALARGA MARCHADOR
(Brazil)

Origins For centuries Brazil and Portugal were closely connected and at one time were under the same ruler, Don Joao VI, in around 1815. It was he who brought quality Portuguese and Spanish horses to Brazil, particularly the Altér Real and Andalusian.

The Mangalarga is a direct descendant of one particular Altér Real stallion which was mated with Criollo mares; later, more Altér Real, Barb and Andalusian was added to improve the breed. The result is neat, lightly-built and strongly reminiscent of the Barb, but with the rolling gait of the Spanish breeds.

It is most often used for riding the enormous *estancias* of Brazil, where its fifth gait, known as the *marcha*, makes it fast but comfortable for the rider. The *marcha* is a cross between a trot and a canter, which the horse can maintain for great distances. The horse's name is a combination of the words Mangalarga, from the name of the *hacienda*, and *marcha*. Today the Mangalarga Marchador is also used for endurance and trail riding, jumping and polo. It is an excellent all-round riding and showing horse.

Appearance The head is high and proud with medium-length ears and intelligent eyes. The nose is straight with flaring nostrils. The back is long with strong loins and neat quarters; the shoulders are sloping with a deep girth and there are well-muscled legs with hard hooves.

The Mangalarga Marchador was strongly influenced by quality Iberian horses which were bred with Criollo mares.

BELOW and RIGHT
Mangalarga Marchadors are neat and lightly built, reminiscent of the Barb, but with a rolling gait.

Characteristics The Mangalarga has incredible stamina which enables it to work all day and cover huge distances.   It is good-natured, willing and obedient.

Colours Bay, grey, chestnut and roan.

Height Usually around 15hh.

MAREMMANA (Italy)

Origins The foundation of the Maremmana originally rested on the now-extinct Neapolitan, with later infusions of Andalusian and other European stock. However, the breed became virtually extinct as it was weakened over the centuries by matings with local semi-wild horses of the Tuscan region of Maremma, as well as with any other horses or ponies that appeared in the vicinity. More recently Thoroughbred blood has been added which has greatly improved the quality, though its hardiness has suffered.

Today the Maremmana is still used on farms and as a general riding horse and is also used by the Italian mounted police.

Appearance The head is rather plain and workmanlike with a straight or slightly Roman nose. The neck is short with a straight shoulder, flat withers and a low-set tail. The legs, however, are strong and sturdy with good tough hooves.

Characteristics The Maremmana is hardy and tough with a calm temperament. It is reliable, obedient and willing to work.

Colours All solid colours including grey and roan.

Height 15–15.3hh.

The Maremmana is used by the Italian mounted police and also in farming.

The Marwari was once a great warhorse and featured in Indian art for centuries. Thanks to renewed interest the breed is once again gaining in popularity..

MARWARI (India)

Origins The Marwari, from the Marwar region of Rajasthan, is similar in appearance to the Kathiawari (page 178), but is of much greater stature, and has featured in Indian art over the centuries. The Marwari is unusual in that it has a fifth gait, called the *revaal*, which is a long, smooth action with little vertical movement and very comfortable for the rider. Marwari numbers declined during the British occupancy of India, but thanks to today's Rajput families and others interested in the continuation of the breed, the Marwari is once again flourishing. It is now used as a dancing horse, popular at weddings and festivals. The dance is a form of *haute école*, which the horse would have been taught when it was a warhorse long ago.

Appearance The Marwari has a high, proud head-carriage with a straight or Roman nose, its trademark ears curving inward until they almost join together in the centre. The eyes are large, bright and intelligent; the neck is of medium length and arches in movement. The coat is fine and silky.

Characteristics The Marwari has a naturally flamboyant presence and the will to perform. However, it is also tough and is able to survive harsh conditions. It is courageous, intelligent and a willing worker.

Colours All colours, including roan, piebald and skewbald.

Height 15–16hh.

Today's Mecklenburg has been strongly influenced by the Hanoverian. Its accurate paces makes it a good dressage horse.

MECKLENBURG (Germany)

Origins The Mecklenburg State Stud at Redefin was founded in 1812, but the breeding of the Mecklenburg horse actually dates back earlier to the start of the 18th century, when horses were bred at Redefin to supply the Duke of Mecklenburg-Schwerin's stables, and destined to improve the quality of horses throughout the country.

The older type of Mecklenburg was a heavy, cob-like animal suitable for the cavalry, but it was the infusion of Thoroughbred which made it famous throughout Europe. Throughout the 19th century the Mecklenburg was further refined with more Thoroughbred; unfortunately, some inferior stock was used and the breed deteriorated in quality, making the offspring more difficult to sell. The breeders attempted to rectify the problem by introducing heavier horses back into the bloodline, but this did nearly as much damage. Eventually, a

happy medium was found and the breed was stabilized.

Today the Mecklenburg has been further developed, making it a horse suitable for leisure and competition riding. It has been heavily crossed with Hanoverian.

Appearance The Mecklenburg is a workmanlike horse, with sturdy limbs and a kind face. It is suitable for most equestrian disciplines.

Characteristics The Mecklenburg has a bold yet tractable temperament, ideally suited to both ridden and carriage work.

Colours Bay, brown, black or chestnut.

Height 15.3–16.1hh.

The Mérens is kind and level-headed, making it a good children's pony. It also works well in harness.

MÉRENS (France)

Origins Ponies remarkably similar to the Mérens, and depicted in ancient cave paintings at Niaux, have roamed the Pyrenees of Andorra since prehistoric times. The native breed has changed slightly over the years with infusions from heavy horses arriving with the Romans and also Oriental bloodlines.

The Mérens has been used for ploughing and hauling for hundreds of years by mountain farmers, where its

stamina and sure-footedness make it suitable for the inhospitable terrain. The Mérens was also used for transporting lumber and also by soldiers in the Middle Ages and Napoleon during his campaigns.

The Mérens, or Ariègeois, is similar to the British Dales and Fell ponies and the Friesian. Breeders still raise their stock the traditional way: the ponies live out all year round and the foals are born in the spring snow. In the summer transhumance occurs when they are herded up high into the mountains where they are allowed their freedom for several months, after which time some are selected for breaking, selling on or breeding. Today they are still used for farming and forestry and also as children's ponies.

Appearance The Mérens is a most attractive pony, with a small, neat head, a slightly dished or straight nose, small pricked ears, and kind, soft eyes. The neck is short and well-developed, and the body strong and stocky with well-developed hindquarters. The legs are shortish with good bone and a little feathering around the fetlocks.

Characteristics The Mérens is well-balanced, level-headed and compliant, as well as energetic. It is tough and can withstand the harshest conditions.

Colours Usually black with a thick mane and tail.

Height 13–14.2hh.

Unlike the Saddlebred, the breed standard for the Fox Trotter bans any artificial aids to improve its natural paces. The foxtrot pace is a cross between a walk and trot and is very comfortable for the rider.

MISSOURI FOX TROTTER
(U.S.A.)

Origins The Missouri Fox Trotter was developed in the 19th century by settlers in Missouri and Arkansas. Initially, its purpose was to be a general riding horse with the speed and endurance to cope with difficult terrain. The foundation stock for the breed was the Morgan, which was infused with Thoroughbred and Arab as well as Iberian blood. As horses with elaborate gaits became more popular, the breed was later mated with Saddlebred and Tennessee Walking Horse which greatly improved its elegance, bearing and paces, including its foxtrot gait; this is basically a diagonal gait like the trot, in which the

horse appears to walk with the front legs while trotting with the hind.

In the early days, before racing was made illegal, the Fox Trotter had been a useful competitor, but after the ban it was once again used as a general riding horse.

A stud book for the breed was eventually opened in 1948. The breed society, however, placed strict guidelines that the Missouri Fox Trotter should have no artificial aids to influence and enhance its gait, such as nicking or setting the tail; consequently its action is not as pronounced or extravagant as, for example, the American Saddlebred. The breed is popular in the United States, where it is used for general riding, showing and endurance.

Appearance The head is a little plain, with a straight nose and a square muzzle with large open nostrils. The ears are medium-length and alert and the eyes have a kind but intelligent expression. The neck is medium-length and fairly well- developed with prominent withers; the back is short, with strong loins and hindquarters. The tail is set fairly low; the legs are long with large joints and well-shaped, strong hooves.

Characteristics The Missouri Fox Trotter has a charming, easy-going nature. It is willing and obedient with excellent stamina and endurance.

Colours All colours as well as part-coloured.

Height 14–16hh.

MORGAN (U.S.A.)

Origins One of America's most famous and versatile breeds, all Morgans can be traced back to just one stallion called Figure, later renamed Justin Morgan after its owner, Thomas Justin Morgan, a tavern keeper and singing teacher who supplemented his income by breeding stallions.

The colt was born in around 1790 in Vermont. It is thought that its sire was called True Briton, probably a Welsh Cob, but little is known concerning the dam; however, it is thought that she had some Oriental and Thoroughbred blood.

Thomas Justin Morgan was so impressed with Figure's looks and personality that he eventually decided to put him to stud. The results were remarkable: it did not matter what mare Justin Morgan covered, a foal the image of its father was produced. Moreover, the performance of each one was second to none, the sire's prowess as a marvellous harness and riding horses having been replicated in its offspring. In fact, it is quite amazing that such a significant and impressive breed developed from just one stallion.

Today Morgans are just as versatile – used in harness competitions, shows, driving, trail riding and driving.

Characteristics Morgans are strong, versatile, hard-working, and have a spirited but tractable nature.

Appearance The head should give immediate evidence of quality, with beautiful and expressive eyes. The muzzle is small and the profile straight or slightly dished. The neck is well-crested and the shoulders strong. The hindquarters are large and strong and the legs sturdy.

Some Morgans are bred particularly for their high-stepping action, a type known as the Park Morgan. The other type is the Pleasure Morgan, whose action is less exaggerated.

Colours All solid colours are acceptable.

Height 14–15.2hh.

The elegant Morgan is a truly remarkable breed in that it orginated from just one stallion. Whatever mare this stallion covered, the foal always minutely resembled its sire.

The Murakosi is a well- balanced small draft horse with a kind and positive attitude to work. It is still used on farms in Hungary.

MURAKOSI (Hungary)

Origins The Murakosi or Murakoz is a relatively recent breed, created in the 1900s to be used in general agriculture and as a draft horse. It was founded on Hungarian native stock, crossed with Brabant, Percheron, Noriker and Ardennais heavy horses. Today, through selective breeding, two distinctive types have emerged, one heavy and one light. Today the breed can still be seen working on farms in Hungary.

Appearance For heavy breeds, both types have good conformation. The head is well-proportioned and large, reminiscent of the Ardennais, with a straight or slightly Roman nose, medium well-shaped ears and a kind, honest look. The neck is muscular with a slight crest and the shoulders are strong; the chest is broad with a deep girth. The body is shortish and well-balanced, with short, clean legs, plenty of bone and a little feathering.

Characteristics Physically very strong, with a good temperament and a positive attitude to work.

Colours Very often chestnut, with a flaxen mane and tail, less often black, brown, bay or grey.

Height Around 16hh.

Murgeses are often ridden by Italian mounted police. They are similar to the Irish Draft in stature.

MURGESE (Italy)

Origins The Murgese comes from Apulia, the region of south-east Italy that extends into the 'heel' of the peninsula and which is known as Puglia in Italian. The original breed is probably about 500 years old and is descended from native Italian breeds intermingled with Barb and later Thoroughbred.

In the 15th and 16th century the breed was used by the Italian cavalry. Over the centuries, however, the Murgese virtually died out, only to be revived in the 1920s; a stud book was opened in 1926. Today the Murgese in a rather inferior light draft horse which has no specific conformity.

Appearance The head is rather plain but with a kind honest expression. The general appearance is similar to that of the Irish Draft in stature, though the hindquarters tend to be weak with a low-set tail.

Characteristics The Murgese has some jumping ability and is used as a general riding horse. It has a kind nature and is a willing worker.

Colours Usually chestnut, but grey or black are also possible.

Height 14–15hh.

MUSTANG (U.S.A.)

Origins Although horses were once present in North America, by the time the *conquistadores* arrived in the 16th century the original prehistoric horses had long been extinct. The Spanish brought Iberian horses with them in their ships, derived mainly from Arabs and Barbs, and many of these sleek, desert-bred and resilient horses were allowed to wander off, spreading into North America and forming feral herds in their new environment.

Native American tribes came to value the Mustang's qualities and many were caught and domesticated by them. They even developed their own breeds based on the Mustang, such as the Appaloosa, the Cayuse Indian Pony and the Chickasaw Indian Pony, also known as the Florida Cracker Horse.

By the beginning of the 19th century there were between one- and two-million Mustangs in existence, many of which ran free, but others were domesticated and used by settlers. Unfortunately, the wild horses were regarded as pests and were culled by the thousands to make room for cattle. But it wasn't only the ranchers who were responsible for the decimation of the population. Thousands were killed in the 20th century, sacrificed to the pet- food industry.

Sadly, there are less than 50,000 Mustangs in existence today and in some areas numbers are dangerously low. Determined efforts are now being made to safeguard the breed for the future and, fortunately for the Mustang, the breed is now considered an important part of the American heritage and a protected species.

Appearance Mustangs come in all colours, sizes and builds, although horses which display Barb characteristics are most favoured by breeders.

Characteristics The Mustang is easy to train, due to its intelligence, and is tough and resilient.

Colours Any colour, but mainly brown, chestnut, bay and dun.

Height 14–16hh.

The Mustang was created from horses which came over with the conquistadors; many were turned loose and formed the basis of the breed as it is today.

*RIGHT and OPPOSITE
New Forest Ponies are plentiful
and can easily be seen when
driving through the New Forest in
Hampshire.*

*BELOW
The New Forest is an excellent
all-rounder for children and
teenagers. It is good-natured and
willing and good at jumping.*

NEW FOREST (U.K.)

Origins It is likely that the New Forest is a
descendant of the Celtic Pony, as are all the
British native breeds, though the earliest
mention of it dates to the time of King Canute
(c.995–1035), who famously sought to stop
the sea's rising tide.

The New Forest is in the county of
Hampshire in southern England and consists
mainly of scrubland, bog and moorland,
which has led to the development of a hardy
animal designed to survive harsh conditions.

Over the years, Thoroughbred and Arab blood were introduced, mainly to increase size and performance and to improve the pony's appearance, but is was not until the end of the 19th century, during the reign of Queen Victoria, that a structured breeding programme was initiated. At the same time, other British breeds were also introduced, such as the Dartmoor, Exmoor, Welsh, Fell, Dales and Highland.

In 1891, the Society for the Improvement of New Forest Ponies was founded to ensure that there was an ample supply of quality stallions living in the New Forest and this in turn led to the official publication of the first stud book in 1910. Nowadays, although still living and breeding in their home environment, many quality New Forest Ponies are also bred in private studs all over the world.

Appearance This is one of the larger breeds native to Britain. It is an ideal child or teenager's pony and excellent for driving. It has a well-proportioned body that is more slender than other British breeds, and well-formed feet.

Characteristics New Forests have a lovely temperament. They are calm, good-natured and a pleasure to own. They are substantial enough for dressage, showjumping, cross-country; in fact, it is often said that a good New Forest Pony can rise to any occasion.

Colours Any solid colour is acceptable.

Height 12–14.2hh.

NONIUS (Hungary)

Origins The Nonius was developed by the famous Mezöhegyes Stud of Hungary which acquired a young stallion when it was captured by the Hungarian cavalry from a French stud in 1813, following Napoleon's defeat at Leipzig. The horse, called Nonius Senior, was of mixed Anglo-Norman and Norfolk Roadster parentage. It wasn't particularly attractive and many conformation defects were present, such as weak quarters and a short neck. Moreover, its plainness was not enhanced by big ears and small eyes. However, Nonius did have an excellent temperament, being willing, obedient and easy to handle. Moreover, the Hungarians must have thought him promising because they began a programme to produce the excellent Nonius breed.

They experimented by putting Nonius Senior to many different mares, such as Arabs, Kladrubers, Normans, Lipizzaners and English cross-breeds. They then selected the best of his daughters to mate with him, with the result that certain traits began to gradually emerge, and which set the breed standard. Nonius Senior died at the age of 22 after an extremely productive career and his sons daughters continued the line with further refinements of Arab and Thoroughbred blood added.

There are two kinds of Nonius: a heavy type suitable for carriage driving as well as farm work, and a lighter version, mainly used as a cavalry or riding horse. Today, both make good all-rounders.

Appearance Nonius Senior's conformation defects have largely been eradicated. The head is rather long, with medium-length ears, large kind eyes, and a straight or Roman nose. The neck is of medium length and well-developed. The chest is fairly broad with a deep girth and sloping shoulder. The back is long and straight with good quarters and long legs.

Characteristics The Nonius is prized for its willing, equable temperament.

Colours Usually black, dark brown or bay with only a little white on the lower legs and face.

Height Large Nonius 15.3–16.2hh.
Small Nonius 14.2–15.3hh.

The Noriker is an ancient breed used for farming and forestry in mountainous regions. It is also used as a general riding horse.

NORIKER (Austria)

Origins The Noriker is also know as the South German Coldblood, the Pinzgauer and the Oberlander. The breed is an ancient one dating back to the Roman Empire, when several heavy breeds, possibly with Andalusian and Neapolitan blood flowing in their veins, were introduced to the province which now equates with modern Austria, but which was then known as Noricum.

The breed which developed from these heavy horses was strong and sure-footed, making it ideal for draft work in difficult mountain conditions where it was used for farming and forestry. By the 16th century the breed was given an infusion of new blood in the form of Andalusian and Neopolitan, which brought a degree of finesse and agility to the breed. By the 19th century a South German strain had developed and this was improved by the addition of Norman, Cleveland Bay, Holstein, Hungarian, Clydesdale and Oldenburg, which made the breed much lighter and more elegant.

As well as the heavy breeds in its bloodline, the Noriker was later refined with additions of Andalusian and Neopolitan, which made it more agile than most draft breeds.

Today there are five different types of Noriker, all of which are lightish draft horses still used for farming in Austria and Germany.

Appearance The head is medium-sized and rather plain, with a straight or slightly Roman nose. It has a placid look. The neck is short, well-developed and strong with a straight shoulder. The body is sturdy with sloping quarters and a low-set tail. The legs are short with good bone, hard hooves, and a little feathering.

Characteristics For a draft horse, the Noriker's breeding has made it quite active and agile. It is strong and its sure-footedness makes it suitable for difficult terrain. It is amenable and obedient and copes well with harsh conditions.

Colours Most commonly chestnut, often with a flaxen mane and tail, also bay, brown, black, roan and spotted.

Height 15.1–16.2hh.

221

Although quite stocky the Norman Cob still manages to look rather refined. It is much larger than most cobs, usually over 15.3hh, which makes it a useful draft as well as riding horse.

NORMAN COB (France)

Origins This comes from Normandy in north-western France, as the name suggests, a region famous for breeding good-quality horses for many hundreds, even thousands of years. The breed was established in the 17th century as an all-round workhorse, suitable for riding, carriage and farm work. Its breeding includes Anglo-Norman, which was a useful base for riding and lightweight harness horses, together with Norfolk Roadster and the native stock of the area.

The Norman Cob is typical of the cob type, with a large head and body and short legs. Its main difference, however, is that it is a much larger animal than the average cob, which stands around 15hh.

In France, Norman Cobs are usually docked, a practice illegal in many countries, particularly the United Kingdom. The breed is popular elsewhere, and French studs are willing to lend their stallions out to private breeders. They are still used for light draft work and are also very comfortable to ride.

Appearance Although the body is stocky, the Norman Cob has a refined appearance, with a high, proud head-carriage, medium-length ears, a straight or slightly Roman nose, and bright, intelligent eyes. The neck is of medium length and well-developed, while the body is strong with a broad chest and stocky legs.

Characteristics The Norman Cob is a quality horse with an active gait. It has great stamina and a charming personality.

Colours Usually chestnut, bay and brown; very occasionally grey or roan.

Height 15.3–16.3hh.

The North Swedish looks rather like an overgrown pony, and like most ponies requires little care or extra feeding. It is full of character and has plenty of stamina.

NORTH SWEDISH (Sweden)

Origins This is another breed that can trace is origins back to the prehistoric Celtic Pony. It shares much of its ancestry with the Norwegian Døle, and has Friesian, Norfolk Trotter, Heavy Draft and Thoroughbred in its make-up.

The breed has split into two distinctive types: the lighter version known as the North Swedish Trotter, which is capable of covering 0.62 mile (1km) in 1 minute 30 seconds, and which is faster than many other breeds recognized for speed. The heavier draft type is of greater stature and is used for general farm and haulage work.

Appearance Like the Døle, the breed resembles a large pony. The head is small and neat with a broad forehead, straight or slightly Roman nose, and a squarish muzzle. The ears are small and alert and the eyes kind and inquisitive. The neck is short and well-developed with a slight crest. The chest and shoulders are powerful, the girth is deep, and the back is long with well-muscled hindquarters. The legs are rather short but sturdy, with good bone, hard hooves, and feathering around the heels. The heavy type has rather more bone and substance.

Characteristics The North Swedish is tough, hardy and can expect a long life. It requires little care and feeding and has great stamina and endurance. It has a well-balanced, springy action; the trotting type has a particularly good turn of speed.

Colours All solid colours.

Height 15–15.2hh.

NORTHLANDS (Norway)

Origins The Northlands is uncommon outside its home territory of Norway. Like most native north-European breeds it can trace its ancestry back to the prehistoric Celtic Pony, though there is also Tarpan blood somewhere in its make-up.

It resembles the Shetland Pony of Scotland and although bred by farmers with no particular thought of keeping the breed pure, it remained remarkably true to type for hundreds of years. However, by the 1940s the Northland was under threat of extinction when numbers dropped to just 43. But due to the efforts of breeders and a well-bred stallion called Rimfaske, the breed has been thankfully rescued.

Today, with riding fast increasing in popularity and a demand for ponies for export, the breed is on the increase and out of immediate danger. The Northland makes an excellent children's pony and is still used for light work on local farms.

Appearance The head is usually in proportion to the body, but can occasionally be a little on the large side. The ears are small and neat and the eyes large and kind. The neck is strong and of medium length; the body is longish and the legs sturdy, with hard hooves and a little feathering around the fetlocks.

Characteristics The Northlands is tough and hardy and can live out all year in the harshest conditions, requiring the minimum of food and care. It is energetic and fun to ride.

Colours Bay, brown, chestnut and grey.

Height 13.2–14.2hh.

OLDENBURG (Germany)

Origins This is the heaviest of the modern German warmbloods, originally bred as a coach horse. It dates back to the early part of the 17th century when keen horse-breeder Count Anton Guenther of Oldenburg, in north-western Germany, began the first breeding programme.

The Oldenburg's earliest ancestors were heavy Friesian horses infused with Spanish and Arabian blood. The breed was stabilized in the 19th century by the introduction of Thoroughbred, Cleveland Bay, Yorkshire Coach Horse, Anglo-Norman and Hanoverian stallions.

Though originally bred as coach horses,

The Oldenburg has a varied pedigree based on Friesian, Spanish and Arabian blood and later refined with Thoroughbred, Cleveland Bay, Yorkshire Coach Horse, Anglo-Norman and Hanoverian.

the Oldenburg was also used by the military as a strong artillery horse. However, as the years passed, the need for such horses diminished and a demand for lighter riding horses for competition and pleasure arose. In the second half of the 20th century lighter breeds were again introduced, such as Thoroughbred, Trakehner, Hanoverian and Westphalian. Nowadays, the Oldenburg excels at dressage and showjumping while retaining its ability as a carriage horse, still used for the purpose today.

Appearance The Oldenburg is distinguished by its noble head and a proud, workmanlike air. It has a high-set neck, long shoulder, strong back, and a well-muscled croup with strong joints. With its large frame and long, active stride, it makes a elegant dressage horse or a powerful showjumper.

Characteristics The Oldenburg could be said to resemble a hunter type. Its character is equable, making it a pleasant horse to handle and own.

Colours Black, bay, brown.

Height 16.2–17.2hh.

The Orlov Trotter is famous above all for its impressive action. It is a well-bred attractive horse and was once the toast of the 19th-century racing fraternity. Today, however, because faster breeds have overtaken it, such as the French Trotter and Standardbred, the Orlov is in imminent danger of decline.

ORLOV TROTTER (Russia)

Origins The Orlov, or Orloff, Trotter is one of the foremost breeds of its type in the world. It was founded in the 18th century by Count Alexey Orlov, whose ambition was to produce a superb trotting horse, and to this end founded a stud at Ostrov, near Moscow. He brought in a large number of Arabians, among them two distinctive stallions – the beautiful, silvery-grey Smetanka, and the brown Sultan I. After one season, Orlov was left with a few progeny from Dutch Harddraver, Mecklenburg, Danish, Thoroughbred and Arabian mares.

Orlov was not happy with his stud and wanted somewhere better with more grazing, which he found in Khrenovoye in the Voronezh region to the south of Moscow, a place he considered perfect for his purpose, with vast areas of grassland, clear, natural springs, and a dry climate.

The Khrenovoye Stud was thus founded in 1778, and the following year produced a colt called Polkan I, which in turn was mated with a Danish mare carrying Spanish blood. The result was a foal called Bars I, which eventually showed exceptional stamina and trotting abilities and became the foundation stallion of the Orlov breed.

The Orlov is a muscular breed famous for its exceptional and impressive action. Its stamina and quality ensured that it reigned supreme on the racetrack until the end of the 19th century, when Standardbreds and later French Trotters were introduced to the Russian racing scene. Unfortunately, the Orlov is now in crisis, due largely to the introduction of these faster breeds.

Appearance The Orlov has a small, elegant head with a noble profile. The ears are highly reminiscent of the Arab's. The hindquarters are powerful and, like many trotters, the shoulders are straight.

Characteristics Energetic, sure-footed and bold. Owing to its swift, balanced trot it is suitable for riding and driving as well as trotting.

Colours Usually grey, black or bay.

Height 15.2–17hh.

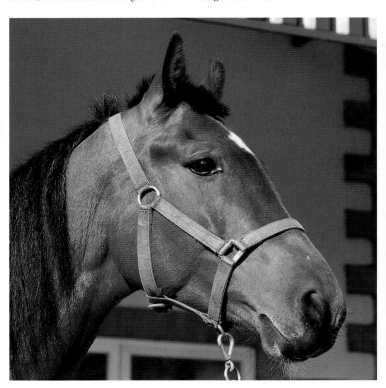

The Paso Fino is famously known for its spectacular gaits – the fino, corto *and* largo *– which are smooth, effortless and comfortable for the rider.*

PASO FINO (Puerto Rico)

Origins The foundation of the Paso Fino is old Spanish or Iberian stock. They have the same bloodlines, inherited from horses brought to the Americas by the Spanish conquistadors in the 16th century; however, different environments have caused slight variations in their evolution in terms of character and conformation.

The Paso Fino is a naturally gaited horse, like the Peruvian Paso or Stepping Horse (page 236) and another lesser known breed from Colombia, and although it is predominantly a working horse on the coffee plantations of Puerto Rico, these gaits make it remarkable. They are spectacular to watch, the main ones being the *fino*, the classic gait of the showring, performed with the horse balanced and collected, the *corto*, executed with only medium collection and light contact on the bit, and the *largo*, the speed form of the gait.

There are another two variants, the *sobre paso*, a much more natural gait in which the horse is allowed a loose rein and is relaxed, and which is used in general riding rather than the showring; the other is the *andadura* which is a fast pacing gait. However, this is uncomfortable and is only performed for short periods. The rest of the time the horse's effortless gait makes it extremely comfortable and smooth to ride, its gliding action making it popular for trail riding. Paso Finos are also in great demand for showing and displays.

Appearance The head is fine, almost Arab-like, with a straight nose and flaring nostrils, longish well-shaped ears and intelligent eyes. The body is very Spanish, similar to the Andalusian's, with a good sloping shoulder, well-developed neck, and medium-length back with slightly sloping quarters and a low-set tail. The legs are sturdy and strong with large hocks.

Characteristics The Paso Fino has an excellent temperament. It has great enthusiasm and is obedient and easy to ride, seemingly enjoying the company of human beings. Despite its small stature it is very strong; in fact, even the smallest will easily carry a man over hills and rough terrain.

Colours All colours.

Height 14–15hh.

The Peneia is a sure-footed, wiry little workhorse.

PENEIA (Greece)

Origins The Peneia is a breed native to the Greek mainland, likely to have been infuenced by Oriental breeds, particularly Arab. For centuries it was used as a packhorse, for light draft work, and also for riding, where its strength, agility and sure-footedness were great assets. Peneia stallions are also bred with female donkeys to produce hinnies.

Appearance The head is of medium size and rather plain with a straight nose, smallish intelligent eyes, and alert ears. The body is small, wiry and underdeveloped. The legs are of medium length, fine though strong, with tough, hard hooves.

Characteristics The Peneia is kind and willing. It is strong with plenty of stamina and endurance.

Colours All colours.

Height 10.1–14hh.

PERCHERON (France)

Origins The Percheron comes from La Perche in Normandy in northern France. The breed is an ancient one dating back to 732, when Arab horses abandoned by the Saracens after their defeat at the Battle of Poitiers were allowed to breed with the local heavy mares of the region. From these matings the Percheron type emerged.

At this time the horse was much lighter than its modern counterpart and was used for riding as well as for light draft work. The type remained popular until the Middle Ages and the Crusades, when Arab and Barb horses from the Holy Land were mated with Percherons. It was also around this time that the Comte de Perche brought back Spanish horses from his forays in Spain; these were also mated with the Percheron, with further infusions of Andalusian added later. By the 18th century, the original breed had become almost completely eradicated by the addition of Thoroughbred and more Arab; in 1820 two grey Arab stallions were mated with Percheron mares, which is responsible for the predominantly grey colour of the modern-day breed.

By now all the heaviness of the ancient breed had disappeared; consequently, heavy mares from other regions were bred with Percheron stallions to make them more suitable for agriculture and to formulate the breed as it is known today. The lighter Percheron still exists and is used as a heavy riding horse, while the heavy version is still used for farm and forestry work and, in some countries, for pulling drays. It is also popular in the showring.

Over the years the Percheron has been heavily exported to other countries such as the United Kingdom, Canada, Australia and other parts of Europe, which has helped its recognization as one of the world's leading heavy breeds.

Appearance For a heavy breed the Percheron's head is proud and elegant, with a straight nose, broad forehead, expressive

The ancient breed of Percheron is now a popular heavy horse the world over. Despite its size, it has a proud and elegant bearing.

eyes, and short shapely ears. The neck is short to medium, well- developed and with great strength. The shoulders are nicely sloping and well- shaped, with a broad chest and a deep girth. The Percheron is fairly short in the back, which adds to its strength, with slightly sloping but broad quarters. The legs are short and sturdy with well-shaped tough hooves with very little feather.

Characteristics The Percheron possesses a good deal of elegance due to large amounts of Arab blood which have been added over the centuries. It has an excellent temperament, is calm, obedient and easy to handle, and has a keen intelligence. It has a smooth but lively action, making it comfortable to ride.

Colours Mainly grey but occasionally black and dark chestnut.

Height Small Percheron 14.1–16.1hh.
Large Percheron 16.1–17.3hh.

There are two types of Percheron the light version is used as a riding horse, while its heavier counterpart is still used on farms and for forestry work.

BELOW and RIGHT
A Peruvian Paso in traditional tack.

PERUVIAN PASO (Peru)

Origins The Peruvian Paso, or Peruvian Stepping Horse, shares much of its descent with the Paso Fino, the national horse of Puerto Rico, the foundation of both breeds

being Barb and old Spanish or Iberian stock brought to the Americas by the *conquistadores* in the 16th century.

The Peruvian Paso has adapted well to its environment and has the ability to carry riders great distances over dangerous mountain terrain in safety and comfort. It has also adapted to the high altitude of the Andes and has a larger, stronger heart and greater lung capacity than other breeds, which enables it to function energetically in areas where oxygen is scarce.

Like the other Paso breeds, the Peruvian has the natural ability to perform the attractive four-beat lateral gaits that make riding long distances so comfortable for the rider without tiring the horse. There are three gaits: the *paso corto*, used for practical purposes; the *paso fino*, an exaggerated slow gait used in the showring and in parades, which has the appearance almost of slow motion; and the *paso largo*, which is fast. These traits are passed from mare to foal and are completely natural, needing no artificial aids. Once a person becomes accustomed to the gaits (it never trots or gallops) the Peruvian makes an excellent riding horse.

Appearance In stature, the Peruvian Paso is similar to its cousin the Paso Fino. The head is fine and resembles that of the Barb, with shapely pricked ears and a proud, alert look. The nostrils are readily dilated, presumably to allow as much oxygen as possible to be taken in. The body has all the evidence of a Spanish inheritance and is similar to the Andalusian's. The legs are sturdy, quite long, and well-muscled with hard hooves.

Characteristics The Peruvian Paso is hardy and energetic, but also equable and intelligent. It is an obedient and willing worker.

Colours Any colour, but usually bay or chestnut, with white on the head and legs permitted. The mane and tail are abundant, with fine, lustrous hair that may be straight or curly.

Height 14–15.2hh.

Like the Paso Fino, the Peruvian Paso has the fino, corto *and* largo *gaits which are passed from mare to foal and which are therefore entirely natural.*

PINTO (U.S.A.)

Origins The Pinto or Paint Horse (from the Spanish *pintado*, meaning 'painted'), like many of the old American breeds, is descended from Iberian horses that came over from Spain with the conquistadors. They are also sometimes called 'calico' horses in America.

In England and other anglophone countries they are referred to as 'piebalds' (black and white) or 'skewbalds' (any other colour and white) because their coats, of any solid colour, are heavily mottled with white; alternatively they are merely referred to as coloured horses, though in the United States the Pinto is regarded as a separate breed.

The original Spanish horses were allowed to revert to a feral condition and gradually extended into North America, where they roamed the Western deserts. Once domesticated by Native Americans, however, they were greatly revered; in fact, the Pinto was believed to possess magic powers.

Ranchers also adopted these hardy horses, as their stamina and agility made them excellent for work over extensive distances. Today they are still used as workhorses but also at rodeos, and for trail riding and showing and as all-round riding horses.

Appearance The Pinto has a fine head and graceful well-defined neck. The ears are alert and of medium length, while the eyes indicate spirit and intelligence. They are usually quite short in the back, with long, strong legs and hard tough hooves.

Characteristics Hardy and agile.

Colours The Pinto is well-known for its striking coat, which can be black, chestnut, brown, bay, dun, sorrel, palomino, grey or roan, patched with large areas of white. There are three distinctive types of coat pattern:
Tobiano, in which the head is like that of any solid-coloured horse, but there are round or oval spots resembling shields running over the neck and chest. One or both flanks may be coloured white or a colour can predominate. The tail is often composed of two colours.
Overo, which is predominantly dark or white, though the white shouldn't cross the back between withers and tail. The head should be white with scattered irregular markings on the rest of the body. At least one leg should be dark and the tail is usually one colour.
Tovero, which is a mixture of the two.

Height 14.2–15.2hh.

The Pinto or Paint Horse came about then Iberian horses which were brought over by the conquistadors turned wild. Their coats are always white with coloured patterning, making them most striking.

239

The Poitevin is an exceedingly rare breed, with only approximately 400 remaining.

POITEVIN (France)

Origins Also known as the Mulassier, and possibly not quite as attractive as the other heavy horses, the Poitevin comes from a low-lying area of west-central France and is the least known of the French breeds; for this reason it is the most endangered.

For centuries it was used for little else than the breeding of very strong mules out of Poitevin mares, the breed having originally been created using Flemish horses which were brought to Poitou in the 17th century to drain the marshes; they also contain Shire and Clydesdale.

The Poitevin once had a rather primitive appearance, but selective breeding has improved it greatly. It is lighter than most draft horses, with a lively, springy gait.

With the advent of motorized transport the mule trade was greatly diminished and with it the Poitevin; it was only saved by the dedication of a few breeders who had been working with Poitevins for a long time and had become attached to the breed. It remains extremely rare, with only around 400 remaining.

Appearance A medium-sized head with a straight nose, small ears, and kindly eyes. The neck is shortish and well-developed, with strong shoulders, a deep girth, and a broad chest. The body is shortish with a straight back and large, rounded quarters. The legs are of medium length and sturdy, with plenty of bone and feathering. The mane and tail are left long.

Characteristics Placid and calm with a quiet intelligence. Poitevans have a rather active gait.

Colours Various shades of grey, dun and black.

Height 15–16hh.

These ponies are most popular with children (though strong enough to carry a small adult), as they are kind, obedient and easy to handle. They also do well in competition.

PONY OF THE AMERICAS (U.S.A.)

Origins This is a relatively new breed dating to the 1950s and is the result of an accidental cross between a Scottish Shetland Pony and an Appaloosa mare with Iberian origins. The resulting offspring, Black Hand I, was a smaller version of its dam and it was this stallion that became the foundation of America's first pony breed.

The breed has the appearance of a small horse rather than a pony, and a little later was further refined with Quarter Horse and Arab blood to produce the showy, high-stepping action popular in the showring. the showring.

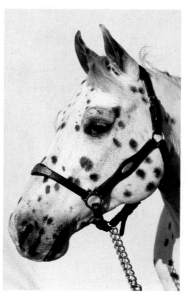

Similar in stature to British Thoroughbred ponies, the Pony of the Americas is most popular with children, who find it easy to handle. It is also strong enough to carry a small adult and is used in endurance, trail riding and showjumping as well as trotting and pony flat racing.

Appearance The head is very Arab with a broad forehead, small pricked ears, and a straight or slightly dished nose. The eyes are large and kind. The body is of medium length with a good sloping shoulder, well-developed quarters, and fine but strong legs.

Characteristics The Pony of the Americas is strong and hardy with a calm but willing disposition.

Colours Similar to the Appaloosa.

Height 11.2–14hh.

The Pony of the Americas is quite refined and similar in conformation to the British Thoroughbred pony. It has a high-stepping, attractive action.

The Pottok is from the Basque region of France and is held in great esteem by the local population. It still lives in a semi-wild condition.

POTTOK (Basque Spain)

Origins The Pottok, or Pottock (which means 'a prehistoric animal hunted by cavemen'), is an ancient native breed with mysterious origins, but it has always inhabited the west of the Basque region as well as Navarra, in Spain, and south-west France, where it remained a pure breed until the 8th century when it was bred with Arabs. Pottoks have been used on farms and as pit ponies in the mines of northern France.

The Basques have a great affection for the pony and it remains an important part of their culture. Many still live in a semi-wild state and some are used as general riding

ponies. They are excellent jumpers, and are also used for trekking, where their sure-footedness and familiarity with the terrain are great assets.

Appearance The head is small and neat with a straight or slightly Roman nose. In winter the Pottok grows a moustache to protect the nose when foraging for food among cold, sparse vegetation. The neck is short and strong with a thick shaggy mane; the chest is broad, and the loins are long with slightly sloping hindquarters. The tail is low-set and very thick. The legs are strong with well-shaped hard hooves.

Characteristics Pottoks have lively temperaments and are willing workers. They are also good-natured, strong and hardy, and have excellent powers of endurance.

Colours All solid and part colours.

Height 12–13hh.

Przewalski's Horse is almost certainly extinct in the wild, but a few survive in captivity. The breed has all the characteristics of horses in prehistoric cave paintings.

PRZEWALSKI'S HORSE (Mongolia)

Origins This is a truly ancient breed, also known as the Mongolian or Asiatic Wild Horse, which is stocky and dun-coloured with a dark-brown erect mane. Primitive horses of this kind were hunted by man 20,000 years ago and the likenesses of similar horses can be seen in prehistoric cave paintings in Spain and France. Now almost certainly extinct in the wild, as no sightings of it have been made for over 30 years, it is the only true wild equine and the ancestor of the domestic horse.

The earliest written evidence of its existence was in the 9th century and later in 1226 when a herd of wild horses are supposed to have caused Ghengis Khan, founder of the Mongol Empire, to fall from his horse.

Because of its isolation and the fierceness with which stallions protect their mares, the Mongolian horse's bloodline remained pure and can be traced back to its primitive ancestors. It gets its modern name from the man who brought it to the attention of the world, Colonel N.M. Przewalski, a Polish explorer, who acquired the remains of a wild horse in 1881 from hunters who had discovered them in the Gobi Desert of western Mongolia. He took them to the zoological museum in St. Petersburg where naturalist I.S Poliakoff examined them and decided that they belonged to a species of primitive wild horse. Following the discovery, some of the living horses were captured and kept in captivity in zoos and wildlife parks in order to save them from total extinction.

The captive population has increased rapidly and is carefully monitored at Prague Zoo, which holds the stud book of the breed. The horses are kept in as natural conditions as possible and some have been released back into the wild in China, Russia and Mongolia, where they are a protected species; there is also a successful population in France.

Appearance The head is of medium size with a broad forehead and a straight or slightly dished nose. The eyes are set high on the head and are rather small with a wild look. The nose tapers to a narrow muzzle with small low-set nostrils. The body is strong, with a longish, straight back, a thick, short neck, and weak quarters. The legs are short and stocky with hard, tough hooves.

Characteristics Przewalskis are never tamed and can be aggressive and ferocious, especially in the presence of their young. They need little care as they are extremely hardy.

Colours Various shades of dun, ranging from yellow to red. They have black manes and tails and black legs, often with zebra markings. There is a black dorsal stripe running down the back. The muzzle and surrounding the eyes is creamy white.

Height 12–14hh.

QUARTER HORSE (U.S.A.)

Origins The first breed to become established in the United States was the Quarter Horse; consequently it holds pride of place in the hearts of all American horse-lovers.

The Quarter Horse's origins can be traced back 500 years to the time when the Spanish *conquistadores* brought Iberian and Oriental horses to Florida. English colonists eventually acquired these horses from Chickasaw Indians, which they crossed with their own English horses, mainly Thoroughbreds, then refined them again with more Thoroughbred blood.

The name Quarter Horse comes from the horse's ability to sprint for short distances over a quarter of a mile (0.4km); before the days of racetracks, the early colonists would race their horses down main streets, which were usually about this distance in length. The powerful hindquarters of the Quarter Horse gave it great acceleration and even today it is faster than the Thoroughbred over short sprints.

The Quarter Horse is truly excellent at herding and cutting cattle which can be seen here at a Rodeo.

247

The Quarter Horse has been strongly influenced by the Thoroughbred, which is apparent from its fine appearance.

Not only was the Quarter Horse good at racing, it also made a good riding horse, pulled wagons, and made an efficient packhorse. However, its most valuable attribute was its natural instinct to round up herds. This was undoubtedly a legacy from its Iberian forebears which already had plenty of cow-sense, having worked the bullrings of Portugal and Spain, and which had nerves of steel and amazing agility. Today, however, racing predominates, but their use in rodeos, trailing and as all-round family mounts is widespread across the United States, Canada, Australia and even parts of Europe.

Appearance Quarter Horses can be quite large due to the influence of the Thoroughbred. The head is relatively small and the eyes are bright and set far apart. The neck, hindquarters and back are extremely muscular, which makes the feet appear small in contrast. The tail is set quite low.

Characteristics The Quarter Horse is easy to maintain, enthusiastic, honest and energetic.

Colours All solid colours are acceptable.

Height 14.2–16hh.

RIWOCHE (Tibet)

Origins The Riwoche was discovered in 1995 by a Frenchman, Dr. Michel Peissel, who was leading an expedition to northern Tibet ostensibly to study another horse, the Nangchen, which he had found two years before.

The Riwoche, named for the location in which it lives, is an incredibly exciting find in that it may be of primary importance in the evolution of the horse, along with Przewalski's horse, with its neolithic origins, and other breeds.

The Riwoche, which is used as a packhorse, has probably existed in isolation for thousands of years, as the 17-mile-long (27-km) valley in which it was found is cut off from the outside world by mountains. Blood samples are being studied to acertain its true origins.

Appearance In stature, the Riwoche bears a resemblance to a small donkey, with a rather heavy head and small ears and nostrils. The mane and tail are bristly.

Characteristics It is very hardy, having survived Tibetan winters, without human intervention, for thousands of years.

Colours Pale brown with the characterictic primitive dorsal stripe from poll to tail and zebra stripes on the back legs. The mane and tail are black.

Height Around 12hh.

SALERNO (Italy)

Origins The Salerno was developed in the Campania region of Italy, based on the sadly now-extinct Neapolitan – a superb horse of Iberian, Andalusian and Arab descent. It was most attractive and so highly prized that a breeding programme was established to further improve it. It is probably the best and most handsome of today's Italian saddlehorses.

By the late-19th century there was deep unrest in Italy and the Salerno's breeding programme was abandoned. However, a few managed to survive and by the 1900s breeding was re-established when the existing horses were crossed with Arabs and Thoroughbreds. The resulting horse was used by the cavalry and as an elegant carriage horse.

The breed continued to develop and more English Thoroughbred was added to produce a superb horse of the highest quality which had excellent paces, jumping ability, speed, stamina and grace.

Appearance The quality head is fine with a broad forehead, straight nose, and flaring nostrils. The ears are medium- length, shapely and expressive. The eyes are indicative of intelligence and spirit. The neck is long and

RIGHT
The Salerno is a highly-prized Italian saddlehorse. It has excellent paces combined with speed, stamina and elegance.

eautifully arched, with sloping shoulders and good broad chest. The girth is deep and the ack straight, with strong loins and well-eveloped hindquarters. The legs are fine, but rong and muscular, with good hard hooves.

Characteristics The Salerno requires an experienced rider as it has a spirited and lively temperament. It does, however, respond well to training, when it is usually obedient and acquiescent.

Colours All solid colours.

Height Around 16hh.

A line-up of Salernos, ridden by Italian mounted police.

The Selle Français is a combination of many breeds, from the heavy Norman to the English Thoroughbred, which was used to improved the breed and to produce a top-flight competition horse.

SELLE FRANÇAIS (France)

Origins Many of the best-known breeds are a fusion of several others and the Selle Français is no exception. Breeders of this beautiful warmblood had been working for many years in their quest for the ultimate competition horse, and used a variety of breeds to achieve their goal. Finally, in the 1950s, the breed was given official status and was named the Selle Français or French Saddle Horse.

Its main ancestor is the Norman, dating back to the Middle Ages, itself a cross between indigenous mares and imported horses such as Arabs and other Orientals. The Norman's primary use was as a warhorse, but the line had also been influenced by German and Danish carthorses, along with Thoroughbred and Norfolk Roadster. Other infusions such as Limousin, Charentais and Vendéen have also played their part in the production of the modern Selle Français.

However, it was mainly Thoroughbred which was responsible for the athletic horse we know today. The breed excels as a competition horse and is particularly talented at showjumping, though it is a good eventer and hunter.

Appearance The Selle Français is an elegant horse. The standard demands a fine head, sloping shoulders, and well-sprung ribs. The legs should be strong and the hindquarters powerful. There are up to five weights to suit individual tastes.

Characteristics Like many of the warmblood breeds, the Selle Français has an even, placid temperament, but is also intelligent, willing and energetic enough for top competition.

Colours Mainly chestnut, although other colours are acceptable.

Height 15–17hh.

Shagya Arabs stem from one stallion, Shagya, which was imported to Hungary from Syria in 1836.

SHAGYA ARABIAN (Hungary)

Origins The Shagya Arabian comes from Hungary's second most famous breeding establishment, the Babolna Stud, founded in the late 1700s; the other one is Mezőhegyes.

In 1816 the military stipulated that all brood mares should be bred with Oriental stallions to provide cavalry and harness horses; stallions with mixed Oriental blood as well as Iberian crosses were also used.

The results, although fairly lightweight, were horses that were tough and with plenty of stamina.

Following this success it was decided that the Bobolna Stud should concentrate on breeding horses with predominantly Arab blood, which was the beginning of the excellent Shagya Arabian.

Today's breed is descended from one Arab stallion, called Shagya, which was brought from Syria in 1836. He was fairly large for an Arab, standing at 15.2½hh, and was from the Siglavi or Seglawy strain. The stallion was typically Arab in conformation with a fine dished nose, a proud high-crested neck, short body, and high-set tail. It was mated with the military-style mares to produce the first Shagya Arabians and subsequent breeding by selection has produced a beautiful, refined riding horse of the highest quality. Today Shagya Arabians make excellent riding and competition horses and are also used for driving. They remain popular in their native country but are relatively rare elsewhere.

Appearance The Shagya is very like the Arab in conformation, but a little heavier. The head is wedge-shaped with a wide forehead and a straight or dished nose. The ears are neatly pointed and alert and the eyes kind. The muzzle is small and delicate with large flaring nostrils. The neck is beautifully arched, well muscled, and set high. The shoulders are sloping, with a broad chest and deep girth; the body is fairly short with well-defined quarters and long, elegant legs which are well muscled at the top with more bone than the traditional Arab.

Characteristics The Shagya has the constitution of the Arab but is bigger and stronger. It is kind, noble and spirited, with great stamina, speed and agility.

Colours All solid colours, though many inherit the Shagya stallion's grey colour. Rarest of all is black.

Height 14.2–15.2hh.

SHETLAND (U.K.)

Origins The Shetland islands lie off the coast in the far north of Scotland. The islands are remote and have a harsh climate, particularly in winter. There is not much shelter for the ponies and food is scarce, but they have adapted admirably to survive on very little and next to nothing during the winter months when they are known to come down from the hills and feed on seaweed that has been washed up on the beach.

It is unclear where the ponies originally came from, but there is evidence that they have been on the islands for a very long time, since Bronze Age remains were found dating from 2,500 years ago. Alternatively, they may have come from Scandinavia across the ice, or even from Europe.

Traditionally, Shetlands were used by islanders as riding, ploughing, pack and harness ponies. In 1870, the Londonderry Stud at Bressay, Scotland, fixed the type and character of the breed and, although no longer in existence, all today's best stock can be traced back to the famous Londonderry sires.

Appearance The head is small and neat and can be slightly dished. The ears are small and the eyes open and bold. The neck, shoulders and withers are well defined; the chest and quarters must be strong and muscular. The mane and tail is profuse, with straight feathering on the legs. The coat is double-layered, a feature unique to the Shetland.

Characteristics The Shetland has plenty of character and can be wilful. Because it is relatively strong for its size, it may be too much for a small child, unless it has been properly trained and has good manners. However, when kept in a suitable environment, with adult help on hand, they make superb children's ponies.

Colours Black, brown, bay, chestnut, grey, piebald and skewbald are all common.

Height Up to a maximum height of 42 inches (107cm).

OPPOSITE and BELOW LEFT
Shetland Ponies have been living on Shetland for at least 2,500 years.

BELOW
Shetlands make good children's mounts and often appear in driving and showing classes.

SHIRE

RIGHT
This is how modern Shires usually appears nowadays, pulling a dray at county shows.

BELOW
Shires stem from medieval warhorses, strong enough to carry knights and their heavy armour into battle.

SHIRE (U.K.)

Origins The Shire is one of the most famous and distinctive of all the draft horses and one of the largest and most majestic breeds in the world. Descended from medieval warhorses, whose immense strength enabled them to carry knights into battle wearing full armour, it was probably based on the Friesian with later infusions of Brabant. It was brought to England by the Dutch to drain the fens of East Anglia. However, it was not until the late 19th century that the best heavy horses in England were selected to develop the breed as it is known today.

to deliver beer locally, using normal mechanized transport for longer distances; the spectacle of these beautiful horses is obviously excellent publicity.

Appearance The Shire's most significant feature is its sheer size and massive muscular conformation. It is the largest and strongest horse in the world and when mature weighs a ton or more. Built ultimately for strength, the chest is wide, the back short-coupled, the loins and quarters massive. The legs, joints and feet are sufficiently large to balance and support the Shire's size; the lower legs are covered with long, straight, silky feathers. In the showring, white feathers are generally preferred as they help to accentuate the horse's action. Even though the Shire is such a large horse, it is not an ungainly heavyweight; in fact it is very much in proportion and quite beautiful to behold. The head is always noble and the nose slightly Roman. The eyes are large and wise.

Characteristics The Shire is well-known for its patient, gentle and placid nature; it is a true 'gentle giant'. In fact, it is quite amazing that such a strong animal that weighs so much can be so easily handled and it is not uncommon to see them ridden or handled by children or small women. Their kindness is legendary.

Colours Bay, black, brown and grey are the recognized colours of the breed. White feathers on the legs are preferred for the showring and white face markings are common.

Height 16.2–18hh.

LEFT
The Shire is the largest and strongest horse in the world, and as a heavy horse is also the most elegant and majestic.

The Shire's strength also made it suitable for agriculture and heavy haulage work, so initially the breed was established in Lincolnshire and Cambridgeshire where strong horses were required to cope with heavy fenland soil; but the Shire soon became widespread in Staffordshire, Leicestershire and Derbyshire until it eventually spread over the whole of England.

Up until the 1930s, the Shire was widely seen across the country, but as farms began to make use of tractors the numbers dropped dramatically until the breed was in danger of disappearing altogether. Fortunately, the problem was realized by a few dedicated breeders who helped to promote the breed and restore its popularity.

The Shire Horse Society has worked tirelessly to raise funds and to encourage the spread of the breed to other countries. Today there are active Shire Horse societies across Europe, the United States, Canada and Australia. Although a few Shires are still used on farms today, it is mainly for the sheer pleasure of working them in their traditional roles. They are also used in ploughing competitions, again, for pleasure, and for the same reason breweries use them in pairs

The Sorraia is an ancient breed with the dorsal stripe and zebra markings of its prehistoric ancestors. The Sorraia itself is a forebear of the Andalusian and Lusitano.

SORRAIA (Portugal)

Origins The Sorraia was discovered in Iberia by a Portuguese zoologist, Ruy d'Andrade, in 1920, when he was fascinated to learn that a wild horse subspecies was alive and well in Europe. However, many disputed that it was a truly wild horse, and some thought it impossible that one could have survived in a pure state, with no contact with horses that man had already had a hand in breeding.

When Andrade researched further into the genetics of the Sorraia he found that it had a similar skull and teeth to those of the Andalusian and Lusitano. He therefore concluded that the Sorraia was the wild ancestor of both of these breeds.

Appearance The Sorraia is a light-coloured pony with a dorsal stripe along the back and zebra stripes on the legs. Due to its rarity, inbreeding has been intense; however, this has not affected its hardiness. At first glance the Sorraia looks a little like a Lusitano.

Characteristics Like many of the world's wild horses, the Sorraia is independent and hardy. It is able to survive on the most meagre pasture and without the provision of shelter in winter. It is a good packhorse.

Colours Dun or grey.

Height 12.2–13.2hh.

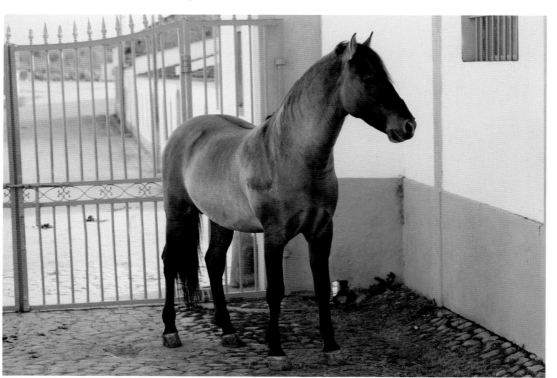

The Standardbred is probably the most successful trotter, used in trotting races all over the world for the past 200 years.

STANDARDBRED (U.S.A.)

Origins The Standardbred is famous for its trotting and pacing abilities and is widely used in harness racing throughout the world. The breed dates back 200 years when trotting races became sufficiently popular to warrant a breeding programme for the purpose.

The founding sire of today's Standardbred was Messenger, a grey Thoroughbred, born in 1780 and imported to Philadelphia in 1788. While Messenger was bred for traditional racing at a gallop, his own sire, Mambrino, had been responsible for a long dynasty of famous trotting coachhorses in England.

Messenger worked at stud for about 20 years and became famous for producing

strong, talented trotters. Meanwhile, during the mid-1800s in New England, the Morgan breed was being used to produce a line of smaller trotters with a straight up-and-down action. The high-stepping action of the Morgan line was then combined with the long-reaching stride of the Messenger line and this increased the performance of the Standardbred no end.

The trot of a Standardbred appears huge in comparison to that of ordinary breeds and is a gait whereby the legs are moved in diagonal pairs. However, the 'pace' is peculiar to this breed and is a gait where the horse moves its legs in lateral pairs. While the trot is natural to all horses, the pace generally has to be taught, although some Standardbreds will offer to pace from birth. Pacing is quicker than trotting as it allows the stride to be longer and more economical.

The term Standardbred was introduced in 1879 and derives from the time standard which was set to test the ability of harness racers. The Standardbred horse is required to cover a mile (0.6km) in 2 minutes and 30 seconds. Since this first standard was set, improved breeding has enabled the modern Standardbred to beat this target easily.

Appearance The head is in proportion to the horse's body and the eyes kind; the ears are indicative of alertness. The horse is muscular overall with a well-sprung barrel, sloping shoulder, and a strong back. The legs resemble those of the Thoroughbred, though are somewhat larger, with large joints; the hooves are large and strong.

Characteristics The Standardbred has an excellent temperament and away from the racetrack is quite placid. However, when

racing it is highly competitive, and displays great stamina and unbounding energy.

Colours All solid colours, but mainly bay, black, brown and chestnut.

Height 14.2–17.2hh.

This Standardbred is in action on the Red Mile Track at Lexington, Kentucky.

SUFFOLK PUNCH (U.K.)

Origins The Suffolk Punch originated in East Anglia in England and takes its name from the county of Suffolk, 'Punch' being an old word for short and thickset. It is thought to date back to 1506 and is the oldest heavy breed in Britain.

The breed was first developed by crossing the native heavy mares of the region with imported French Norman stallions.

However, modern-day Suffolks can be traced back on the male side to a single, nameless stallion, foaled in 1768 and belonging to Thomas Crisp of Orford, near Woodbridge, Suffolk; even though the breed is relatively pure, infusions of Norfolk Trotter, Thoroughbred and cob were added during the centuries that followed.

The Suffolk Punch is immensely strong, but due to its relatively small size is also quite agile. These qualities, combined with a lack of feather on the legs, like the Percheron, made it ideal for working the heavy clay soils of East Anglia. Moreover, food consumption, in proportion to its size, is also small, which enabled it to work long days on farms without stopping.

As with many of the heavy breeds, numbers fell dangerously low when farm tractors became widespread. Today Suffolks are rare, even though there has been a concerted effort in recent years to increase numbers. Today, Suffolks are shown, used in ploughing competitions, or are owned by breweries.

Appearance The Suffolk Punch is always chestnut in colour (the traditional spelling for this particular breed is chesnut, without the 't'). The breed is well known for its great strength and has an extremely powerful, muscular body with relatively short legs providing a low centre of gravity, which in turn helps the horse to pull ploughs or vehicles more easily. Suffolks mature very early and can do light work at 2 years old, with full work at 3. Their working life lasts well into their 20s.

Characteristics The Suffolk is well known for being easy to train, docile and hardworking. It is capable of almost any kind of work and is easy to maintain.

Colours Various shades of chestnut.

Height 16.1–17.1hh.

The Suffolk Punch is Britain's oldest breed, dating back to 1506. Sadly, they are quite rare today.

The Sumba has the dun colour and dorsal stripe, which means that it has not evolved very far from its primitive state.

SUMBA (Indonesia)

Origins The Sumba is primitive in appearance, and with dorsal stripe and dark points is not dissimilar to Mongolian and Chinese natives that were probably descendants of the Asian Wild Horse. Sumbas are ridden by small boys in their native Indonesia in competitions of equestrian dancing with jingling bells attached to the horses' knees.

Appearance These ponies are not without charm, with largish but rather pretty heads. They have small, black-tipped ears, slightly dished noses, and large attractive almond-shaped eyes which are soft and expressive. The neck is rather short with a compact straight-backed body. The quarters are also small, and the shoulders straight. The legs are long and rather fine. There is a black dorsal stripe from poll to tail, an indication of its primitive heritage.

Characteristics Sumbas are kind and willing. They are tough and hardy with good stamina and make good children's ponies.

Colours Usually dun, with dark points.

Height Around 12hh.

*Bred to be a cavalry horse, the
Swedish Warmblood is now a
quality competition horse.*

SWEDISH WARMBLOOD (Sweden)

Origins Like many European warmbloods the
Swedish Warmblood was developed to
produce a supreme cavalry horse, with
strength, stamina, intelligence and courage.

In the 17th century the Royal Stud at
Flyinge mated indigenous coldblooded stock
with many European breeds, most specifically
Iberian, Friesian, Barb and Arab. This
produced the breed's foundation stock and a
Swedish Warmblood stud book was eventually
opened in 1874.

It was necessary for horses to undergo stringent tests before they could be registered to ensure that their conformation was up to standard; action, stamina, temperament and performance where also rigorously tested.

Over the next 100 years or so the breed was refined and improved with infusions of Hanoverian, Trakehner, English Thoroughbred and more Arab. Consequently it could almost be said that the quality warmblood we know today was especially designed for the purpose, that is, to excel at competition; this includes dressage, eventing, showjumping and carriage-driving.

Appearance The head is rather fine and long, with a straight nose and a well-defined muzzle with flared nostrils. The ears are long, giving an impression of alertness, and the eyes are bright and intelligent. The neck is long and elegant with a well-developed crest. The shoulders are muscular and sloping with a good broad chest and deep girth. The back is medium-length with strong loins and well-developed quarters. The long legs are muscular with large joints and the hooves are strong and shapely.

Characteristics These horses are respected for their jumping ability and excellent paces. They are willing, obedient and intelligent and have a lively and spirited demeanour.

Colours All solid colours.

Height 16.1–17hh, though some are smaller.

SWISS WARMBLOOD (Switzerland)

Origins The Swiss Warmblood is based on Switzerland's highly respected Einsiedler breed which dates back at least to the 11th century; in fact, there is evidence that Benedictine monks in Einsiedeln were breeding the horses as early as 1064.

For many centuries the Einsiedler, which is strong and athletic, was used as a riding and driving horse. Gradually the breed was enhanced when Norman and Hackney blood were added and a little later infusions of Anglo-Norman were also introduced.

But it was in the 20th century that the breed really took off when Selle Français and Anglo-Arab were added, making the horse much finer and warmblooded. Then in the 1960s the Swiss decided that they wanted their own performance and competition horse, so using the remodelled Einsiedler they introduced other European warmbloods such as Hanoverian, Holstein, Trakehner and Thoroughbred.

The result was the Swiss Warmblood, a high-quality sports horse that excels at dressage, showjumping and carriage-driving competitions. In its early stages, the National Stud at Avenches used imported stallions, but now that the breed has developed its own standard Swiss Warmbloods are used.

Appearance The head is of medium size and good quality with a straight or slightly dished nose, intelligent eyes and alert medium-length ears. The neck is long and elegant with a slight crest. The body is of medium length with a good strong sloping shoulder, broad chest, and deep girth. The legs are long and well developed with well-shaped hooves.

Characteristics These quality horses are known for their excellent paces and superb jumping ability, having had many successes in international competition. They are kind, willing and easy to train.

Colours All solid colours.

Height Around 16hh.

TENNESSEE WALKING HORSE (U.S.A.)

Origins The Tennessee (or Plantation) Walking Horse originated in the deep south of the United States and was recognized as the ideal utility breed to transport plantation owners around their large estates. The smooth, gliding gait of the 'Walker' (as the breed is also known) provided hours of comfort in the saddle; the movement is performed from the elbow rather than the shoulder, thus transmitting the minimum of movement to the rider. Although still widely ridden for pleasure, the Walker is nowadays extensively bred for the showring, and is also used as a general riding and harness horse.

In fact there are two or three characteristic gaits, the flat-footed walk, the running walk, and the canter. The first horse perceived to have this natural talent was foaled in 1837, but it took another 50 years or so to establish the breed as it is today. The Thoroughbred, Standardbred, American Saddlebred, Narragansett Pacer and Morgan bloodlines all played their part in establishing this distinctive breed, but it was one stallion, foaled in 1886, that became the foundation stallion, possessing all the qualities such as the delightful temperament and the characteristic gaits. Nearly all the offspring inherited their sire's traits and he subsequently enjoyed many successful years at stud. Once a breed association was well-established, approximately 300,000 horses were registered.

Appearance The Walker has a large head with a straight profile, gentle eyes, and pointed ears. The neck is arched and muscular, with a broad base which enables the horse to carry its head high and elegantly. The breed has plenty of bone, which adds to its sturdiness, and has a short-coupled and level topline. The limb joints are well-made, with particularly powerful hocks that allow the hindlegs to step well under the body. The tail is often nicked and set artificially high. It is usually left long.

Characteristics Walkers are naturally gentle and calm, but it is their unusual gaits for which they are most famous. Although the gaits are inherited they need to be developed by further training. The flat walk, running walk and canter are natural to the breed. The running walk has several variations: the rack, the stepping pace, the fox-trot and single-foot.

Colours Nearly all colours, but especially black, chestnut, brown, grey, roan or bay.

Height 15–17hh.

The Tennessee Walking Horse is famous for its unusual gaits. It is now used extensively for pleasure and also in the showring.

The Tersky is one of Russia's finest breeds. It has a good deal of Arab and Thoroughbred in its make-up which enhances its capabilities in competition.

TERSKY (Russia)

Origins The Tersky or Tersk is a true performance horse, specializing in endurance, racing, jumping and dressage. Not only has it excellent sporting and athletic capabilities, it is also one of the most beautiful of the Russian breeds.

Originating in the northern Caucasus, the breed is now concentrated at the Stavropol Stud. Once, breeding and rearing took place on the steppes, with the result that weaker stock succumbed to wolves or died of disease. Survival of the fittest has consequently made the breed incredibly tough.

The modern breed is a product of the early 20th century, based on the Strelets Arab, which was produced by crossing Anglo-Arabs with Orlovs, and developed by crossing Arabs with old-type Terskys to which Thoroughbred blood had also been introduced.

There are three variations of Tersky: the first is lightweight, fine and Arab-like in appearance, and is known as the Eastern type. There is also a middleweight, and one that is sturdier and longer in the back, with a frame that is thicker-set. The heavier types have received infusions of Trakehner.

Appearance The Tersky is a horse of medium height and great beauty, based on Arabian bloodlines which is reflected in its appearance. The head is finely chiselled with a dished profile. The eyes are large and intelligent and the nostrils flared.

Characteristics The Tersky has a wonderful temperament. It combines kindness and intelligence with courage and stamina.

Colours Predominantly grey, usually with a metallic sheen to the coat. Black, chestnut and bay are also possible.

Height 15–16hh.

THOROUGHBRED

Origins The Thoroughbred is probably the most important breed of all and is the best known of all the British breeds. Its history dates back to the 17th century when farmers and landowners in England became increasingly interested in racing. Until that time, local horses not specifically bred for the purpose were raced, and it soon became apparent that in the quest for success a selective breeding programme was required. This was all the more pressing when gambling became popular with the public at large.

The wealthier landowners recognized the fact that the native horses had stamina but were lacking speed, so between 1689 and 1729 horses were imported from the Middle East to improve the racing stock. It is generally accepted that the modern Thoroughbred stems from three such stallions: the Byerley Turk, the Darley Arabian and the Godolphin Arabian, all of which had long careers working at stud. Between them, they established the three bloodlines of Herod, Eclipse and Matchem, which were pivotal to the British Thoroughbred, though the name was not applied to the breed until 1821.

Although initially bred with racing in mind, the qualities of the Thoroughbred make it an ideal horse for all other equestrian disciplines, e.g. eventing, showjumping, dressage, etc. The Thoroughbred has been exported far and wide to improve racing stocks, but has also been used to improve hundreds of other breeds as well.

Thoroughbreds reached the United States in the 1730s – all direct descendants of the

three famous foundation stallions, where they were generally similar to those elsewhere; recently, however, a distinctive American type has emerged, with longer hindlegs and longer stride, making its quarters appear higher by comparison.

Appearance The Thoroughbred is a truly beautiful and athletic animal, with long, clean limbs, a fine, silky coat, an elegant profile and a muscular body. The eyes are always large and intelligent, the ears finely

OPPOSITE
Thoroughbreds are produced all over the world, particularly for racing. This stallion is standing at stud in France.

LEFT
Thoroughbreds are naturally good at jumping and many are used for steeplechasing and at point-to-points. This Thoroughbred is from New Zealand and is an eventer.

BELOW RIGHT
An American Thoroughbred
taking part in a flat race.

OPPOSITE
Kentucky is the centre of horse-
racing in the United States; this
mare and foal are grazing the
famous 'blue' grass.

sculpted. Built for toughness, stamina and speed, the Thoroughbred is the ultimate racing machine.

Characteristics Thoroughbreds are courageous, honest and bold. In fact, one has only to watch a steeplechase or hurdle race to see that this is the case. Often the Thoroughbred is described as 'hot-headed'. While this is probably true of some individuals which may be more sensitive than others, most are a pleasure to own and ride.

Colours All true colours are acceptable.

Height 15–16.2hh.

The Trakehner has a chequered history, but today is popular as a competition horse, excelling in top dressage and eventing.

TRAKEHNER (Germany/Poland)

Origins The Trakehner is the most elegant and most Throughbred-like of all the warmbloods. Nowadays, because of its athleticism and paces, it is predominantly used for competition, particularly dressage and eventing.

The Trakehner's history is a chequered one dating to 1732 when the first Trakehnen stud was founded in East Prussia, now part of Poland but then in Germany. The stud became the main source of stallions for the whole of Prussia and the area quickly became famous for its beautiful and elegant coach horses.

The Trakehner came into being when native horses of the region were bred with Thoroughbreds and Arabs, infusions which gave it both speed and endurance. Within 50 years, however, the emphasis had shifted from producing coach horses to the breeding of chargers for the cavalry, which continued until the Second World War, when the Trakehner stud was completely destroyed. Fortunately, towards the end of the war, about 1000 horses were saved when they were trekked west with refugees escaping from the Russian invasion. Although some of the horses died on the way due to the harsh conditions, sufficient survived to continue the breed. Today, breeding of the Trakehner is again taking place in its place of origin as well as in other countries.

Appearance In terms of appearance, the Trakehner resembles the middleweight Thoroughbred. The head is fine with an intelligent and interested expression. The profile is straight and similar to that of the Thoroughbred. The neck and shoulders are shapely, the back short and strong, and the quarters powerful. The legs are strong and straight, producing a powerful, straight action.

Characteristics The Trakehner has an excellent temperament, being amiable, obedient and courageous. Although it resembles the Thoroughbred, it is without the 'hot' temperament associated with that breed. For this reason, breeders looking for an infusion of Thoroughbred without this trait often select Trakehner stallions instead.

Colours All solid colours are acceptable.

Height 16–16.2hh.

RIGHT
In its present form, the Ukrainian Saddle horse is only around 50 years old. It was bred specifically as a performance warmblood.

OPPOSITE
The Vladimir Heavy Draft has all the fine attributes of a heavy horse, with an alert and proud bearing and lively attitude.

UKRAINIAN SADDLE HORSE
(Ukraine)

Origins This is a relatively modern breed, in fact, only about 50 years old, formed by crossing Hungarian mares (Nonius, Furioso North Star, Gidrán), with Trakehner, Hanoverian and Thoroughbred stallions.

The development of the breed was monitored so closely that an extremely useful warmblood was developed in a relatively short space of time, one that was suitable for all disciplines.

Horses are rigorously performance-tested early in their lives before they are sold on, and only the best are retained for breeding purposes.

Characteristics Like most warmbloods, the Ukrainian Saddle or Riding Horse has a kind and obliging nature and a positive attitude to work. It is also courageous and bold.

Appearance The breed is refined and elegant, its Thoroughbred blood immediately apparent. The eyes are large and bright and the expression intelligent. The profile is straight.

Colours Most solid colours, particularly bay, chestnut and black.

Height Up to 16.1hh.

VLADIMIR HEAVY DRAFT (Russia)

Origins The Vladimir originated at the turn of the 20th century in the provinces of Vladimir and Ivanovo to the north-east of Moscow.

Local mares were mated with imported heavy breeds, mainly Clydesdales, but were also crossed with Shire, Cleveland Bay, Suffolk Punch, Ardennais and Percheron. The result is a horse suitable for all heavy draft work.

The breed was officially recognized in 1946 and from then on only horses which satisfied strict conformation criteria and performance tests were registered.

A horse that matures early, the Vladimir Heavy Draft can be put to work and stud when it is 3 years old.

Appearance The Vladimir has all the hallmarks of a heavy breed, with a muscular body, broad chest and strong neck. Its legs are sturdy and well-muscled.

Characteristics The breed is remarkable for its proud posture and majestic appearance. Unlike some of the other heavy breeds, its paces are forward-going, making it suitable for pulling troikas. Today, the Vladimir is still used for work on farms and in transportation.

Colours Mainly bay, back and chestnut.

Height 15.2–16.1hh.

*The Welsh Mountain Pony
(Section A) is the oldest of the
Welsh breed of ponies.*

THE WELSH BREEDS (U.K.)

Horses were present in Wales as long as 10,000 years ago. The indigenous breed which inhabited the hills was the Celtic Pony and it is thought that all Welsh breeds known today derive from them.

It is recorded that native stock was being bred in Wales in around 50 BC when Julius Caesar founded a stud in Merionethshire and was responsible for introducing Arab blood into the breed. The first mention of Welsh Ponies and Cobs were noted in the laws of Hywel Dda, written in AD 930.

Through the centuries, variations of the original wild ponies were developed. Early on in the 20th century, the Welsh Pony and Cob Society identified four clear types, described below. These are the original, once wild, Welsh Mountain Pony not exceeding 12hh (Section A); the Welsh Pony not exceeding 13hh (Section B); the Welsh Pony of Cob Type up to 13.2hh (Section C); the Welsh Cob of 13.2 –15.2hh (Section D).

WELSH MOUNTAIN PONY (SECTION A)

Origins The Welsh Mountain Pony is the oldest of all the Welsh breeds. As the name suggests it is tough, resilient, sound in limb as well as constitution. Known for its intelligence, agility, endurance and hardiness, the Welsh Mountain Pony is capable of surviving the harshest of winters. These ponies are now found all over the world and are highly regarded as quality children's riding ponies, and also perform well in harness.

Appearance The head is refined, with a small tapering muzzle and small, pricked ears. The eyes are large and bold. These qualities, as well as a dished face, give the Welsh Mountain a distinct resemblance to the Arab which was introduced into the breed. The neck, well-defined withers and quarters are in proportion to the rest of the pony's body, while the tail is set quite high. The limbs are set square with well-made joints and the feet are small, rounded and hard.

Characteristics The Welsh Mountain is a pony of great personality and charm, having inherited intelligence and quick-wittedness – traits which the original wild ponies seemed to have possessed in abundance. When in

action, the gaits must be smooth and the hocks well flexed.

Colours Mainly grey, but all true colours are acceptable.

Height Not exceeding 12hh.

WELSH PONY (SECTION B)

Origins The Welsh Pony has all the best attributes of the Welsh Mountain Pony, though breeders have accentuated its talents as a riding pony. Moreover, because the Welsh Pony was used for generations on farms for herding sheep, it is also tough and agile.

These qualities, when combined with good looks, jumping ability, and superb conformation for riding, makes them perfect as children's mounts.

Appearance The Welsh Pony shares many similarities with the Welsh Mountain Pony. The head is refined, with small pricked ears and the face may be slightly dished. The eyes are large and intelligent. The neck, back and quarters are muscular and in proportion, with the tail set high. The limbs are straight and strong and the hooves strong and rounded.

Characteristics The Welsh Pony is willing, active and enthusiastic and will always give of its best.

Colours Mainly grey, but all true colours are acceptable.

Height Not exceeding 13.2hh.

The Welsh Pony (Section B) has refined looks combined with strength and toughness. It is an excellent choice for children.

WELSH PONY OF COB TYPE (SECTION C)

Origins Originally used for farm work, the Welsh Pony of Cob Type was also used for carting slate from the mines. It is the same height as the Welsh Pony, but sturdier and capable of taking the heavier rider. It was developed more as a harness pony than for ridden work and has a naturally pronounced action, probably inherited from the Hackney which was introduced into the breed.

Appearance The general appearance should be that of a small cob. The eyes are spaced widely apart and the expression is intelligent. Like the other Welsh breeds the ears are small and pricked. The body and legs are sturdier and more cob-like than that of the Welsh Pony, and the feet are also slightly larger. The mane and tail are full.

Characteristics The Welsh Pony of Cob Type is similar in temperament to the other Welsh breeds, being lively and enthusiastic. It performs well in harness and is also a natural jumper.

Colours All true colours are acceptable. For the showring, however, ponies are preferred with plenty of white on the lower legs.

Height Not exceeding 13.2hh.

WELSH COB (SECTION D)

Origins Of all the Welsh breeds, the Welsh Cob is the most famous. Known for its stunning looks and extravagant paces, it is not only the ultimate working cob, but is also guaranteed to be the centre of attention in the showring.

OPPOSITE
A Welsh (Section B) mare and foal at stud.

LEFT
The Welsh Pony (Section C) should resemble a small cob in appearance. However, it tends to be a little larger than the first two types.

The Welsh Cob (Section D) is also very cobby in appearance. It is rather larger than the other three types and is most striking in appearance with extravagant paces. Its size means that it can be ridden by the whole family.

The breed dates back to the 11th century when it was known as the Powys Cob or Powys Rouncy. Welsh Cobs not only possess Welsh Mountain Pony blood, they were also influenced by imports from all over the Roman Empire. Breeds from Spain, such as the Andalusian, and the Barb and Arab from North Africa, were all crossed with the early Welsh Cob variety. Later in the 18th and 19th centuries other breeds such as Hackney and Yorkshire Coach Horse were also introduced.

Traditionally, Welsh Cobs were used by the military as well as by farmers; they were so versatile that they could be used by anyone needing transport or light haulage.

Appearance The Welsh Cob is compact, well muscled, well balanced and strong. It has a fine head with large, intelligent eyes and the usual small, pricked ears. The neck is arched and muscular, the back is short-coupled for strength, and the quarters are powerful and rounded. The legs are sturdy and straight and the feet are in proportion to the animal's body, hard and rounded.

Characteristics The Welsh Cob is proud, courageous, and extravagant in action. It is suitable for all disciplines and for all members of the family.

Colours All true colours are acceptable.

Height 13.2–15.2hh.

WESTPHALIAN (Germany)

Origins Like most European warmbloods the Westphalian is based on an older, heavier breed which was once native to Westphalia for hundreds of years. This native coldblood was bred with Thoroughbred to produce a warmblood which was first registered as a Westphalian in 1826, when the stud book was opened.

For many years the horse was used for riding and light carriage work until the end of the Second World War when measures were taken to improve the breed. Westphalian stock was infused with more Thoroughbred and Arab blood to increase its speed and endurance, as well as intelligence. Hanoverian was also used to ensure good sense and obedience.

The result was a superb quality riding horse which received its true recognition in the 1970s as a competition horse, particularly in showjumping. Nowadays it not only excels at dressage but also eventing.

Appearance The head is handsome and broad, with medium wide-apart ears, a straight nose

and clever eyes. The neck is long and well developed with fairly prominant withers, a straight back, strong loins and well-muscled quarters. The shoulders are sloped with a broad chest and deep girth. The legs are well porportioned and strong with good bone.

Characteristics The Westaphalian is well known for its courage and spirit. It is also obedient and easy to handle.

Colours All solid colours, with white on the lower legs and head allowed.

Height 15.2–16.2hh.

The Westphalian is another German success story, originally bred as a carriage and riding horse. However, it now excels at dressage, eventing and showjumping.

*RIGHT and OPPOSITE
Like its close cousin the
Malopolski, the Wielkopolski is
another Polish Arab type. It is
kind and obedient and as useful
working on farms as it is in
competition.*

WIELKOPOLSKI (Poland)

Origins The Wielkopolski shares much of its
heritage with the Malopolski, which is
another breed of Polish Arab, both originally
bred as general riding and driving horses also
capable of work on farms. Both are based on
native Polish Mazuren and Posnan stock,
breeds which now barely exist, having
become almost totally subsumed into both
the Malopolski and Wielkopolski.

The Wielkopolski was established after
the Second World War when the native stock,
which also contained Konik, was bred with
Trakehner, Hanoverian, Thoroughbred and
Arab to produce a horse of excellent quality,
which was a middleweight used for riding
and driving.

There are stringent guidelines to protect
the quality of the breed in which all stallions
must undergo conformation tests before
being allowed to breed.

Appearance The Wielkopolski has the Arab
wedge-shaped head, though it is somewhat
plainer. The nose is straight with a neat
muzzle and large open nostrils. The ears are
medium-length and well shaped and the eyes
are lively and intelligent. The neck is high-
set, long and elegant, with a slight crest. The
shoulders are sloping, with a broad chest and
a deep girth. The hindquarters are well
muscled, and the legs are long with good
bone and well-shaped hooves.

Characteristics This is a good all-round
competition horse also used for driving. It
is strong with plenty of stamina and
endurance, used on farms and for light draft

work in its native land. It has a kind and
quiet temperament and is a willing and
obedient worker.

Colours All solid colours.

Height 15–16.2hh.

TYPES

BELOW and RIGHT
In most countries the Albino is
regarded as a genetic mutation. In
the United States, however, it is
considered a breed and is actively
bred for its lack of colour.

ALBINO (U.S.A.)

Albinos occur naturally in nearly all species and the horse is no exception. Albinism is a genetic mutation in which the horse is born without the ability to produce the body's colouring pigment, melanin, and is therefore pure white. This is a rare condition, and can unfortunately mean that the horse is not always totally healthy. The lack of pigment means that it is easily sunburned and it is prone to other skin disorders. Some are born with poor eyesight or are deaf, while others are more subject to disease.

In the United States, however, the American Albino is regarded as a breed and is deliberately bred as such. It is said to be

descended from one stallion, an American Saddlebred, born in 1906 and called Old King. Today Albinos are carefully bred for strength, colour and conformation and are controlled by the American Albino Horse Club.

Albino horses are pure white with pink skin and blue eyes which can vary in intensity. Today, like the Palomino, Albinos are favoured for their striking beauty and therefore make suitable circus, parade and show horses.

AMERICAN WARMBLOOD (U.S.A.)

For many years, high-class warmblooded horses were imported into the United States to be used as sports horses for both professional and amateur competitors. These horses came from many sources and from all over the European continent. Desiring to establish a warmblood of their own, American breeders instigated a breeding programme to produce a horse with a broad genetic diversity distinctive to the United States. For this purpose, the American Warmblood Registry, in Jackson, California was founded in 1981 and now controls and encourages the breeding of high-performance, athletic and even-tempered horses suitable for all equestrian disciplines.

Only mares and stallions of the highest quality are used and all are inspected and certified for breeding purposes. With only 20 or so years of breeding history behind it, the American Warmblood as a type is still in its infancy; consequently, it is yet to be recognized as a specific breed. The huge gene pool used to make up this newcomer means that the American Warmblood can vary widely in looks depending upon which breeds have been introduced and when, remembering that the use of Thoroughbreds, Arabs and heavy horses can greatly influence size, colour and shape. Whatever the case, the American Warmblood is certainly proving its worth, and excels not only at showjumping but also at dressage.

BELOW LEFT and BELOW
The American Warmblood Registry was opened in 1981 to encourage the breeding of American performance horses.

BELOW
Cobs are strong and reliable and make excellent all-rounders, this show Cob being a fine example.

OPPOSITE
The Hack should be light, graceful and refined.

CANADIAN CUTTING HORSE
(Canada)

Not a breed in itself, this is an extremely important type which has been developed over many years to work on the huge cattle ranches of Canada. It can also be seen in rodeos and cattle-cutting contests all over Canada.

As the name suggests, the Canadian Cutting Horse was developed and bred for separating specific cattle from the main herd and for the speed and agility required for the task. The main influence is the Quarter Horse, whose own work and therefore breeding has given the Cutting Horse many of its useful qualities. However, the Cutting Horse is much larger even though it is just as quick and agile. Its temperament is such that it is easy to train and, like the Quarter Horse, has good cow-sense.

COB (U.K.)

Like the Hunter, the Cob is not a breed but a type and must not be confused with actual breeds such as the Welsh Cob. Originating in the British Isles, the Cob was developed largely by crossing Thoroughbreds with some of the heavier breeds.

The Cob is a relatively small horse, ranging from 14.2–15.1hh, but very strong and powerful and characterized by a deep, short body. The legs are short and sturdy and the neck short, deep and elegantly arched.

Dating to the 18th century, Cobs have traditionally been bred in Britain and Ireland, although nowadays they also come from many other countries too.

They are known for their soundness, reliability, calmness, and suitability as perfect family pets. They are sufficiently strong to carry a grown man, yet small and steady enough to accommodate a child. They can also be trusted with disabled or elderly riders, which is a virtue almost exclusive to the Cob type. However, their generous, placid nature does not mean that they are lacking in performance; in fact, they make excellent hunters, harness horses and showjumpers. Generally speaking, it is usual to hog the mane to show off the Cob's fine head and neck.

HACK (U.K.)

Although a distinct type, the Hack is not a breed. It is essentially a horse of quality and in Britain, where it is unique, it is usually a Thoroughbred or Thoroughbred-cross Arab type. It is usually comparatively small and light, graceful and refined, though not without substance, usually standing between 14.2 and 15.3hh.

Its conformation should be impeccable and its manners perfect. The heyday of the Hack was in the 19th century, when horses were selected and trained for ladies and gentlemen to be seen out and about on. They were not expected to gallop, hunt or jump; they were merely for pleasure.

Today, in Britain, Hacks are produced mainly for the showring and are judged for their conformation, manners and paces. The gaits should be easy, elegant, smooth and straight. In other countries different breeding criteria may apply; in the United States, for example, the Saddlebred, rather than the Hack, is considered to be the ultimate riding horse.

HUNTER (U.K.)

The Hunter can be any type of horse, as long as it has the stamina to carry a rider for a day's hunting accompanied by hounds. Being largely a British invention, the original Hunter had to feel comfortable in the type of landscape found throughout the British Isles. Consequently, various other kinds of Hunters have been developed in other parts of the world, and their breeding reflects the terrain and surroundings in which they work.

The Hunter must be tough, versatile, safe and mannerly. It must also be capable of jumping any obstacles it may encounter, such as gates, ditches and hedges.

Notable breeds used in the production of Hunters range from the Thoroughbred through to Irish Draft and Cleveland Bay. As the Hunter is a type rather than a breed, it can consequently be of any size, ranging from 14.2 through to 17.2hh, and can also be any colour and weight. As well as performing in the hunting field, Hunters can also be shown and used for general pleasure riding and jumping.

A Hunter must be well-proportioned, with a good sloping shoulder, strong hindquarters, and a deep chest. It must also be sturdy and powerful.

PALOMINO (U.S.A.)

Despite the efforts of breeders, the Palomino is still regarded as a type as the colour cannot be bred to order but occurs spontaneously in nature.

Rare and beautiful Palominos have been in demand since ancient times and the colour crops up in most breeds. In Spain, they are known as Ysabellas, after Isabella of Spain, who during the Middle Ages made great efforts to produce them. Some were taken to the Americas and one was presented by Cortés to Juan de Palomino, hence the name.

Today, in the United States, Palominos can be registered, provided that their colour and conformation is acceptable to the Palomino Society whose aim is to establish a unique breed type and colour for the future.

The two most common Palominos in America are the Quarter Horse and Thoroughbred types. In Britain, Palominos occur in many of the native breeds, but particularly in the Welsh Mountain Pony. The Palomino should have a lovely gold-coloured coat, described as resembling a newly minted gold coin. The mane should be white, light cream or silver, with no other colour present. White can occur on the head or lower legs. Famous as 'The Golden Horse of the West', the Palomino is one of the most beautiful and famous colour types in the world.

OPPOSITE
The Hunter must have excellent manners, substantial size, and the ability to jump large obstacles.

LEFT
The immense beauty of the Palomino's golden coat makes it much in demand. This is an American Quarter Horse.

POLO PONY (Argentina)

Although referred to as a pony, suggesting an animal of 14.2hh or less, the Polo Pony is actually a horse, usually measuring about 15.1–15.2hh. Moreover, it is a type rather than a breed, developed specifically for the game of polo.

One of the oldest games in the world, polo originated in Persia (Iran) some 2,500 years ago, though it has since spread throughout the world and is now popular in England, India and North and South America. Polo is a hard, fast and tough ball game, performed on horseback, from where goals are scored using a long-handled mallet. Consequently the ponies must be able to react immediately to the rider's wishes, be fit, fast and fearless, have great acceleration, and be capable of sharp, sudden turns. It is therefore not surprising that the very best Polo Ponies are said to have an instinct for the game.

Polo Ponies have been developed all over the world by using many different breeds noted for their stamina and agility, the Arab being a good example. Today, however, the most successful horses come from Argentina, now the polo centre of the world, where they are infused with Criollo and Thoroughbred bloodlines. Though its main resemblance is to the Thoroughbred, the Polo Pony is slightly shorter in the leg and rather smaller and more nimble. It should have natural balance, powerful hindquarters, a short back and a sloping shoulder.

RIDING OR PLEASURE HORSE
(U.S.A. and U.K.)

As a type, the Riding or Pleasure Horse is halfway between a Hack and a Hunter in size and build. It is not usually a specific breed, but when shown in competitions must bear all the hallmarks of good conformation, careful training and obedience to the rider's aids.

The Riding Horse should have a distinct air of quality about it and this usually means that it has quite a lot of Thoroughbred in its make-up, rather than the heavier breeds which tend to dominate the Hunter types. Having said this, the Riding Horse should still have plenty of bone and substance. As a class, the Riding Horse is always popular and well-supported, probably because so many horses fit the category.

OPPOSITE
The best of today's Polo Ponies come from Argentina, where they usually contain Criollo, Arab and Thoroughbred bloodlines.

LEFT
The Riding or Pleasure Horse is often used in the United States for display riding.

RIGHT and OPPOSITE
The Show Pony is one of Britain's
prized possessions, produced by
crossing native breeds with
Thoroughbred and Arab to
achieve fine quality.

SHOW PONY (U.K.)

The English Show Pony is a breeding success which is the envy of the world. It was developed in the 20th century to provide children with a mount that bears all the hallmarks of a quality hack, but which is still pony-sized.

The original Show Ponies were bred by crossing British native species with Arabs and Thoroughbreds. The purpose of this was to obliterate the heavy, cobby looks associated with many of the native breeds, and to introduce the more refined appearance of the Arab and Thoroughbred.

Some of the early Show Ponies were rather highly strung and consequently unsuitable for small children, but over the past few decades temperament has been enormously improved. Nowadays, as well as taking pride of place in Britain, it is exported to ride and compete all over the world. High prices can be commanded for winning ponies, but it is usually the rider-pony combination that makes a true winner.

STABLE MANAGEMENT

Experienced equestrians are only too aware of the importance of a well-designed stable yard: errors of layout, drainage, lighting, as well as badly-sited entrances for pedestrians and vehicles, cause many difficulties, leading to a greater and more time-consuming workload. If you are lucky enough to own land where you can establish a new yard from scratch, take the time to plan it carefully.

RIGHT
*This well-organized feed room
has a blackboard displaying each
horse's feeding requirements.
The feed bins are vermin-proof
and have easy access.*

BELOW
*These sturdy brick stables were
built at the turn of the last
century and are most attractive.
They offer warmth in winter and
coolness in summer.*

Stabling

Stables should preferably be built in rows
or around a central courtyard. Make sure
there is enough space between rows to
allow horses to be easily moved from one
location to another. It is also important
to provide an area where horses can be
tied up safely. Horses should not be tied
up too near to one another, as a squabble
may lead to one or other of them being
kicked or bitten. The stables themselves
should be of adequate size and, if the
location is exposed, should have their
entrances facing away from the prevailing
winds. The stables should be airy but free
from drafts. Horses are happiest in loose

boxes where they have sufficient space to
move around. A medium-sized horse
requires a stable 12-ft (3.7-m) square; if a
horse is particularly large, 14 x 12ft (4.3 x
3.7m) is recommended. Ponies can be
accommodated in a 10 x 12-ft (3 x 3.7-
m) loose box. In larger yards an isolation
stable for sick horses is recommended,
well away from the main yard; should an
infection break out, the risk of the other
horses becoming infected is thereby

reduced. Loose boxes should be located
in a well- drained site and all roofs
should be meticulously maintained.
Stables prone to flooding are a great
inconvenience, as bedding has to be
constantly replaced during wet weather
and they are uncomfortable and
unhealthy for their occupants.

Types of Stabling Today, the most
popular stabling is made of wood, which

arrives ready to assemble. There are variations in quality, and it is wise to shop around before selecting the type suitable for your requirements.

Brick-built stables are best: they are strong, airy but warm in winter and do not rot. Indoor stabling in a large barn partitioned with panels and bars is also popular; the horses are kept warm in winter out of the elements and cool in summer when ventilation can be introduced. These are preferable for horses which are being kept in countries that have extreme climates. The drawback is that natural light may be at a premium; moreover, horses may feel uneasy with only bars separating them from their neighbours.

Bedding

Straw A straw bed is the most popular, as it is relatively cheap, warm and comfortable. However, straw should not be used to bed down horses with allergies to dust or fungal spores.

Stabled horses must be mucked out

BELOW
These indoor stables provide first-class accommodation. They are particularly beneficial in countries where extreme variations in temperature are the norm, i.e. they are warm in winter and cool in summer.

thoroughly each morning and droppings should be removed regularly throughout the day (skepping out). An old laundry basket makes a suitable skep. It is easier to muck out an empty stable so, if possible, secure the horse outside the stable in a tying-up area. Use a four-pronged fork to sift through the bedding, removing all droppings and wet straw. Start from one side of the stable and work methodically through the whole. Pile all the straw up in one corner and sweep the floor thoroughly. If convenient, let the floor dry for a while before putting the bed back down. From the pile in the corner, fork the straw into the centre of the stable, laying the bed down and flattening it. Shake up a new, clean bale of straw and spread it over the whole bed, placing the bulk of it around the edges of the stable in the form of banks. These will help prevent drafts and shield horses from injury when lying down. Make sure you add an adequate amount of clean straw, as a deep, clean bed is more economical in the long run and will be warmer and more comfortable. Some horses develop the habit of eating their beds. This should be discouraged as impacted straw in a horse's stomach may cause colic. To stop this, try mixing the new with the existing straw, which will make it less palatable. Finally, it is a good idea to regularly remove (perhaps once a week) all the straw from the stable and disinfect the floor. Once the floor is dry, the bed can be put back again.

Wood Shavings and Paper Beds Both varieties come in plastic-wrapped bales which are convenient and clean to handle, so much so that they can be transported in the back of an ordinary car without making a mess. Depending upon how much your horse dirties his bed and how often he is turned out to grass, you will find that approximately one or two bales a week will suffice. Price will vary from place to place, but generally speaking the cost will be slightly more than keeping a horse on straw. It is most important that the horse is very thoroughly mucked out in the morning and that all wet patches and droppings are removed. The bed must then be shaken up to prevent it from becoming impacted. As with the straw bed, regular visits to skep out must be made throughout the day in order to keep the bed clean and fresh. Both beds are great for horses with dust or fungal spore allergies. Make sure you only buy the best product available; the cheaper brands tend to be more dusty, while wood shavings may contain sharp splinters.

Auboise Bed This is a fairly new and entirely natural product made from the hemp plant. It is particularly absorbent and, like shavings, is suitable for horses with allergies. It is expensive to start off as quite a few bales will be needed to establish a decent-sized bed: however, absorbency is so good that the result is ultimately economical.

Equipment for Mucking Out

Wheelbarrow

Shovel

Four-pronged fork, with blunted prongs

Skep

Hosepipe

Shavings fork

Rake

Broom

LEFT
A selection of tools for mucking out beds made of straw and shavings.

OPPOSITE
A wood-chip bed is easy to maintain and beneficial for horses with dust allergies. It produces less waste so is cheaper overall.

be fitted with grilles (for horses which are liable to jump out or are liable to bite passers-by) or anti-weaving grilles. Hayracks, if required, should be fitted at a safe height, but not so high that they allow dust from hay to fall into a horse's eyes. Salt licks are also useful, being ready and to hand when horses need them. Traditionally, water is supplied to horses in buckets, but if they are often knocked over, an automatic, self-filling system can be installed. Toys are available from various sources and are designed to alleviate the boredom of a horse confined to a stable.

Tack Room A neat, tidy and well-planned tack room is essential for storing and cleaning tack. Hot and cold running water must be laid on and power points provided. Veterinary equipment can also be stored here and, if space permits, boots, exercise bandages and rugs. Most important is storage for saddles and

Deep Litter Bed This is economical as less bedding is used than in a conventional bed. The bed can be started off using either straw, shavings or paper. At every opportunity, the droppings should be removed and the bed topped up with clean bedding. It will not need shaking up, but when using shavings very wet patches must be dug out and removed. This type is less suitable for horses which are kept stabled and not turned out, as the continuous heat from the bed can cause foot infections such as

thrush. It is essential that the feet are kept as clean and as dry as possible. Provided that the bed is very carefully maintained, a deep litter bed will stay comfortable and odour-free throughout the winter. However, once spring arrives, the bed must be completely removed and the stable floor given a thorough disinfecting.

Stable Fittings Stables should have specially made latches, mangers, haynet tying rings and, where necessary, should

Tack rooms should be free from damp and equipped with plenty of saddle racks and pegs for bridles. As tack is a valuable commodity, it is wise to fit strong doors, sturdy locks and a burglar alarm.

bridles which are often the most valuable pieces of equipment. This makes them particularly attractive to thieves as they have a good secondhand value. You will therefore need as much security as you can afford. All windows and doors should be barred or reinforced and alarms and closed-circuit TV are further possibilities. All tack should be permanently marked: in the event of it being stolen and recovered by the police, it can then be promptly returned to its owner.

Flooring The traditional stable floor is usually concrete, but it is becoming increasingly popular to cover the concrete with rubber. This provides a warm, slip-proof base; because of this, bedding can be reduced.

Water Supply In the stable yard, a good, easily accessible water supply is essential; it is also important that a drain is sited at this location as the cleaning of boots, buckets and other equipment, as well as hosing horses down, will produce a lot of excess water which needs to run away. Ideally, the tap and hosepipe should be in a frost-free location and all pipes leading to the tap should be lagged to prevent them from becoming frozen in winter.

Electricity Supply As with all electrical fittings situated outside, a circuit-breaker, installed within the main fuse box of the electricity supply, will reduce injury in the event of wires becoming wet or damaged. Outdoor sockets and switches designed for the purpose are the only ones which should be used. Do not be tempted to economize by using regular indoor fittings.

Fire Prevention Most stable yards store hay and straw which is a perennial fire risk. Store these in a barn well away from stables so that, in the event of fire, there will is no danger to horses. Make sure there is an adequate amount of extinguishers located around the yard and that you and others are aware of the drill to evacuate people and animals in the event of a fire; plan at least two different exits out of the yard. Smoking in stableyards should be strictly prohibited and 'No Smoking' signs prominently displayed in strategic positions.

Security These days, theft is still on the increase; but there is much you can do to minimize the risk. Closed circuit TV is expensive but effective but alarms also act as deterrents. Make sure all valuable items are securely under lock and key. It is worthwhile investing in strong reinforced padlocks and chains. Fortunately stealing horses is relatively rare when compared to the theft of property, particularly where horses are freeze-marked (page 322).

Storage Areas where hay, straw and bedding are to be kept should be perfectly dry and free from vermin. They should be located well away from areas where animals are housed.

Muck Heaps These should be positioned well away from stables, as they smell unpleasant and encourage flies. They can

LEFT
Have plenty of clean bowls, scoops and utensils to hand.

Equipment for Feeding
Feed bins (plastic dustbins are rot- and vermin-proof)
Feed scoop (to measure quantities)
Scales
Rubber feed bowls
Water buckets
Haynets

also be a nuisance to neighbours and passers-by, so think carefully when you decide where to position them. A pit or bunker is ideal for the purpose: it is best if it is contained on three sides, which will help keep the area tidy. For a fee, an agricultural contractor will regularly remove the muck, so there must be easy access for large vehicles. Do not be tempted to burn the muck: although this is a cheap method of disposal, the resulting smell and smoke is unpleasant and will annoy your neighbours; in some areas burning may even be against the law. Muck must not be spread onto grazing land used by horses as the process may cause re-infestations by parasites which will ultimately be passed back to horses.

Insurance Policies Make sure you are well insured for every eventuality. Accidents, theft or storm damage can prove costly. It is a wise precaution to insure your property for public liability.

Pest control Rats and mice are particularly attracted to stable yards and can be controlled by using traps and poisons. Handle poisons carefully and follow all instructions to the letter. Rats, in particular, can cause damage and spread diseases, some of which are fatal to human beings. It is essential that numbers are controlled.

A Typical Daily Stable Routine

7.00am
1. Check horse over for general health and that no injury has occurred during the night.
2. Put the horse's headcollar on and tie him up.
3. Pick out his feet and change or adjust rugs as necessary.
4. Muck out the stable and lay the bed down for the day.
5. Provide a haynet and the first feed of the day.
6. Remove the headcollar.

9.00am
1. Tie horse up. Remove droppings from the stable.
2. Give a short grooming. Tack the horse up and then exercise him.

10.30am (or on return from exercise)
1. Remove tack from horse.
2. Give a thorough grooming, making sure feet are picked out and shoes are in good condition.
3. Put on day rugs.
4. Give haynet.
5. Remove headcollar.

12.00pm
1. Tie up.
2. Check water.
3. Remove droppings.
4. Give second feed.
5. Clean tack.

2.00pm
1. Turn horse out in paddock, if available.

4.30pm
1. Bring in horse from field.
2. Groom off mud.
3. Pick out feet.
4. Give haynet.
5. Give third feed.
6. Remove headcollar.

8.00pm
1. Tie up.
2. Remove droppings.
3. Check rugs.
4. Top-up water, if necessary.
5. Refill haynet, if necessary.
6. Give fourth feed.
7. Remove headcollar.

NOTE: *If you are a busy person and have sole charge of your horse, the above stable routine can be condensed into a morning and evening visit with turn-out during the intervening period.*

OPPOSITE
Take time out with your horse; a good relationship is beneficial to both of you.

HORSES KEPT AT GRASS

This horse is so at home in his paddock that he feels confident enough to stretch out for a good rest.

Horses are at their happiest out in a field. This is no surprise, as a grazing horse is as close as he can get to his natural environment. Horses kept in stables for hours on end, particularly with insufficent exercise, often suffer from boredom and develop stress-related habits such as wind-sucking and weaving. Ideally, horses should be turned out on a daily basis, where they can exercise freely: this means that they will be fitter than the stable-kept horse, and not overfresh when they come to be ridden.

However, there are disadvantages in keeping a horse at grass, which is why the majority of people prefer to keep them partly in a stable and partly out to grass, as it is difficult to regulate the weight of a grass-kept animal. During the spring and summer, when the grass is rich, horses put on weight rapidly, which can interfere with the exercise routine for two reasons. Firstly, it is dangerous for a horse to be ridden with a bellyful of grass; secondly, an overweight one will be more subject to strains. In the winter, grass-kept animals grow thick coats which protect them from the elements. This can make fast exercise difficult, as the thick coat causes the horse to sweat profusely when ridden in excess of walking for any length of time. Clipping in winter is not really advisable as the horse needs to retain all his natural protection. Horses at grass are often muddy and greasy: while this may seem undesirable to the owner, the horse is likely to be perfectly happy and healthy. Grass-kept animals should not be overgroomed as this removes the natural oils in the coat which are a horse's defence against harsh weather.

In most countries, horses are quite happy to be kept at grass all year round. This is not an excuse for neglecting them. In fact, a grass-kept horse needs to be carefully monitored and checked over at least twice a day.

All horses need extra attention in winter in terms of food and shelter, but native horses and ponies out at grass tend to fare better than other breeds, as they have already become acclimatized. Other breeds such as Thoroughbreds and other lightweights are not really adapted to living out in winter, and will require even more attention in the form of supplementary feeding, extra rugs and a field shelter.

In summer, horses need to be protected from hot sun and biting insects. Sprays and potions can be bought or made for the purpose. If the sun is extremely strong, it may be necessary to bring the horse into the stable during the hottest part of the day. Sometimes, a summer drought can destroy much of the grass. If this happens, you may have to provide extra food.

When grass is in abundance, horses tend to put on weight rapidly and disorders such as laminitis can appear, making it necessary to restrict grazing. Electric fencing is suitable for dividing fields into smaller sections. Horses with a tendency to weight gain or laminitis can be restricted to smaller areas than those without these problems.

When out all year, horses require plenty of space, with each provided with at least 1 acre (0.4 hectare).

Horses are herd animals, so are happiest in the company of others. Avoid keeping a horse alone in a field; he may fret or even jump out to look for company.

Horses benefit greatly from a spell in the paddock for a few hours a day.

Thoroughbreds and lighter breeds are less able to cope with adverse weather conditions. This is because their coats are often thinner and their skins more sensitive.

Taking Care of Grazing Land

Good management of grazing land brings its own rewards, but it is a year-round task to keep pastures in good condition.

It is best to divide the grazing into sections (electric fencing is ideal for this purpose), ideally three; however, two will do if a limited amount of land is available, but the aim is to have one or two paddocks rested. While one paddock is in use the others can be rested, topped and rolled. Weeds can be killed or dug up and the grass can be fertilized.

Rotating grazing land can control worms; resting land interrupts the worms' life cycles, helping to reduce infestation. All horses must be regularly wormed; it is best to treat all horses in a field at the same time, making sure that new arrivals are wormed before entering the paddock.

All droppings should be regularly removed from the paddock, which will help to prevent the grass from becoming sour, break the worm cycle, and generally improve the appearance of the paddock. This is particularly important where a lot of horses are grazing on a small area.

All horse owners should be aware of plants poisonous to horses. Some cause serious illness, while others can be fatal (see page 321). All poisonous plants and weeds which smother the grass should be dug up by the roots and burned to prevent their seeds spreading. Do not neglect this: unwelcome plants spread quickly, so regular checks should be made of the entire paddock, particularly during the spring growing season.

Water Supply Horses at grass need constant access to clean, fresh water. Ideally, a galvanized metal self-filling trough is the best choice. For safety's sake the ballcock apparatus should be protected by a lid. Provide plenty of space around the trough to avoid the possibility of horses becoming trapped between fence and trough. Site the trough in a well drained location and away from trees so that leaves cannot accumulate in the water. All troughs should be regularly scrubbed clean, then rinsed out. A cheaper option to a purpose-built trough are containers with rounded edges, filled with clean water, which you will need to check, clean and refill daily. Avoid

RIGHT
Make sure your horse always has access to a plentiful supply of clean, fresh water.

BELOW
This purpose-built field shelter will provide a horse with extra protection from the elements, especially if the paddock has no natural shade, when the shelter becomes a necessity.

receptacles with protruding metal or sharp corners. Remember that horses need large quantities of water, particularly in hot weather. Do not allow them to drink from streams which run through farmland, as they may be contaminated with chemicals; stagnant ponds or any other unsafe source of water should also be fenced off.

Shelter Horses living out require shelter, both from the sun's rays and flies in summer, and from harsh weather in winter. A well-designed field shelter should provide sufficient space for the number of horses using it, with a wide enough entrance to enable them all to freely come and go. Make sure the shelter is positioned in such a way that horses

RIGHT
This beautiful grey horse is a
picture of contentment, enjoying
the sunshine and sniffing the air.

RIGHT BELOW
Make sure that field gates
are firmly padlocked.

cannot be trapped between boundary fence and shelter. It should be sited with the entrance facing away from the prevailing winds. High hedges are also good protection from strong winds, but it is important that they have been sited correctly.

New Zealand Rug In winter, horses should be kitted out with New Zealand rugs, as only the hardiest will get through winter without one. There are many different kinds and prices vary. Modern fabrics have made them light, waterproof and tough, and providing you purchase a good-quality rug, your horse should stay warm and dry all winter. It is a good idea

to have a spare in reserve to allow for repair to damage.

Gates and Fencing These are a must if horses are to be kept safe and protected from injury.

The best is wooden post and rail which, with a hedge behind it, will provide shelter as well. Beware of poisonous trees, e.g. laurel or laburnum, which should be removed or completely fenced off.

Hedges are a safe option and provide shelter all-year-round; however, they do require maintenance and the boundaries should be reinforced with electric fencing in the event of weak spots occurring.

Post and wire is an acceptable option. However, it is less strong and can cause injury if allowed to get slack.

LEFT
Horses are happy to stay out in cold weather provided that they are adequately rugged up.

BELOW
Learn to recognize poisonous plants, which should be dug up and burned.

Poisonous Plants

Ragwort

Yew

Hemlock

Privet

Foxglove

Laurel

Laburna

Young horses are turned out for a few years to allow them to mature and grow. Once they are three or four years old they can then be broken in.

Electric fencing in relatively cheap and very versatile as it can be moved around where needed. It is best used in its widest form so that it can be easily seen by horses. If electric wire is to be used, hang strips of plastic from it at regular intervals. It should not be used as an external boundary fence as horses could easily escape if it were to fall down or the electricity supply fail.

Fences made from sheep wire or barbed wire are dangerous and should be avoided at all costs.

Security Horse theft is sadly a fact of life: make sure that all external field gates are fitted with tamper-proof chains and padlocks. These are worth the expense for peace of mind. Chains and padlocks should be fitted at the opening and also where the gate or gates are fastened to the hinges to prevent thieves from lifting them right off. Never leave headcollars by gates or on horses: this is an open invitation to thieves. Place a sign on the gate to the effect that all horses have been security-tagged.

It has become apparent that the most effective form of security is to have horses freeze-marked. This is a painless procedure whereby the skin is branded with a number using a very cold substance. This causes the damaged skin to produce white hairs which outline the shapes of the numbers for ever. It can be placed out of sight in the saddle area or on the shoulder. The number is registered in a national data base, enabling it to be recognized not only at sales and slaughterhouses, but also at customs posts and border checks. Moreover, the horse cannot be passed on to anyone else without the permission of the owner and all the relevant paper work.

Another security method is to mark a hoof with your post or zip code: this can be done by a farrier, but is not ideal and will eventually grow out. Identi-chipping is excellent for small pets, but is not as effective for horses as there is the possibility of the chip migrating to a dangerous location in the body.

A Typical Routine for a Grass-Kept Horse

8.00am
1. Remove New Zealand rug, if wearing one (depending on weather).
2. Check horse over for injury and general condition.
3. Pick out feet and sponge eyes, lips, nose and dock.
4. Lightly groom body to remove loose mud.
5. Check water supply and fencing.
6. Dig up poisonous plants.
7. Remove droppings from the field.

10.00am
1. Exercise horse.
2. After exercise, make sure that the horse is cool and dry and brushed off before rugging up.
3. Pick out feet and check shoes for condition.
4. Give supplementary feed, if necessary.
5. Use sun block and fly repellent, if necessary.
6. Turn out into field.

5.00pm
1. Remove New Zealand rug, if wearing one.
2. Check horse over for injury.
3. Pick out feet and sponge eyes, lips, nose and dock.
4. Give supplementary feed, if necessary.
5. Use fly repellent, if necessary.
6. Rug up and turn out into field.

GROOMING HORSES

Grooming removes dust and dirt from the coat, stimulates the circulation, and helps tone the muscles.

All stabled horses require a daily grooming, which includes care of the coat, mane, tail, skin and feet. Horses at grass also need attention but require a modified grooming session (see page 327).

A well-groomed horse has a much better appearance than an ungroomed one. The action of grooming also stimulates the circulation and tones the muscles while eliminating the dirt. It is best to groom after the horse has been exercised; however, you will need to give him a preliminary grooming to tidy him up prior to exercise. This is known as quartering.

Quartering

Work over the horse with a body brush, using a curry comb to remove dirt from the brush. Brush the mane and tail and pick our the feet. Sponge the eyes, nostrils and dock.

When grooming the coat in winter, fold the horse's rug back halfway, exposing only the areas you wish to groom rather than removing the rug completely. In this way you will prevent the horse from getting cold before he is tacked up.

The Full Groom

Before starting to groom, it is best to stand your horse in a well-lit area where he can stand quietly.

Hoof Pick This is a vital piece of equipment. First pick out the feet and while doing this check each shoe for wear, the presence of thrush, or bruising to the sole. Always use the hoof pick in a downward direction to avoid damaging the softer parts of the hoof, thoroughly removing debris from the deep grooves either side of the frog where disease can form. When going for a ride, carry a pocket hoof pick with you; removing a troublesome stone immediately could save weeks of discomfort.

Dandy Brush The dandy brush, which has hard bristles, is for removing mud and sweat marks. Do not use on horses with sensitive skin or on clipped areas, as it is far too harsh. However, it is ideal for grass-kept, hardier animals. Plastic or rubber curry combs can also be used for removing mud, but as with the dandy brush, care must be taken not to scratch the skin.

Body Brush The body brush is used next. This has soft, closely-set hairs and must be used in conjunction with the curry comb for removing dirt from the brush. Start with the mane, which can be brushed through in sections to remove all tangles. Once the mane is shiny and clean, groom the whole body using short, circular movements of the brush. After every few strokes, clean the brush with the curry comb which should be occasionally tapped on the floor to clean. Groom along the lie of the coat: horses do not enjoy being rubbed up the wrong way. Take care when grooming the belly and around the back legs. Some horses

are extra sensitive in these areas and may kick out or bite in anger.

Groom both sides of the horse thoroughly and when finished use the body brush on the tail. It is unwise to use a harsher brush, such as a dandy brush, as the tail hairs may be pulled out, thus damaging its appearance.

Finally, using a body brush, groom the head; but first untie the horse's headcollar and temporarily tie the head

LEFT
The feet need special attention and should be picked out daily, presenting a good opportunity to check the shoes for wear and tear.

BELOW
Keep a separate sponge for cleaning around the eyes and face.

RIGHT
Keep your grooming kit in a handy tray which is easily portable.

BELOW
Use a mane comb to gently remove tangles and dirt from the mane.

strap around the neck so that it is possible to groom the whole head. When grooming the head, make sure you shield the horse's eyes with one hand so that dust does not fall into them.

Sponges Keep two sponges, one for the dock area, the other for cleaning around the eyes and face. Use a damp sponge to wipe these areas clean. When cleaning under the dock, make sure you do not stand directly behind the horse or in a position where you are likely to be kicked.

A water brush can be used damp to 'lay' the mane and tail. Brush the hairs gently into the required position; in the

case of the tail, a dry tail bandage can be applied and left for a while to allow the hair to set neatly.

The stable rubber is a cotton cloth used to give a final finish to the coat. Polish in the direction of the lie of the coat to bring up a brilliant shine.

Hoof Oil This can be used for cosmetic purposes to make the hooves shine. It is debatable whether it has any effect on the hoof for good or bad, but used

occasionally should do no harm. There are other products said to aid hoof growth and strength. However, these should not be relied upon; a good diet and regular shoeing is the only way to achieve healthy hooves.

Massage Horses benefit from a massage. Traditionally, this is done with a 'wisp', which is tightly woven hay or straw twisted together. However, it is now more usual to use a leather-covered massage pad to tone the muscles, which should be slapped in a regular rhythm along the lie of the coat. Each area should be slapped about 5 times. Once the horse is accustomed to massage, he will begin to enjoy it.

Grooming Horses and Ponies at Grass

Much of the above grooming procedure will apply to the grass-kept animal. However, avoid the prolonged use of the body brush on the coat, as vital waterproofing oils will be removed, making it difficult for the horse to stay dry in wet weather.

Bathing

Washing the Mane Horses' manes can become very dirty and greasy and providing that the weather is warm enough, can be washed. There are various shampoos for the purpose and some contain fly repellents. Dampen the mane with lukewarm water and wash it with shampoo, starting at the head end and working downwards. Make sure that shampoo does not get onto the horse's face, or into the ears, eyes and nose. Rinse thoroughly, then dry with a towel, making sure the shoulders are dried as well.

Washing the Tail As with the mane, use lukewarm water and a mild shampoo. Soak the tail and work in the shampoo. Rinse well, then brush out with a clean body brush. Swing the tail around to remove excess water and apply a dry tail

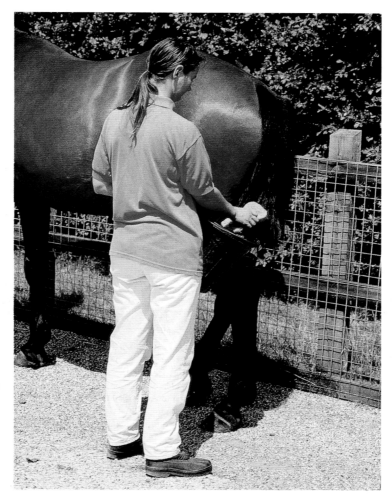

When washing the tail, be careful not to startle the horse and don't stand directly behind him in case he kicks out.

Hosing the legs is a good way of cleaning them, but it is also useful for reducing inflammation when a leg has been injured.

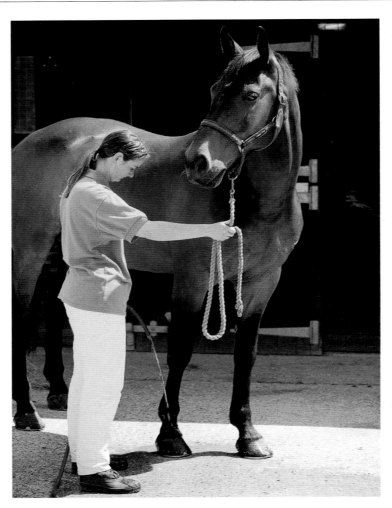

bandage to neaten its appearance. This can be removed later.

Washing the Body It is not really advisable to wash a horse as you run the risk of removing the natural oils which are a protection against the elements. Soaking the coat right down to the skin will make the horse vulnerable for days on end until the skin has had a chance to replace the protective oils.

If the weather is warm, however, and you feel a bath is necessary, use a special horse shampoo and a sponge to wash the coat. Rinse thoroughly, then remove the excess with a sweat scraper before drying with a towel (all this should preferably take place in bright sunshine). Once dry, groom and apply rugs, if necessary, as extra protection will be needed for a few days.

Pulling the Mane

Most horses have naturally thick manes, though only Thoroughbred types seem to have manageable ones. For this reason, it is necessary to thin and shorten the mane by 'pulling' it. Cutting a mane with scissors or clippers should not be attempted on any account. This will ruin the appearance for many months and will make it look even thicker.

It is best to pull the mane after the horse has been exercised when the pores are open and the hair will come out more easily. First make sure the mane is well brushed and free from tangles. Starting at the top end, take a few hairs at a time

from underneath, wind them around a mane comb and pull sharply downwards. Work down the mane, repeating the process until it all looks even. If the horse is particularly sensitive, pull just a small area each day over a week or two. A well-pulled mane will lie flatter and be easier to plait.

ABOVE LEFT
This horse's mane is in its natural state.

ABOVE
Pulling the mane.

LEFT
A pulled mane.

For some breeds of horses and ponies, it is traditional to leave manes and tails in their natural state. If you have one of these breeds and it is your intention to show it, you will need to leave the mane and tail strictly alone.

This beautiful Saddlebred has been trimmed for the showring.

Hogging the Mane

Hogging is when the whole mane is removed with clippers. Most horses have a nice enough mane for it to be left natural; however, some have either a very ragged mane or one that is thin and patchy. In such instances, complete removal is the only way to tidy it up, but it will have to be trimmed with clippers every few weeks. When hogging a mane, make sure the clipper blades are sharp and in good order. Finally, it should be noted that once the mane has been hogged, it may take years for it to grow back to normal.

Pulling the Tail

Only pull the tail of a stabled horse: by removing hairs from the tail, you will be reducing the horse's natural resistance to wind and rain. Pulling, however, dramatically improves the appearance of the tail. As with pulling the mane, pull the tail after exercise when the pores are likely to be open. Pull a few hairs at a time from both sides of the tail. Keep your work even. When finished, and if required, the tail can be 'banged' (cut squarely) 4-in (10-cm) below the hock. Finally, apply a tail bandage which will help maintain the shape. As an alternative to pulling, the tail can be left natural but plaited. (See page 408 et seq. for shows.)

Trimming

It is best to leave the grass-kept horse untrimmed as the hair around the fetlocks, ears, jaw etc. provides natural

protection from the elements. Use trimming scissors for the stabled horse. Comb against the lie of the coat to trim up areas such as the fetlocks and jaw. When trimming the ears, only remove long unsightly hairs, do not remove hair from inside. Also, never remove hair from around the horse's eyes. It is better to leave the whiskers, too, as you will be reducing the horse's natural defence against flies if you cut them off.

Clipping

During the winter, all horses grow thick winter coats for protection against the cold. For horses which are not exercised, this is fine, but it will be impossible to exercise those that are worked throughout the winter months without them becoming overheated. When an unclipped horse gets hot he sweats profusely, which can be debilitating as well as distressing. As a result he will begin to lose condition if worked regularly in this manner. Another disadvantage is that he will take a long time to cool down after exercise and may remain wet for some time, which is not a good idea when the weather is cold. Clipping alleviates the distress caused by getting too hot: the horse will cool down quickly and will be easier to clean off after being ridden.

Traditionally, the first clip should be carried out in autumn and then when necessary (usually every 4–6 weeks) until the end of winter. Clipping should not take place thereafter, as once spring arrives the summer coat will have

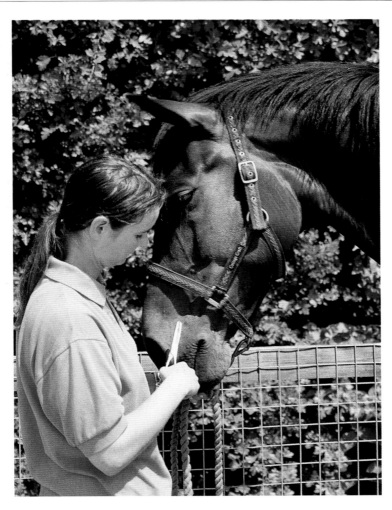

Always use scissors with rounded ends when using them to trim a horse.

begun to grow and the new coat will
be damaged

Depending on the type of horse and
its workload, you can choose which type
of clip you require.

Belly and Gullet Clip

Clips which remove a small area of hair
are either for horses which are not in
hard work or for those out at grass. In
this clip, the hair on the belly, between
the front legs and underneath the neck, is
removed. In light exercise the horse can
still lose heat, but still retains the bulk
of his natural protection. Horses with
this kind of clip may be turned out
with adequate shelter or in a New
Zealand rug.

Trace Clip

In the trace clip, more hair is removed
than in the belly and gullet clip, but the
horse is still left with a degree of natural
protection. It is not a recommended clip
for horses wintering out, but they can be
turned out during the day with a New
Zealand rug and given stable rugs at
night. This clip will suffice for horses
which are in moderate work, but is not
suitable for faster workers, e.g. hunters,
eventers etc.

Blanket Clip

This is so-named as the clipped area
takes the shape of a blanket laid over a
horse's back. This is a useful clip as
enough hair is removed to permit fast
work; but the back area is left unclipped,

leaving a modicum of protection and making it suitable for horses which feel the cold. This clip is only recommended for stabled horses and they will require adequate rugs.

Hunter Clip

All hair is removed except for that of the saddle area and the legs. The saddle area is left intact to prevent the saddle from rubbing the skin; the hair is left on the legs for protection against wet and muddy conditions which may result in mud fever and cracked heels. This clip is only recommended for stabled   horses and they will require adequate rugs. When being exercised, and if the pace is slow, always use an exercise rug to ensure that the horse's loins do not get cold.

Full Clip

This is similar to the Hunter clip, but hair from the saddle area and the legs is removed. The horse will need to be extremely well rugged up and must be stabled.

How to Clip
Preparation

• Select a well-lit, draft-free location in which to clip: if the horse is in a location he knows well, he is more likely to be relaxed. Always have an assistant standing by.

• Wear overalls, a hard hat, tie hair back and wear sturdy rubber boots to protect

OPPOSITE
This horse has a Hunter clip, allowing it to work hard during the winter months without overheating. Any sweat and dirt will dry quickly and be easy to clean off.

BELOW
Clipping equipment.

BELOW LEFT
A blanket clip.

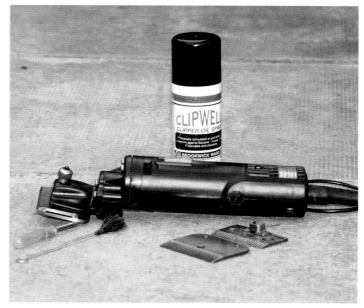

RIGHT
This horse is having his second clip of the season, which will be much easier this time, as the existing pattern left by the first clip can be followed.

BELOW
A full clip.

against the possibility of an electric shock.

• Always use well-maintained clippers with sharp blades. Blunt blades pull at the coat and upset the horse.

• The horse should first be thoroughly groomed.

• Mark the line of the clip with chalk, making sure the line is even on both sides.

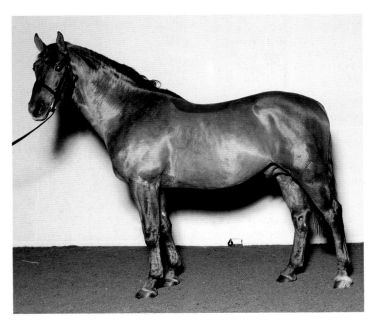

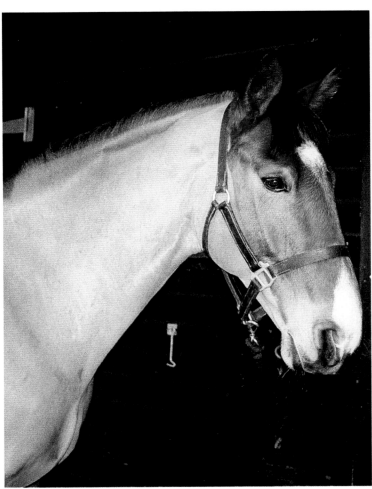

• Make sure the loop handle of the clippers is threaded over your wrist; they are sure to break if accidentally dropped. When clipping, make sure the spare flex is kept well out of the way.

• Use a tail bandage to keep the tail out of the way.

• Have rugs to hand. You will find that while you are clipping the front of the horse you can keep the back half-covered, and vice versa.

Most horses are quite happy to be clipped, while young horses being clipped for the first time will usually stand quietly once they have become accustomed to the sensation and noise. When clipping a horse you do not know, make sure you approach him carefully. Ask a handler to hold him in a bridle and try to reassure him. Allow the clippers to run for a while without touching the coat. Once he is used to the noise, turn the clippers off and put them against the horse's shoulder. If he remains calm, turn the clippers on and begin work. However, clipping may be impossible because the horse is so frightened, in which case you may need a vet to sedate him.

Clip against the lie of the coat, the clippers parallel to the coat. Be extra careful when clipping between the back legs or under the elbows as it is easy to accidentally nick the skin. Take care to avoid being kicked or bitten.

Clipping the Head You can choose between clipping the face completely, clipping half of the face or clipping just under the chin, when it is preferable to use a smaller pair of clippers. When clipping half the face, you can use the horse's bridle as a guide. Clip up to the cheekpieces, making a clean straight line from behind the horse's ears down to the muzzle area. On no account clip inside the horse's ears or interfere with the long hairs around the eyes. Leave the whiskers around the muzzle intact.

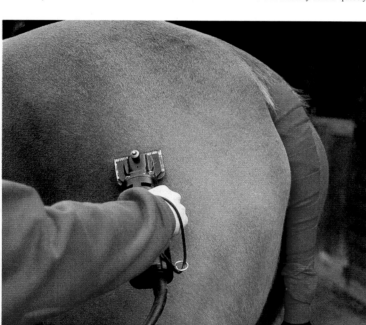

LEFT
Hold the clippers parallel to the horse's side, clipping against the lie of the coat.

THE HORSE'S HEALTH

RIGHT
This horse and his rider are
enjoying a pleasant day out in
the countryside.

Keeping a horse healthy isn't exactly
rocket science: it is a matter of getting the
balance right between feeding, exercise
and good stable management, as well as
vigilance and the ability to recognize
when something is wrong. Much of this
comes down to experience, which you will
gain in your day-to-day contact with your
horse. However, there are rules which
must be followed if he is to lead a happy
and healthy life. These are outlined in the
chapters on Stable Management, Feeding,
and Fitness, all of which are vital to your
horse's well-being.

This chapter explains how to prevent
certain diseases from occurring and
how to recognize the signs of ill health.
A runny nose or eyes could well be a
symptom of something more serious,
so follow these guidelines and remember
to call the vet if you have any worries
or doubts.

Daily Health Check

Grooming presents a good opportunity to
check your horse over for disease and
injury. Tie him up and stand well back to
look at the overall picture: firstly, does he
look happy? Ideally he will be standing
there, quite relaxed, perhaps resting one
leg. Wake him up and get him to stand
square. He should be able to do this easily,
but if he persists in resting a leg it could be

A fit and healthy animal should be happy, alert and full of vitality all year round.

Find time, preferably twice a day, to look your horse over for signs of injury or disease.

a sign of injury. Check that his eyes are bright and shining and free from discharge, likewise his nose. Look at his flanks: in a relaxed state breathing should be barely perceptible.

Now start to groom him, following behind with your other hand to check for lumps or abrasions, working your way down each leg in turn to check for puffiness. This could indicate a strain or injury caused by a kick from another horse in the field. Also examine the skin:

it should appear clean with no raw patches indicative of skin disease or a rub from a piece of tack. Pick out the feet at least twice a day or as often as necessary, checking that there is no damage such as puncture wounds, bruising from stones, or signs of disease of the frog, such as thrush, foot rot, or sore spots caused by overreaching. Finally, give him a quick trot up to check for lameness.

Preventive Medicine Like us, horses are subject to many diseases: however, maintaining them in good health helps to reduce the risk of more serious conditions. Many opportunist diseases affect either the very young, the elderly, or horses in a poor neglected state. Tetanus and equine influenza can be contracted by any horse and are potentially lethal, so it is vital that there is yearly vaccination against them. Horses are also susceptible to worms, picked up while grazing, which if left untreated can seriously undermine their constitution and even cause death. To avoid this, a regular worming programme must be introduced: your local vet will be able to advise you regarding treatment, but the general procedure is to worm every 6 weeks and more often at certain times of year. Wormers come in powders which can be mixed into feed; some horses will happily eat this, others may reject the strange taste. Although they are easy to administer, you must watch when they are consumed to make sure that the required dose has been taken. The other type is a

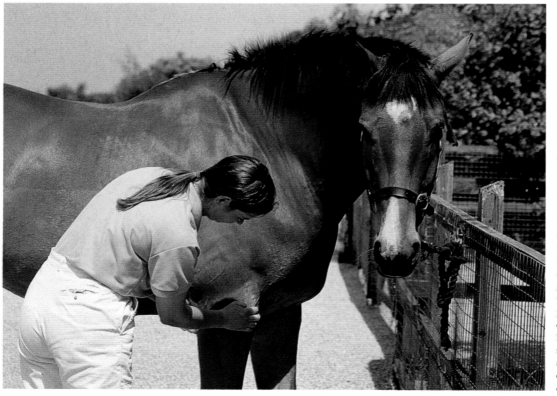

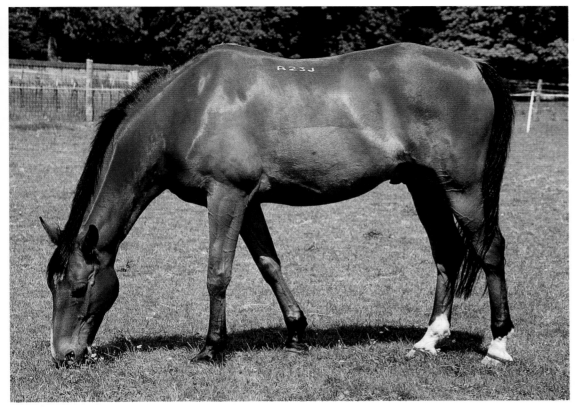

In good weather, horses are at their happiest and healthiest out at grass. Make sure, however, that the horse's weight is carefully monitored and that he is not prone to laminitis.

paste which comes in a syringe: this is rather more problematical as it has to be inserted into the horse's mouth and discharged very quickly before he gets the taste of it and spits it out; a bowl of feed close at hand has to be eaten afterwards to ensure that it all goes down.

Another way of preventing disease is regular shoeing, which is necessary every 4–6 weeks depending on how quickly the feet grow. It is tempting to neglect this as the process is expensive; but feet left to grow too long can cause enormous problems, resulting in navicular syndrome, laminitis and tendon injury.

Make sure that teeth are checked for rough areas of growth which may cause discomfort, and which may require rasping down so that the horse can continue to chew properly.

The Vital Signs Learning to recognize your horse's normal breathing pattern is important and will alert you to any abnormalities. At rest, a horse's respiration is 8–16 breaths per minute, a breath being one movement in and out. The breathing should not be clearly defined but can by felt by placing your hand on the ribcage. Rapid and obvious

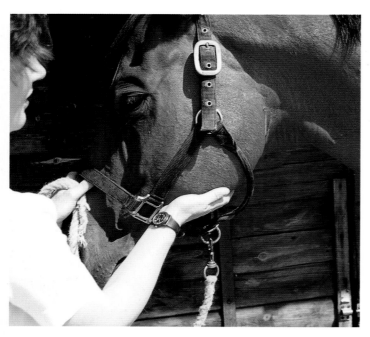

Signs of Disease or Injury

An important part of horse ownership is being able to recognize when your horse is unwell. This becomes easier with experience and as you get to know him. Many know instinctively when their horse is ailing when others can see nothing wrong at all. At the first inkling of a problem, watch him carefully. Any of the symptoms listed below could be an indication of a serious problem, such as colic, respiratory trouble or an injury. First of all, try to ascertain if the symptoms are caused by external damage such as a strain or a kick, then call the vet.

- Sweating
- Rolling of the eyes
- Discharge from eyes and/or nose
- Heavy breathing
- Tucking-in at the flanks
- Looking towards or pecking at the stomach
- Excessive rolling
- Inability to move without pain
- A dejected look
- Loose or no motions
- Reluctance to stand on all four legs

movement is a sure indication that the horse is stressed, either from internal pain or external injury, which is likely to be accompanied by a dejected look. If, however, he is alert and agitated, he may merely be reacting to something he can either hear or see in the distance.

Taking the Temperature A veterinary thermometer is an important part of the first-aid kit. Read the instructions before using. Give the thermometer a good shake down and apply a little petroleum jelly. Standing to the side of the horse's rear, gently lift the tail to one side and insert the thermometer, holding it against the wall of the rectum. Hold it in place for the prescribed amount of time. A

horse's normal temperature should be 37.5–38°C (99.5–100.4°F). A rise of a degree or more should be taken seriously.

Checking the Pulse The pulse is strong and can be taken at various sites, i.e. behind the pastern, either side of the fetlock, where it is known as the digital pulse, or you may use a stethoscope behind the elbow. However, the easiest and most convenient place to take the pulse is where the artery crosses the inside of the jawbone. Remember to use your fingers only as your thumb has a strong pulse of its own. At rest, the normal pulse rate is 36–40 beats per minute. Increased pulse and respiration when at

This Anglo-Arab is in the peak of condition and enjoying his exercise period.

rest may indicate that the horse is suffering, due to pain or illness, stress or excitement.

Simple Flesh Wounds Horses are prone to infections, so once a wound has been identified, act quickly. Most flesh wounds can be treated at home. Flush the wound out with clean water, removing all dirt and debris. Next boil up some water, let it cool slightly, and add either salt or an iodine-based scrub. Dip a ball of cotton wool into the solution and give the wound a thorough cleansing – be as thorough as the horse will allow. Repeat until you are confident that the wound is clean. Using more cotton wool, dry the wound and apply antiseptic. If not too serious, let the air get to the wound, which will aid the healing process; if more serious, apply a dressing. If in any doubt, or if the wound becomes inflamed or has a foul-smelling discharge, call the vet.

Serious Wounds It is usually quite obvious when a wound is serious; it may have blood pouring from it, or there may be a large gash or tear which requires veterinary attention and sutures. Other wounds may appear superficial but could in fact be potentially serious. All wounds which are adjacent to or on a joint will require urgent veterinary attention, as infection could easily spread to the joint causing irreparable damage. Likewise puncture wounds, which can be very deep, concealing internal damage. As with all wounds, the most important

FAR LEFT
Wounds should be cleaned
meticulously, using a sterilized
bowl with boiled water, cotton
wool and antiseptic.

CENTRE LEFT and LEFT
Correct bandaging requires skill
and experience, and the novice
handler should seek advice if
possible. The hock (left) is one
of the most difficult areas to
bandage and care must be taken
that it is not done too tightly and
that there are no pressure points.
Do not bandage over the point of
the hock.

thing is to get them as clean as possible,
using clean fresh water; don't apply any
treatments until the vet sees them. If
bleeding is excessive, plug the wound
with cotton wool and hold it in position
with a bandage to stem the flow. Call the
vet urgently: he may apply sutures and
prescribe antibiotics to combat infection.

A first-aid kit to cover almost any eventuality.

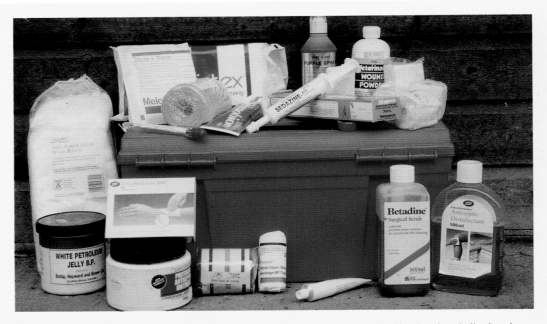

First Aid

All horse owners should have a comprehensive first-aid kit, which should be kept in an airtight container and placed where it can be easily located. It is advisable to take a second kit along when the horse is away from home, i.e. at competitions.

First-Aid Kit

• Large roll of cotton wool
• 3–4 rolls of gamgee
• 3–4 rolls of crêpe/self-adhesive bandage
• 3–ß4 wound dressings (non-stick)
• Poultices (for inflamed puncture wounds)
• Poultice boot or tape to hold a dressing in position
• Wound powder/antiseptic cream or spray
• Salt
• Liquid antiseptic or iodine-based scrub
• Anti-inflammatory analgesic sachets (on vet's advice only)
• Elastic support bandages for joints
• Surgical tape
• Tweezers
• Blunt-ended scissors
• Veterinary thermometer
• A clean bowl
• A torch

Being aware and taking preventive measures to protect your horse will pay dividends in the end.

THE IMPORTANCE OF THE FEET

RIGHT
The feet of horses likely to be involved in fast work, such as eventing, must be well-formed and in good condition.

BELOW
The points of the foot.

OPPOSITE
Short periods of galloping on the beach are excellent for getting horses fit without injury; the soft sand helps to protect limbs and feet from strain.

The horse is a grazing animal, not designed to travel great distances at speed, except when fleeing from predators. However, once it was domesticated, it became apparent that its hooves were unsuited to a punishing workload without some form of protection. For centuries, the basic design of the horseshoe has changed very little, with only minor modifications of shape and better use of materials, together with stronger, lighter metals.

New technology has also contributed to the development of shoes to alleviate particular foot problems, such as the egg-bar, which offers support for weak heels or navicular syndrome. The new lightweight shoes can be glued to hooves

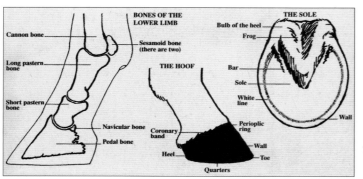

BONES OF THE LOWER LIMB

Cannon bone

Sesamoid bone (there are two)

Long pastern bone

THE HOOF

Short pastern bone

Navicular bone

Coronary band

Pedal bone

Heel

Quarters

THE SOLE

Bulb of the heel

Frog

Bar

Sole

White line

Wall

Periople ring

Wall

Toe

where the horn is weak, and which cannot hold conventional shoes.

Gone are the days when it was necessary to take your horse to the local forge for hot shoeing. In those days, if it was impossible to get to a forge, the farrier would have had to come to you when, with no heat source at his disposal, he would have had to cold shoe the horse; this is obviously inferior as a cold shoe cannot be shaped as accurately to fit a horse's foot. Most farriers are now fully mobile, with gas-operated forges in the backs of their vehicles. This has two main advantages: firstly, the farrier can come to you; he can hot shoe all the horses in a yard at the same time, which may affect the price to your advantage. Secondly, this has almost totally eradicated cold shoeing.

The job of shoeing has become quite a science: would-be farriers undergo an intense period of training, when they get to know as much about a horse's feet as any veterinary surgeon. They will also be able to offer corrective shoeing as an important extra. Over time, given careful trimming and shaping, an ill-shaped foot can be corrected to produce a healthier one, less likely to be affected by diseases such as navicular syndrome or pedal ostitis.

Regular shoeing plays an important part in your horse's overall care and goes a long way to prevent disease and general lameness. Shoeing should take place every 4–6 weeks, depending on how much horn has grown; even if the shoes

Remember that however easy it may look to you, the farrier's job is highly skilled; under no circumstance attempt to shoe or make corrections to the shoes yourself.

Cold Shoeing

This is virtually unheard of nowadays and was mostly used when people couldn't get their horses to a forge. It is not ideal as the shoe cannot be properly shaped to the foot, making any form of corrective shoeing virtually impossible. The invention of the mobile forge and better awareness of the benefits of corrective shoeing has largely eradicated this form of shoeing.

Hot Shoeing

This is by far the best method, as the shoe can be manipulated to closely fit the shape of the horse's foot. As the shoe is heated beforehand, it is more malleable and it is therefore easier to fit it accurately to the horse's foot.

Types of Shoe

Fuller This is the most common, named because the part of the shoe which comes into contact with the ground, which has been provided with a groove, has been 'fullered'. This has the advantage of making the shoe lighter and allowing more grip. Fullers come in two types: the *hunter* which is the most common and the *wide-web* which is commonly used on heavier breeds or those with sensitive feet. These shoes are used on horses whose feet are healthy.

OPPOSITE
It is a good idea to ask your farrier to check a new foal's feet; certain deformities can be corrected by trimming if they are dealt with early enough.

LEFT
The mobile forge allows the farrier more flexibility as he can travel from yard to yard, hot shoeing as he goes. The invention of the mobile forge has largely eradicated the need for cold shoeing.

aren't worn, the farrier will need to trim and reshape the feet. Some will offer a refit, where the old shoe is removed, reshaped and fitted to the newly trimmed feet. This is a less expensive option and you are only paying for the farrier's time.

Feet which have been left too long between shoeings can develop a number of conditions: shoes may become tight, causing corns and discomfort; they may fall off completely, damaging the wall of the foot in the process; or they may come askew or twist, causing more injury and pain. Feet which are allowed to grow too long are likely to become unbalanced which can put strain on the ligaments and tendons of the lower leg, as well as affecting the small delicate bones of the foot, leading to chronic lameness.

Make regular checks of your horse's shoes, making sure they are still fitting properly, with no twisting or looseness, and that all the nails are present; check also for uneven wear. Call your farrier out the minute you detect a problem, even if the horse isn't yet due to be shod.

If you regularly hack out on rough terrain, or do a large amount of road work, you may be seeing your farrier more often. However, the average time between visits for a horse in ordinary work is between 5–6 weeks.

Egg-Bar or Straight-Bar Should only be fitted on the advice of a veterinary surgeon as a method of correcting a foot problem, such as navicular syndrome. The bar at the back supports the heel, relieving pressure on the affected area. Being remedial, these should only be worn for light work at a walk.

Extra-Grip A horse's shoes will have adequate grip for everyday work, provided that he is regularly shod. If hacking out usually occurs on hard, hilly roads, however, you may wish to have road nails fitted for extra grip. These are similar to an ordinary shoeing nail but have a small round tungstan tip which is very hard.

When competing, particularly on slippery grass, good grip is essential. Ask your farrier to fit shoes with stud holes. Studs come in a variety of sizes according to the amount of grip required and can easily be screwed into the hole and tightened using a spanner. Only fit studs for soft ground as they stand proud and can cause strain if used on hard ground.

Removing a Shoe

Only attempt to remove a shoe in an emergency, i.e. if the shoe is hanging off and likely to cause injury or panic.

Removing a Front Shoe The farrier supports the foot between his knees so that his hands are free. Using a hammer and buffer he will then knock up all the

clenches. Next, using a pair of pincers placed between the shoe and the foot wall, he will prise the shoe off from heel to toe, using jerking movements; this is repeated on the other side until the shoe is off. In some cases the shoe may not come off so easily, in which case a pair of pliers are used to pull out the clenches to release the shoe. This is all done quickly and calmly and the shoe and nails are moved safely out of the way before the foot is returned to the ground.

Removing a Back Shoe Standing with his back to the horse's head, the farrier holds the leg up and over his thigh, pressing his side against the horse's hock which will prevent it from kicking out. The hoof is then allowed to rest on the inside of the farrier's knee. He would never attempt to hold a hindleg between his knees as this is extremely dangerous. The shoe is than removed in the same way as the front.

Tools Used for Shoeing

Keep a hammer handy to knock back raised clenches and clips when required. This will not harm the hoof and may prevent cuts. A buffer and pincers are also useful for removing a shoe in an emergency. Watch the farrier closely to see how he does this; he may even teach you how to do it if you ask him nicely! The following make up a farrier's tool kit:

The Farrier's Tools

Buffer – Used in conjunction with a hammer for knocking up clenches.

Clenching Tongs – Used to pull over nail-ends to make clenches.

Drawing Knife – For paring and trimming the hoof and frog.

Hoof-cutter – For trimming the hoof wall.

Nail-puller – For removing nails.

Pincers – For removing the shoe.

Pritchel – For carrying a hot shoe.

Rasp – For removing horn and tidying the hoof at the end of shoeing.

1 The farrier removes all the shoes, which will usually be taken away for recycling. In the case of refits he will remove the nails and clean them up for later. He will then clean up each foot in turn, removing loose matter and filing off uneven horn.

2 Using the hoof-cutter, he trims away the hoof wall to bring the hoof back to its original size. He will probably cut more off the toe that the heel as this grows quickest. It is at this stage that he will concentrate on any rebalancing or re-shaping which needs to be done: this can only be done very gradually over months of shoeing.

3 Using the rasp, the foot is then filed to remove any loose horn and to even up the foot.

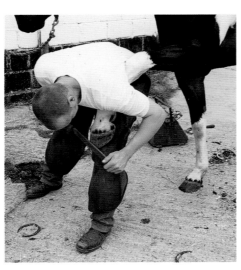

4 The correct size shoe is then selected and placed in the furnace: if the horse is having old shoes refitted, these are also heated. They are left until they glow red-hot. Holding the shoe with the pritchel he then shapes the shoe over the anvil to fit the horse's foot.

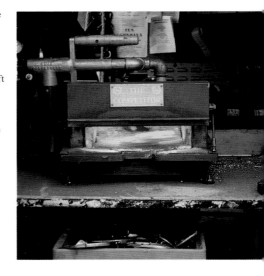

5 Once he is happy with the shape of the shoe, he will hold it in position against the hoof. The burn mark which remains will reveal any unevenness which will require further rasping, and confirm that the shoe is correctly shaped to fit the foot.

6 If all is well, the shoe is cooled in water and nailed into place. A shoe has eight nail holes, though not all are usually required. Three on the inside and four on the outside is the most common arrangement.

7 Next, the nail ends are twisted and bent over to form a clench using the clenching tongs. To make it easier for himself, the farrier will usually rest the hoof on a metal tripod.

8 Using the rasp, the hoof is tidied up: all rough edges are filed down and smoothed off. Finally the clips, small tags which are part of the shoe, are hammered into position. These help keep the shoe securely in place.

HOW TO HANDLE HORSES

RIGHT
During competition, the horse may become restless and excitable before the event. It is all the more important that you handle him confidently; this is where a bridle will offer extra control.

BELOW
A horse at home in familar surroundings is usually calm, obedient and can be handled in a headcollar.

Handling your horse frequently is the best way of relating to him. He has been handled since he was a foal, but he will need to get used to you and your ways. Speak to him often in a quiet but purposeful way and let him smell your hand so that he learns to recognize your scent. Approach him head-on, slightly to the side, and speak to him as you advance so that he is aware of your presence, then give him a gentle reassuring pat. Never approach from behind or jump out at him: a horse's natural instinct is to flee, which could cause him damage,

When catching a horse in a field, always be cautious and alert. It is wise to wear a hard hat and gloves just in case an accident occurs. Most horses are accustomed to this happening every day, so catching them should not present a problem.

particularly in a stable. Always be gentle and tactful so that he quickly learns to trust you.

Horses become very good at recognizing their owners and have a way of sensing their approach. Some even recognize the sound of their car arriving and can get very excited, particularly if a mealtime is approaching.

Handling your horse confidently can only be learned by experience; by keeping to the following guidelines you can be sure that a safe and happy relationship will ensue.

Catching a Horse in the Stable Approach from the front, then quietly move to the nearside of the head. Slip the lead rope around the neck to form a loop; this will offer some control if the horse decides to move away. Then hold the headcollar on either side and slip it over the nose; then, using your right hand, flick the strap over the head and secure the buckle. Should the horse move at this stage, don't give up, go with him so that he cannot get away; he will soon learn that it is a fruitless exercise and stand still for you.

Catching a Horse in the Paddock
Approach the horse slowly from the side with the headcollar hidden behind your back. When you are close enough, speak to him in a soothing voice and extend your hand for him to sniff. Move to the

nearside of his head with your back to his quarters. Proceed as for applying a headcollar in the stable. If the horse is difficult to catch, offer a tidbit to coax him. Never raise your voice in anger: this may frighten him, causing him to run away. Don't be tempted to chase him for, after the initial shock, he may come to regard this as a great game.

Fitting a Headcollar The noseband should be situated half-way between eyes and muzzle. It should be neither too loose nor too tight. A good guide is that you should be able to insert three fingers between the noseband and the nose. Only put a headcollar on a horse to lead him or as a means of restraint. Take it off when he is in the stable or paddock, as it could easily get caught up, causing fright or injury.

Tying-Up When tying a horse up, it should never be directly to a ring: horses are immensely strong and in the event of them breaking away can panic and do considerable damage. Tie a piece of baling twine to the ring and secure him to that; it will break before doing any damage. Never under any circumstances tie a horse to a door hinge, gate or any other unsuitable object as this is extremely dangerous.

Tie him up using a quick-release knot (see right), which is easy to undo if the horse panics. Don't leave him tied up for long periods: this is not only boring, but he may become stiff and cold. Do any

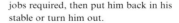

jobs required, then put him back in his stable or turn him out.

Other Restraints At certain times in your horse's life, other forms of restraint will be the only option, e.g. for clipping, veterinary treatment or worming. When a

horse discovers there are unpleasant things in life, his natural reaction is to run away; at times like these a firm hand may not be enough.

Start off gently: you could try simple distractions, such as a tasty tidbit, while lifting a front leg up may disable him

temporarily, allowing for quick treatment; but a bridle or lunge cavesson will offer more effective control. However, when all else fails you can resort to a metal twitch. Fitted carefully and firmly to the nose, it appears to induce a trance-like state, making a horse oblivious of the unpleasant procedure. There is scientific evidence to suggest that the process triggers the release of endorphins, natural painkillers, which are released into the bloodstream and produce a calming effect. Sometimes, however, even this isn't enough: ask your vet to administer a mild sedative.

Leading a Horse

In the Yard Your horse should be taught to behave when he is being led; a headcollar is fine in the stableyard. Because most people are right-handed, it is usual to walk on the horse's nearside, which means that your controlling arm is nearest the horse; if you are left-handed you may feel more comfortable the other way round. Place your controlling arm on the lead rope about 12in (30cm) from the headcollar, your left hand holding the end. Never ever wrap the rope around your hand; should the horse flee in panic you could be dragged along and easily break fingers. Always wear gloves when performing this operation as rope burns can be very painful.

Don't pull a horse around sharply: horses aren't supple enough to cope and may be injured. If he stops and refuses to go forward, don't pull on him

LEFT
Fitting a headcollar. You should be able to insert three fingers between the noseband and the nose.

RIGHT
A horse can be safely led in a
headcollar, but only within the
confines of his stableyard.

as if it were a tug o'war; stand beside him and encourage him forward with pushing motions, speaking to him in a gentle voice.

On the Road Before attempting to lead a horse onto a road, make sure he is accustomed to traffic. Choose a safe area beside the road and let him look around. He should be showing interest while remaining calm. Practise leading him during quiet periods of the day when traffic is lighter until you are confident he can cope. Remember that a horse which is traffic-shy is not only a danger to himself but to you and motorists.

Leading a horse on the road is potentially dangerous and should be avoided whenever possible; when there is no other option but to do so, more restraint is required. Always lead him in a bridle with the reins over the head and held as you would a lead rope (don't wrap it around your hand). Walk in the same direction as the traffic, keeping your body between the side of the road and the horse. For your own safety always wear gloves and a hard hat. If you lack confidence, ask another person to accompany you; they will be useful for slowing down the traffic should a problem occur.

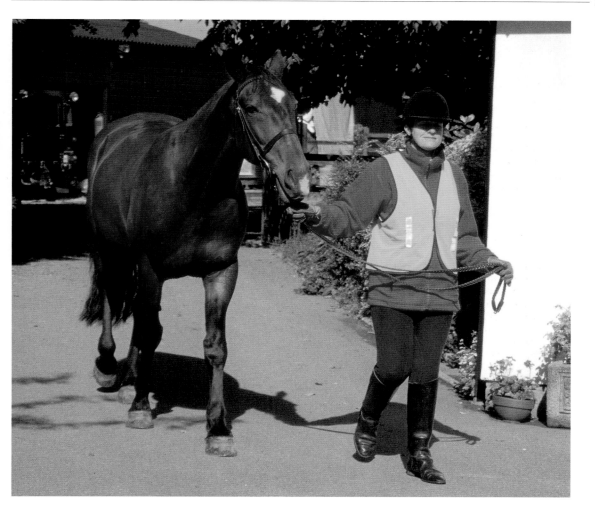

When leading a horse on the road always wear a hard hat and gloves. It is also important that you can be seen by other road users: either wear bright clothes or a reflective tabard. The horse should always wear a bridle.

CORRECT FEEDING

RIGHT
Horses usually enjoy their feed and look forward to it with enthusiasm.

BELOW
A stabled horse needs some fresh fruit and vegetables each day to give him the vitamins he requires for perfect health.

Horses are grazing animals. Their natural method of feeding is to browse over a wide area, eating little and often. A wild horse nearly always has food in its stomach, but not so much that it cannot run away to escape from danger. Stable-kept horses, on the other hand, have an artificial lifestyle: consequently, it is our responsibility to make their lives as near natural as possible. The more successful we are in achieving this, the happier and healthier the horse will be.

Redland Insurance Company

Instead of grass, stabled animals are fed hay. This should be made available to them day and night so that they can feed or rest as they choose. Concentrated feeds should be given in small amounts at regular intervals
throughout the day, and according to a strict timetable.

Every horse has its individual feeding requirements: some need more food than others, depending on size, personality, workload and metabolism. It is essential, therefore, that a close eye is kept on weight and condition, with adjustments for extra nutrition when necessary. In fact, correct feeding is quite a science, and the many different kinds of feeds and supplements on the market, all backed by powerful advertising promising increased performance, rather add to the complications.

If you are considering a horse's diet for the first time, or are worried about that of an existing one, make sure you consult an expert or at least the previous owner. Every horse is different: one may require surprisingly little food, while another may need more than usual for its size, workload and weight.

Roughage

Hay This is the main source of roughage and is the mainstay of a horse's diet, vital to the digestive process. Hay has a low nutritional content, but due to its digestive system it is possible for horses to extract goodness from it. Make sure that it is of good quality. It is false economy

OPPOSITE
This showjumper is full of vitality and enthusiasm. His owner has planned his diet to fit him for the work he actually does.

LEFT
Hay makes up the bulk of the diet of this stabled horse. It should always be of top quality and free from dusty particles.

to buy cheap, low-grade, dusty hay as it is less than useless nutritionally and may cause health problems. Dusty hay contains fungal spores which can damage a horse's lungs. Dampening the hay will control the dust, but the fungal spores will still be present and if eaten may damage the liver. Good hay should be greenish-brown, smell sweet, and should shake out freely. If it clumps together, it

means that it was baled wet and should not be fed to horses.

Hay should be harvested in the late spring when the grasses are starting to flower. It should then be stored for the remainder of the summer until early winter, after which time it can be used.

Meadow Hay This comes from permanent pasture which is cut yearly for hay. Good

Hay can be soaked in a simple plastic tub.

quality meadow hay is greatly enjoyed by horses as it usually contains a variety of grasses, e.g. rye, timothy, cocksfoot, meadow fescue and crested dog's tail. Horses also love clovers and other herbs. Make sure there are no poisonous plants present, such as ragwort. If possible, and if there is any doubt regarding quality, inspect the pasture before the hay is cut and baled.

Seed Hay This, as the name implies, is grown from seed as a crop. Seed hay has a higher nutritional value than meadow hay and is very good for horses, provided the quality is good.

Soaked Hay This should be fed to horses allergic to dust and spores and is also beneficial for those suffering from coughs or colds. The easiest way of soaking hay is to contain it in a haynet before submerging it in a tub for approximately 12 hours, when the haynet can be hung up to drain. Make sure it is properly drained before tying it up in the horse's stable; this will avoid making the bedding wet. Discard uneaten hay which, because damp, will rapidly deteriorate after about 12 hours. Never be tempted to use water which has been used before for another purpose.

Haylage or Vacuum-Packed Grass This is a substitute for hay and is suitable for horses with dust allergies. After the hay has been cut, it is left for a while to wilt before being baled into air-tight polythene wrappings where cold fermentation takes place. Haylage is more nutritious than hay and should therefore be fed it slightly lower quantities: as the protein content is higher than in hay, the amount of concentrated feed may also have to be adjusted. The disadvantage of feeding this is that, once the polythene pack has been opened, all the haylage must be fed immediately as it goes sour very quickly,

particularly when the weather is warm. A good idea is to share a bale between several horses, when it can be used up quickly without wastage. Should you discover that the polythene wrapping on an unused bale has been pierced or damaged, the whole bale must be discarded.

Silage This is the least common form of roughage. However, the kind of silage commonly fed to cattle must not be fed to horses, as it may contain harmful bacteria. Silage is made by a process in which grass is preserved by hot fermentation before being enclosed in airtight bags. As with haylage, once bags are open deterioration is rapid, and they must consequently be used up immediately. As the protein content of silage is quite high, it should be introduced into the diet over a period of about three weeks and should be fed in smaller amounts than hay.

Alfalfa This is highly nutritious and therefore suitable for resting or convalescing horses.

Chaff This is chopped hay, oat straw or alfalfa and can be bought mixed with molasses to make it more palatable. Mixed with concentrated feeds it aids digestion as it encourages the horse to eat more slowly and chew more thoroughly. It is essential for horses which bolt their food. Add a few large handfuls to each feed.

Concentrates

Hardy breeds and horses not in work can be kept healthy on grass and/or good quality hay. However, the physical demands we make on horses means that extra nutrition must often be provided.

Calculating the correct amount and balance of concentrated feed can be difficult to gauge; to overfeed can be just as dangerous as to underfeed. A horse that is overfed can either become too fat, when undue pressure is put on limbs and vital organs, or it may become too spirited and difficult to ride: one that is underfed may become thin and susceptible to disease. It is important to take expert advice.

These days, however, the situation has become rather easier, with feeds that are ready-mixed and which can be fed according to a horse's type, breed, nature and weight. For example, there are prepared mixes low in calories and suitable for 'good doers' and native breeds. If a little more nutrition is needed, but your horse needs to be prevented from becoming too spirited, there are mixes for this purpose. There are also mixes for showing horses, mares and foals, old horses, riding horses, event horses and finally for racehorses which need high nutrition to provide sufficient energy for hard, fast work. Clear instructions on how to feed these mixes are marked on the packaging. Make sure you select a well-known and respected brand as you are trusting the manufacturer to provide the correct

balance of nutrients. Usually, these proprietary brands have extra vitamins and minerals added, so you will not need to buy these separately.

Before mixing your own feed, you will require detailed knowledge of all the various feeds available.

Oats Nutritionally, these are a good food source. They can be fed whole, but to aid digestion they are better bruised, crushed or rolled. Avoid oats that are dusty and stale, as once they have reached this state they will have lost most of their nutritional value. Some horses and most ponies become excitable if fed oats, and should be avoided if this is the case. Horses in rest should not be given oats.

Barley Like oats, this can be crushed or rolled but should not be fed whole unless well cooked. Micronized barley (cooked in a microwave oven) is also an option. Boiled barley is easily digested; firstly, it should be soaked in water for three hours, then brought to a boil. It should then be simmered for a further two hours. Once cooked through, the husks will split and the grains will become soft. However, care should be taken, as some horses are allergic to barley and may break out in a rash.

Cubes (Nuts) and Coarse Mixes These are formulated from many ingredients, the advantage being that the ingredients

Horses in ordinary work do not need large quantities of concentrates. This horse is largely kept at grass and thrives on very little in the way of additives.

have already been pre-mixed with the necessary extra minerals and vitamins. These feeds do not have a long shelf life, so make sure they are used by the date shown on the packaging.

Maize Has the appearance of thick cornflakes and is sweet-smelling. It is high-energy and can be mixed with chaff and other grains. It is useful for fattening and generating warmth. Use sparingly.

Bran A low-energy feed consisting of the husks of wheat grains. Bran is the only form of wheat which can be fed to horses. It has little food value, but is valuable as a mild laxative. Fed dry it has the opposite affect and can be constipating. It can be fed as a mash to ill, tired or old horses as it is soft and easy to eat. It should only be mixed in small quantities with other feeds.

How To Make a Bran Mash

Put about 2–3lb (900–1350g) of bran into a clean bucket. Pour on boiling water and stir. (The bran should be wet but not sloppy.) Add some salt and possibly a handful of oats to taste. Place a sack over the bucket and let it steep until cool. Add a few carrots cut up lengthways, supplements (if required), and serve.

Linseed This is the seed of the flax plant. Fattening, and with a high oil content, it is good for the coat and can also be added to a mash. Feed 8oz (225g) dry weight 2–3 times a week.
Preparation: Care should be taken when preparing a linseed mash as it is poisonous if not handled correctly. Soak linseed overnight in cold water, then bring it to a boil for at least 10 minutes before simmering until the seeds are soft. If mixed with a larger quantity of water it can be fed as a tea; with less it will be more like a jelly.

Sugar Beet This is a good source of digestible fibre, has a high calcium

Make yourself familiar with the different types of horse feed. After a while, experience will tell you which combinations are most suitable for your horse.

Oats	Mix	Cubes
Bran	Sugar Beet	Chaff

RIGHT
Ponies need regulated diets: overfeeding is as dangerous as underfeeding.

BELOW
Horses are herbivores and have a digestive system geared to a high-fibre diet.

OPPOSITE
Three-day-eventers require a high-energy feed.

content, and is energy-producing. It can be bought dried in either pulp form or cubes. Follow the instructions on the packaging carefully and do not overfeed. The pulp needs soaking for 12 hours – the cubes, which are more dense, for 24 hours. Use the soaked mixture the same day; if it is left for any length of time, particularly when the weather is warm, fermentation will begin, making it harmful to horses.

Succulent Foods Horses confined to a stable require some fresh produce every day. Grass is the most natural food source for a horse, so try to imitate nature as much as possible by taking him

OPPOSITE

It is essential that your horse is neither too fat nor too thin. As the horse is put to harder work, his feeding régime will need to be adjusted accordingly.

to graze in-hand for 10 minutes each day. Carrots and apples should also be provided. Make sure these are sliced lengthways to avoid the possibility of choking; remember not to feed too many apples as they can cause colic if consumed in large quantities.

Supplements There are various types designed to be added to feed. Some are intended for show horses, which need to be in top condition with shiny coats, others for horses with poor feet, or old horses. In fact, there is a supplement available for almost every eventuality.

Amounts to Feed

Type & Height	Approx Weight		Total Feed	
	kg	lb	kg	lb
13.2hh pony	255	560	6.5	14
14.2hh cob	400	880	10	22
15.2hh horse	450	990	11.5	25
16.3hh horse	500	1100	12.5	27½
(Thoroughbred)				
16.3hh horse	600	1320	15	33
(Hunter)				

1kg = 2.2lb

Consider carefully the type of work your horse will be doing. As a rule, the harder and faster the horse works, the more concentrate he will require. Refer to the Rules of Feeding (page 365) and the chart (left) for the bulk to concentrate split.

Feed Chart

Whatever kind of horse you have, generally speaking it will need to eat 2½ per cent of its body weight daily.

- Use a weigh-tape (or if possible a weighbridge) to determine your horse's weight.

- The chart below is designed to give a rough idea of the amount of food required for different sizes of horses and ponies.

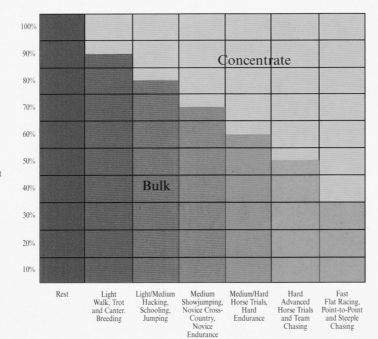

Concentrate

Bulk

100% 90% 80% 70% 60% 50% 40% 30% 20% 10%

Rest | Light Walk, Trot and Canter. Breeding | Light/Medium Hacking, Schooling, Jumping | Medium Showjumping, Novice Cross-Country, Novice Endurance | Medium/Hard Horse Trials, Hard Endurance | Hard Advanced Horse Trials and Team Chasing | Fast Flat Racing, Point-to-Point and Steeple Chasing

Remember that carrots, apples, cod liver oil and garlic are natural supplements which provide many vitamins and minerals and are often cheaper than their manufactured equivalents. When using proprietary brands, follow the manufacturer's instructions to the letter as excessive use of vitamins and minerals can be injurious to horses.

What to feed? All horses are different, so it is important to determine whether your horse is a 'good doer' or a 'bad doer'. The former is a horse which eats up all its food, seems to thrive on very little, and has a tendency to put on weight. The latter is the opposite: it will be difficult for him to maintain condition and he will lose weight during cold weather or when worked hard despite all the care and attention he has from his owner. Bad doers need special feeding: it may be necessary to consult a vet who may be able to find a reason for the problem.

Feeding Example

for a 16.1hh middleweight all-rounder in medium work, stabled in winter.

Weight	500kg (1100lb)
Total feed	12.5kg (27½ lb)
Good Quality meadow or seed hay (65%)	8.2kg (18lb)
Concentrates (35%)	4.3kg (9½lb) Oats 2.7kg (6lb) Barley 900g (2lb) or medium-energy mix 3.6kg (8lb) Alfalfa chaff 450g (1lb) Sugar beet 225g (½lb) Carrots

EXERCISING FOR FITNESS

RIGHT
This three-day-eventer is fit and in 'hard' condition.

BELOW
Although a picture of health, this horse is in 'soft' condition. In this state he is lacking in speed and stamina and would also be prone to strains.

Before beginning any kind of fitness programme, the horse's general state of health needs to be assessed, as any kind of unsoundness or underlying disorder will be accentuated once the horse starts to exercise.

A horse in good condition should be alert and confident with a happy disposition. It should stand evenly on all four legs, though it is normal to

Unfit horses are prone to injury, in which case protective boots should be worn.

RIGHT
Walking on the roads is an
excellent way of building up
fitness. However, it is essential
that both you and your horse are
clearly visible to other road
users.

OPPOSITE
Short periods of galloping will
help maintain fitness, but do not
allow the horse to become tired
or stressed or his condition may
suffer.

occasionally rest a hindleg. The skin should be clean, the coat glossy, and it should lie flat. The eyes should be wide and bright with no discharge. A healthy horse will have a good appetite and should be able to chew his food normally. The body should be well filled out but not too fat and should have pleasing proportions. The limbs should appear clean and there should be no heat or swelling. The horse should be able to urinate and defecate regularly without difficulty. It should be sound in all paces. The breathing rate should be even and when at rest should be 8 to 12 inhalations per minute. The body temperature should be 38°C (100.5°F). The pulse should be 36 to 42 heartbeats per minute.

Once confident that your horse is well and sound, you can then begin to plan an exercise routine to bring him to fitness. At this point it is a good idea to check that injections for tetanus and influenza are up to date, and that the worming programme has been regularly carried out.

A horse in 'soft' (unfit) condition, while healthy, well rounded and pleasing to the eye, is not fit enough to undertake strenuous exercise. It will usually be carrying an excessive amount of fat, not only on the surface of the body, but also around the vital organs, and will lack muscle. In order to bring it to a peak of fitness, it is important that the horse is introduced to an increased workload slowly, as overworking it too soon can cause injury. While steady work is important, it is necessary to allow a horse

BELOW RIGHT
During a cross-country competition, the horse will be required to jump and cover the ground at speed. It is therefore essential that it is properly fit.

OPPOSITE
Riding the horse in the manège will improve suppleness and balance as well as fitness.

one rest day per week. This is beneficial to the horse's mental as well as physical state. On its rest day, if the horse is permanently stabled, it should be walked in hand for a short period around the yard to stretch its legs, or be allowed to graze for a while in a safe place. Ideally, try turning him out in a field for a couple of hours a day, including the rest day.

A careful feeding plan will need to be worked out. As the horse increases in fitness, the amount of concentrated, high-energy feed should be increased and the amount of roughage decreased (see previous chapter).

Begin the fitness programme with walking only. Walking on roads is good for horses as it helps harden the muscles and tendons without causing strain. Make sure you are well versed in all road safety procedures. Get some training and take the necessary examinations to prepare yourself for road work. Adequate fluorescent gear is needed at all times on both horse and rider to make them fully visible to motorists.

Walking exercise should last for three weeks. Begin with about 20 minutes and build up gradually to about $1\frac{1}{2}$ hours. Make sure the horse is encouraged to walk purposefully, as to allow him to dawdle will hardly contribute to making him fit. During this period, keep a close eye on his appearance. Check that tack is not rubbing and that his limbs are hard and cool; any swelling or heat could indicate injury.

Once the walking only period is complete, you can begin to combine walking with short periods of slow trotting. This can be built up over the following three or so weeks. Trotting uphill is good exercise and helps prevent the horse's front legs from jarring on the hard ground. However, avoid prolonged trotting on hard surfaces, as too much can put excessive wear and tear on the limbs and feet. During this stage, the horse can be schooled in a field or manège and some short periods of cantering can be introduced.

At six weeks your horse should be fit enough for more strenuous work. If you

are fortunate to have access to open country or gallops, more cantering can be introduced. After warming up in walk and trot, start with a quarter of a mile (0.5km) in canter and slowly build this up to 1 mile. The strength of the canter can be built up, but do not be tempted to gallop flat out. After fast work, make sure the horse is walked so that it can cool off.

Work in the manège can also be increased. This is quite taxing, so start with 20 minutes and build up to about one hour. Concentrate on suppling movements, including plenty of circles and serpentines. Trotting over poles and gymnastic jumping exercises over grids

will improve balance and athleticism and also add variety.

Make sure you don't push your horse too hard. Once he has achieved fitness, have some relaxing hacks and remember to allow him his rest day.

Lunging
Lunging is an alternative to ridden exercise and most horses enjoy the change. But remember that working in a tight circle puts strain on the horse's limbs, so don't be tempted to overdo it. Avoid prolonged periods of trot or canter and remember to change the horse's direction regularly; time yourself so that

he is lunged for equal periods on both sides. The horse should wear a lunge cavesson which is attached to a long lunging rein. He should be encouraged to move in a circle around the person lunging him. Make sure both you and your horse are wearing the correct equipment. The lunge whip is for gentle encouragement and must not be used severely.

Side-reins should initially be long and should only exert a very slight influence on the horse's outline. Once he has become accustomed to working in them they can be shortened. However, he should still be able to reach forward into

This horse is going freely forward in a soft, natural outline. The handler is positioned correctly.

contact with them. Side-reins must never be used to force a horse's head into a position. The head must be positioned in front of the vertical and be unrestricted. Do not lead a horse in side-reins or use them to walk him for long periods, as he could become uncomfortable and develop a restricted walk.

The Rider
Hard Hat
Gloves

Boots
Lunge whip

The Horse
Brushing boots on all four legs
Lunging roller or saddle
Lunge cavesson
Lunge-rein
Side-reins
Bridle with mild bit
 (remove reins and noseband)
Overreach boots

LEFT
When lunging, the handler should always wear a hard hat, gloves and stout footwear.

FAR LEFT
This horse is wearing a correctly fitted lunge cavesson, snaffle bridle and side-reins. The stirrup leathers should be rolled around the irons to prevent them from slipping down.

BELOW LEFT
The side-reins should be secured to the girth straps.

RUGS & SADDLERY

Horses in the wild do not need rugs. Their coats grow thick and long in winter to protect them from the cold. However, in the artificial world which we have created for them, horses tend to be more dependent on us. In summer they need protection from heat and flies, in winter they need to be kept warm and dry. There are many kinds of rugs which come in different styles and fabrics. Recent technology has created modern materials, which means that rugs can now be warm and waterproof but still 'breathe'.

The best rugs usually have cross-over straps to keep them in place. If the rug is not equipped with these, a roller can be used. Make sure that it is used in conjunction with a wither pad to protect the spine. The roller should be fitted firmly around the horse's girth, but not so tight that it causes discomfort. Rugs without leg straps must be fitted with a fillet string.

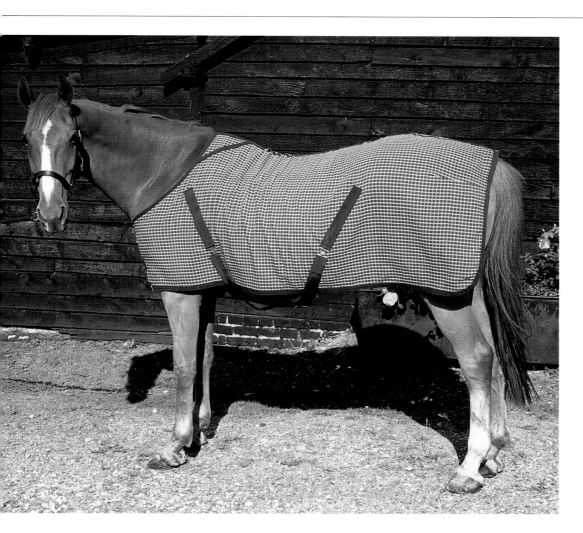

OPPOSITE, LEFT and RIGHT
This horse is wearing a quilted night rug with cross-over straps. Rugs come with optional extras such as this cosy neck cover (right) for extra cold winter's nights.

LEFT
A summer sheet helps to protect horses from flies and keeps the coat clean in summer.

RIGHT
This woollen day rug has the
distinctive gold, red and black
stripes.

BELOW
A quilted night rug.

Night Rugs

These should be thick and warm. It is a good idea, however, to have a few rugs of different thicknesses which will allow them to be changed according to weather conditions. Night rugs can also become quickly soiled when the horse lies down at night, so have a change of rugs ready while the dirty set is being washed. Traditionally, the best rugs are made of natural fabrics which are more comfortable for the horse; jute and wool are both warm and durable. However, quilted, synthetic rugs lined with cotton

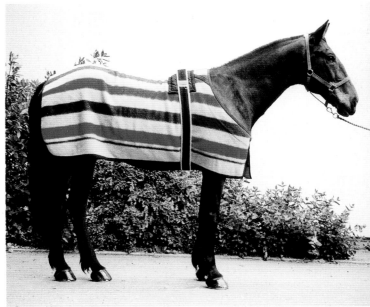

are now popular as they are easy to wash and dry.

When the weather is very cold, an under-rug can be provided, or a blanket may be put under the night rug.

Day Rugs

In the morning, the night rug should be removed and replaced with a day rug. Traditionally, day rugs are made of wool and should be of good quality. Synthetic materials are now increasingly used, and the technology is so good that even though the fabrics are artificial, they can still 'breathe'. Day rugs can also be used for keeping horses warm on cold days at shows or while travelling.

Anti-Sweat Rugs

Made from cotton mesh, this resembles a string vest. Used in conjunction with a light rug on top, the anti-sweat rug is useful for horses which sweat after work, as the air pockets help trap warm air, helping the horse to dry out.

of thickness, ranging from little more than a windcheater to thick quilts to be used in the coldest of weather. All can usually be fitted with a neck cover for extra protection against wind and rain.

New Zealand rugs take a lot of wear and tear, so it is advisable to have a spare in the event of the other needing to be dried out or cleaned.

Leg Straps

It is important that leg straps are correctly fitted. They must be crossed over and not secured too loosely or too tightly.

LEFT
An anti-sweat rug.

BELOW LEFT
When fitting a New Zealand rug, pass the leg straps between the hindlegs and loop them through one another before attaching them to the clips provided.

BELOW
A New Zealand rug.

New Zealand Rugs

These days there are many types of New Zealand rug, traditionally made from tough canvas and lined with a woollen blanket. They come with or without a surcingle and also with or without leg straps; but those with leg straps tend to stay in place better. Although the traditional rug is durable and warm, it takes a long time to dry when thoroughly wet and can also be heavy when waterlogged.

The synthetic alternatives available today are made from tear-resistant fabrics, extremely waterproof and lightweight. They dry out easily but still 'breathe'.

Turn-out rugs come in many grades

383

ABOVE
A summer Sheet.

RIGHT
An exercise Sheet.

OPPOSITE
Putting on a rug.

Summer Sheets

These are used in warm weather to protect horses from flies, and are useful at shows to prevent the coat from becoming dusty. The rug, traditionally made from cotton, should be secured with cross-over straps and a fillet string.

Exercise Sheets

As the name implies, these are used on horses during exercise. They are traditionally woollen, but can also come in a fluorescent material which is waterproof and affords good visibility during road work. The rug must be fitted under the saddle and secured by the girth. Care must be taken that it lies smoothly under the saddle; any folds in the material could injure the horse's back.

Washing and Cleaning Rugs

Stable rugs are best cleaned in a washing machine, but remember to following the manufacturer's washing instructions, as shrinkage can be a problem when rugs are made from natural fibres. Large rugs may be too bulky to wash at home, but can be sent to laundries which specialize in washing such items. If this is not an option, lay the rugs out on a clean area of concrete and scrub them until they are clean, then rinse and hang them out to dry.

Washing New Zealand rugs is a tricky problem as detergent removes the fabric's waterproofing properties.

Scrub or machine wash with tepid water and detergent. Once dry, the rug will have to be re-proofed using a special spray purchased from a saddler's or camping store. Pay particular attention to the seams.

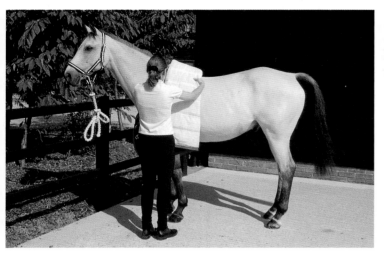

Putting on a Rug

During this procedure, great care must be taken to avoid being bitten or kicked.

• Make sure the horse is securely tied up.

• Pick up the rug and make sure that all straps are tied up and not dangling, so as not to alarm the horse.

• Always put the rug on from the 'nearside' of the horse. Gather the rug over your left arm before gently throwing it, well forward, over the horse's back. Make sure the rug is roughly in position, but still well forward. Do up the front buckles, then gently pull the rug back into its correct position. Then secure the other straps and finally make sure the fillet string is in place.

• When removing a rug, make sure all the buckles and straps are undone before gently removing the rug from the horse's body.

RIGHT
Points of the bridle.

Saddlery

Saddlery is often referred to as 'tack', which is a generalized term for saddles, bridles, girths, martingales, bits, etc.

It is important to familiarize yourself with the many different types of equipment you will need; it is also important to be able to fit it, as ill-fitting or inappropriate tack can cause injury.

Well-made, high-quality tack is expensive, so it is important to make an informed choice from the outset. Do not be tempted to buy cheap, shoddy items, as sudden breakage could be dangerous. It is also important that tack fits both you and your horse.

Make sure all items are checked for quality before making a purchase and be especially careful when buying second-hand. However, it is possible to make great savings by buying second-hand tack; for instance, you may be able to save up to 25 per cent off the new price by buying a saddle or bridle that is only a few months old.

Finally, always seek expert advice before selecting or fitting saddlery.

The Bridle

There are a variety of styles and makes of bridle, and you must select the one that best suits your horse. You may wish to match the colour of the bridle and saddle for extra smartness. Some bridles come with fancy leatherwork and stitching, so if you intend to use it for show purposes, check that the one you choose is correct for the type of showing

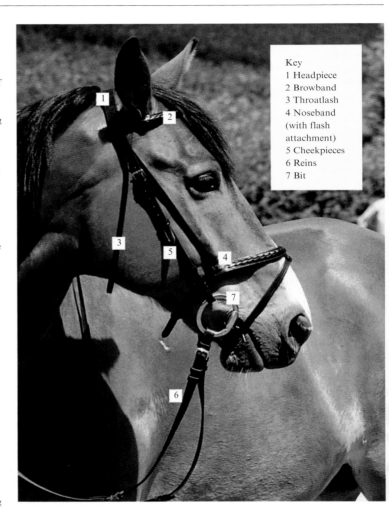

Key
1 Headpiece
2 Browband
3 Throatlash
4 Noseband
(with flash attachment)
5 Cheekpieces
6 Reins
7 Bit

you intend. It is usual for bridles to come in three sizes, fo pony, cob and horse, and it is sometimes possible to get extra large. All bridles have some degree of adjustment to enable them to be fitted to the precise size once they have been tried on the horse.

Bits

There are a multitude of bits which can be divided into three categories: the snaffle, the pelham and the curb-bit, which is used in the double bridle.

The Snaffle This is the most common,

and in general is used in training. Ideally, it should be made from stainless steel which is clean and strong and does not corrode. The mouthpiece, however, can be made of rubber, vulcanite, plastic, as well as metal. Always choose a good quality make and if purchasing a second-hand bit, check that it is not worn or bent.

Aim for the mildest and simplest snaffle and make sure it is expertly fitted. Only introduce a new bit when you feel it is really necessary and always seek expert advice. If your horse is not working to your satisfaction, it is more likely to be the fault of the rider than a problem with the bit. However, if the horse genuinely appears to be suffering mouth discomfort, it may be that the bit you are using is fine but it is the horse's teeth which need attention. In either case, the opinion of a vet should be sought before the bit is used again.

Generally speaking, the thicker the bit, the milder it is. Thin bits can be very severe as they exert a greater amount of pressure over a smaller area. However, make sure the bit is not so thick that the horse finds it difficult to accommodate it in his mouth. The bit should lie comfortably in the mouth and should cause a small amount of wrinkling at the corners, but not excessively so. The width of the bit is important: if it is too narrow, it can pinch the horse and if too wide will be able to move around too much, causing mouth soreness.

LEFT
A correctly fitted snaffle bridle.

RIGHT
A correctly fitted double bridle.

BELOW
A selection of bits and a bitless bridle.

OPPOSITE
It is usual for a double bridle to be worn in Working Hunter classes.

Reins

There are many different kinds of reins. They come in different lengths, widths, colours and styles. Select reins which are comfortable for the size of your hands.

Leather Reins These are smart and pleasant to hold. Their drawback, however, is that they can become slippery in wet weather, so wearing gloves is essential to prevent your hands from slipping through the reins.

Rubber Reins In this case, leather reins are partly covered with rubber to provide an excellent grip.

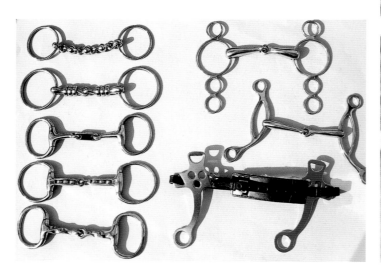

Plaited or Laced Reins These have a good grip but are quite difficult to clean.

Continental Reins Made of webbing, they usually have bars made of leather to prevent the reins from slipping through the fingers.

Nosebands

Cavesson Noseband This is the standard type of noseband found on a bridle and is fitted around the horse's nose above the bit.

Drop Noseband This is fitted below the bit and is used to prevent the horse from resisting the bit by opening its mouth too wide. The noseband must be very carefully fitted so that it does not interfere with the horse's breathing.

Flash Noseband This is a combination of the cavesson and drop nosebands.

Grakle Noseband Prevents the horse from crossing its jaw.

The Double Bridle

This is a form of bitting which should not be used until the horse is working correctly and comfortably in an ordinary snaffle bridle. It should not be used on a horse which has mouth problems. There are two bits: the bridoon bit acts as an ordinary snaffle and is worn in the usual way, the curb-bit is worn slightly lower. Both bits must be fitted well clear of the teeth. The curb-chain should sit

This horse is wearing a pelham bit, which is more severe than an ordinary snaffle. It also has a running martingale and breastplate.

comfortably in the chin groove and under no circumstances should it be twisted.

Generally speaking, the double bridle is used in dressage and in some showing classes. The combination of the two encourages flexion and helps to keep the horse's jaw relaxed.

Pelham This is a bridoon and curb-bit combined in one mouthpiece. Some horses prefer the pelham to the double bridle. Ideally, it should be used with two sets of reins, but can be used with one if 'roundings' are attached. This is not the best scenario as the effectiveness of the pelham is diminished.

Kimblewick This is a modification of the pelham which can be used with one set of reins. The bit is often suitable for strong ponies and young riders.

Bitless Bridle Also known as a hackamore. Instead of exerting pressure in the mouth, the bitless bridle acts on the poll, nose and chin groove. It is very severe and should only be used by expert riders.

Martingales

Standing Martingale The standing martingale should be fitted to the cavesson noseband (on no account should it be fitted to a drop noseband) and should be used to prevent the horse from throwing its head beyond a controllable level. It must not be used to hold a horse's head down.

In this case the bridle has been fitted with a mild, plastic snaffle bit, which is very kind to the mouth and therefore ideal for young horses.

First select the correct size of bridle for the horse, making minor adjustments to the buckles. There should be four fingers' width between the throatlash and jawbone and two fingers' width between the cavesson noseband and the nose. The noseband should lie halfway between the corners of the mouth and the angle of the cheekbone. Check the height of the bit; with a jointed bit, you should be able to see one or two wrinkles at the corner of the mouth.

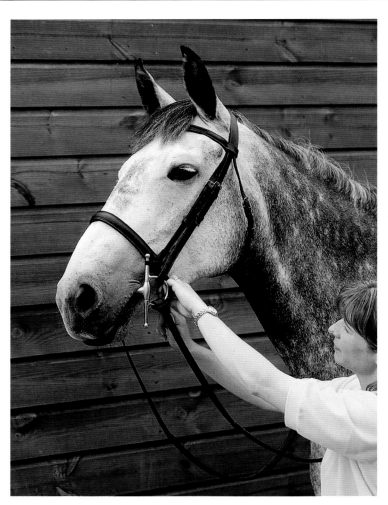

Running Martingale This should be fitted to prevent the horse from throwing its head beyond a controllable level. Like the standing martingale, it should not be used to hold the head down.

Irish Martingale This is a simple device to prevent the reins from going over the horse's head.

Breastplate A useful piece of saddlery which prevents the saddle from sliding back. This is useful for horses in fast work when they gallop and jump. When fitting, make sure it is not done up too tightly; when a horse is in full gallop or jumping, it needs plenty of room to stretch forward. The breastplate can be fitted with a running martingale attachment.

Care of Tack

All tack should be cleaned and checked for wear after use to satisfy yourself that it remains in sound condition as well as remaining smart and comfortable.

Cleaning the Bridle When cleaning, check the bridle for cracks in the leather which could indicate deterioration and weakness; also check that the stitching is sound. Any part which needs mending should be dealt with immediately by a reputable saddler or a new one purchased. Take the bridle apart to clean it. Use a damp sponge to remove all the old saddle soap, dirt and grease. The bit should be washed separately in soapy

RIGHT
The girth straps must be in excellent condition for safety's sake. If signs of deterioration are discovered, discard the straps immediately and replace them with new ones.

BELOW
Clean your tack regularly to keep it clean and supple. Use the opportunity to check for wear and tear, such as worn stitching and cracked leather.

water before being rinsed and dried thoroughly with a clean cloth. Do not put metal polish on any part that comes into contact with the horse's mouth. Once satisfied that the leatherwork is spotlessly clean, the bridle can be polished with saddle soap and a cloth. Finally, put the bridle back together, making sure that it is adjusted to the particular horse's requirements.

Cleaning the Saddle Strip the saddle of stirrup leathers, irons, girth strap and numnah. If you have one, place the

saddle on a saddle horse (a worthwhile investment). If you do not, you can work on the saddle while it is held over your lap. With a damp sponge, clean all the dirt, grease and old saddle soap from the saddle. While you work, check it over carefully for wear. Clean the stirrup leathers in the same way. These are particularly susceptible to wear, so check for cracks. Wash, dry, then polish the stirrup leathers. Brush the numnah and girth to remove loose dirt. If very dirty, wash the numnah and girth in soap and water and hang them out to dry. Polish the saddle with saddle soap and a cloth, then put everything back together again. Do not apply saddle soap to suede-covered kneerolls as this will stain and cause the suede to go shiny. Protect the saddle with a cover to keep it clean and free from dust while it is being stored for use next time.

Different Types of Saddle

It is essential that a saddle is fitted by a qualified specialist; if the saddle does not fit properly, extreme damage can be done to a horse's back.

It is also important that the saddle fits the rider, as a saddle that is too small or too large will upset the rider's position and balance which, as a consequence, will be uncomfortable for the horse. As well as the size of the rider, the saddler will take many other factors into account, such as the horse's age, size and breed.

Once the new saddle has been fitted, remember to have it checked over every

This German-made, general-purpose saddle is fitted with knee- and thighrolls for comfort. It can be used for all disciplines and if kept clean and well-serviced will last for many years.

six months by the saddler. Horses can rapidly change shape, depending upon age, breed and general condition, and a saddle can quickly fail to fit properly.

General-Purpose Saddle This is the most popular type and is designed for those needing just one saddle for flat work, jumping and hacking. While it is adequate for day-to-day use, more specific saddles are required by those interested in particular aspects of equestrianism, e.g. dressage or jumping.

The general-purpose saddle is ideal for riding out in the countryside and will feel comfortable for many hours.

Dressage Saddle This has a straighter cut than the general-purpose saddle. The cut of the saddle allows for the rider's leg to hang longer and encourages him to sit

OPPOSITE RIGHT
This straight-cut dressage saddle is being used in conjunction with a square, white numnah, which is traditionally used in dressage competitions.

LEFT
The dressage saddle encourages the rider to sit deeper and taller in the saddle and allows the legs to hang longer.

The jumping saddle is forward-cut to allow the rider to remain balanced when using a shorter stirrup length for jumping.

taller. Generally, for dressage, the rider uses a longer stirrup than when using a general-purpose or jumping saddle. For those serious about dressage and flat work, a dressage saddle is a worthwhile investment.

Jumping Saddle Riders who showjump regularly will benefit enormously from a jumping saddle. The flaps have a more forward cut than those of a general-purpose saddle. This means that the rider can have a shorter stirrup length which will aid balance when jumping.

Racing Saddle The racing saddle is designed to be small and lightweight. Even so, the saddle will have to be strong enough to endure the rigours of the race course.

Girths There are many kinds of girths made from a variety of materials such as webbing, leather, nylon string, and other synthetic materials. Look for a comfortable girth with plenty of strength to it and remember to immediately discard girths which show signs of wear and tear.

Boots and Bandages

These are used to either support or protect the legs and there are many different kinds. For horses which have never worn boots or bandages, make sure you introduce them gradually so that you do not cause unnecessary alarm. When removing boots, always check the horse's legs for rubs or sores. Boots should be fitted just tightly enough to prevent them from falling down; the straps should

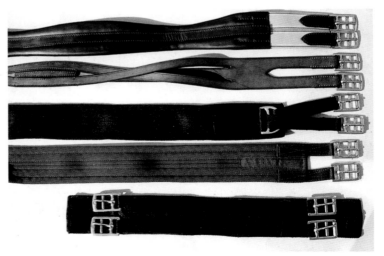

OPPOSITE RIGHT
*The top two girths are made of
leather, the second two are of a
lightweight webbing material,
and the bottom one is a web
dressage girth*

LEFT
*This jumping saddle has padded
kneerolls to support the rider's
legs when jumping.*

FROM LEFT TO RIGHT
Brushing boots, tendon boots,
bandages, knee boots, overreach
boots.

always face to the back. Clean the boots thoroughly after use; caked dirt or sweat are likely to cause sores.

When putting on boots and bandages, care must be taken as the handler is in a vulnerable position and could easily be kicked. Adopt a crouching position so that it is easier to step back if required. Boots are used to prevent injury and should only be used for relatively short periods as they can cause rubbing and sores on the legs. Only the best quality should be used as

cheaper, badly-cut boots can wrinkle, causing pressure points and leading to serious injury.

Brushing Boots Used to prevent injury to a horse caused by one of its legs knocking or 'brushing' against another. The padding on the inside of the boot softens the impact of the blow, thus preventing injury. Horses which move with their legs close together and also those being lunged or ridden in tight circles are all at risk from brushing injuries. Boots can be made from leather or man-made materials

and can be lined with softer material to prevent rubbing. Fetlock boots also prevent brushing injuries.

Tendon Boots Usually open-fronted, they protect the tendons of the front legs from a strike from a hind foot. They also act as brushing boots.

Overreach Boots These are bell-shaped, made from rubber or plastic. They should be fitted over the front hooves to prevent injury from a hindleg striking the heel

applying bandages; it is important that the pressure is even and not too tight. Badly applied bandages can cause injury.

Hock boots are used for protection while travelling, but should not be worn during exercise.

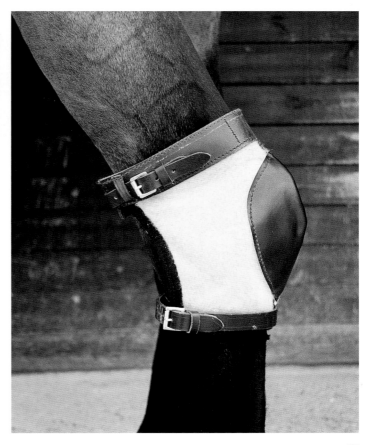

area of a foreleg. They can be fitted with Velcro or straps to fasten them. If not fitted with straps, they can be pulled on over the hoof.

Knee Boots Generally used to protect horses while travelling. However, they are invaluable for horses working on roads or hard ground and those which are prone to stumbling. During a fall, it is likely that a horse will fall onto its knees; these boots cushion such blows. The top strap must be fitted securely, but the bottom

strap must be loose enough to allow the horse to move freely and bend his knee with ease.

Hock Boots Used for travelling, they must be fitted in the same way as knee boots.

Medicine Boots These wrap around the lower leg, offering almost total protection to the entire area.

Bandages Great care must be taken when

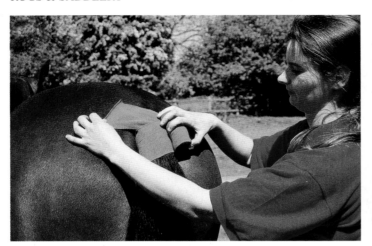
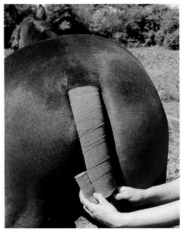
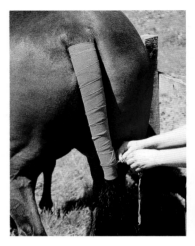

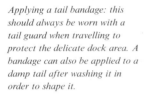

Applying a tail bandage: this should always be worn with a tail guard when travelling to protect the delicate dock area. A bandage can also be applied to a damp tail after washing it in order to shape it.

OPPOSITE
This polo pony's legs are well-protected with exercise bandages.

Tail Bandages These are crêpe bandages which can be applied to the tail to protect it when travelling or to keep it out of the way while the horse is being clipped. They can be applied to improve the appearance of the tail as, once removed, the tail will have acquired a tidy and smooth appearance. On no account put tail bandages on too tightly or leave them on overnight.

After grooming the tail with a body brush, use a water brush to dampen it. Apply a dry tail bandage. Start at the top, unrolling the bandage evenly, then tie the tapes just below the dock. Finally, bend the tail gently into a natural outline, taking care not to cause discomfort..

To remove the tail bandage, undo the tapes and slide the whole bandage off in one go.

Stable Bandages These are an aid to circulation and help warm up tired and cold horses. They are useful for horses which are unwell or on box rest. They must be applied with great skill and not too tightly; always use a suitable padding such as gamgee underneath, and do not use it too often. Once it has become flattened, discard it and start again with new padding. The gamgee must be cut to fit and wrapped around the leg to lie flat, as wrinkles cause uneven pressure on the leg. Begin rolling the bandage just below the knee, or in the case of the hindleg, the hock. Roll the bandage down the leg evenly, applying even pressure as you go.

When the coronet is reached, turn the bandage to roll it upwards until you reach the top where the tapes must be tied and tucked in. Tie the tapes at the side of the leg, not at the front or the back, where uneven pressure could result in soreness.

After removing the bandages, give the legs a thorough check over for sore spots or excessive marks caused by the bandaging.

Travelling Bandages These are the best form of protection for a horse's legs when travelling in a horsebox. They have the advantage over travelling boots in that they stay put and do not easily come off. Basically the same as stable bandages, travelling bandages must be wound down just over the coronet to protect a horse in the event of it treading on itself or being trodden on by another horse. Bandaging can also extend to just below the coronet band.

Exercise Bandages Used to protect the horse's legs during work, they are often used for cross-country events. They must be expertly applied as they can cause damage to the legs if wound too tightly or unevenly. Use a crêpe bandage with gamgee for padding. The bandage must be applied evenly from just below the knee or hock to just above the fetlock joint; it must then be wound upwards to just below the knee where the tapes should be tied and tucked in at the side of the leg. The tapes can be covered with electrical tape or sewn in to prevent them from coming undone during fast work. The bandages must only be tight enough to prevent them from falling down. Remember that the horse's circulation must not be interfered with in any way whatsoever; the tendons must not be subjected to undue pressure.

TRANSPORTING HORSES

This horse is correctly attired for travelling in a horsebox or trailer.

At some time in their lives, most horses need to be transported from one place to another, whether it is to a new owner, a horse show or a veterinary hospital. For this reason it is a good idea to get them used to the procedure in advance. Horses which travel regularly by trailer or horsebox soon become accustomed to the motion of a vehicle and, provided that the driver is sympathetic, they should never be alarmed or frightened; many owners claim their horses even enjoy travelling.

It is important to practise loading and unloading before actually going anywhere; even during practice sessions the horse should be correctly attired in full travelling gear as follows:

Poll guard
Headcollar
Bridle
Lead-rein
Anti-sweat rug with a day rug on top, if necessary
Roller and pad
Knee boots
Hock boots
Travelling bandages or travelling boots
Tail bandage
Tail guard

It is important to provide the horse with maximum protection while travelling, and it should never go into a vehicle unless it is wearing the recommended gear. It is also important that all rugs, boots and bandages are well secured; a rug without a roller or a loosely-tied bandage could easily fall off causing the horse to panic. In cold weather, the horse will need to be rugged up, but be careful not to cause overheating as this will lead to anxiety. To avoid this, use an anti-sweat rug with a day rug, made from natural fibres, on top. The small holes in the anti-sweat rug will allow the

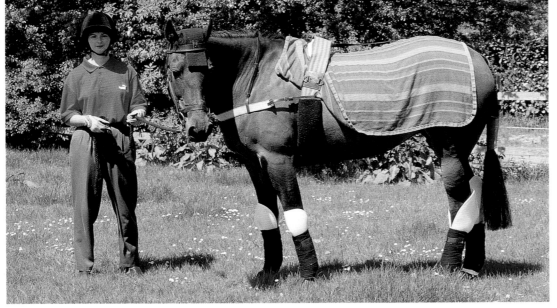

air to circulate beneath the top rug, preventing the horse from becoming too damp.

Short Journeys If you are only going a short distance, horses can be loaded partially tacked up with the saddle and bridle. However, the reins and any other straps must be secured so that they do not fall on the floor or get caught up. Do not transport tacked-up horses over long distances.

Long Journeys Horses should be rested every four hours and offered water; weather permitting, the ramp should also be lowered to allow air to circulate.

To accustom a horse to the inside of a trailer or box, allow him inside and

The handler is leading her horse quietly and positively into a trailer. The more regularly horses are transported, the quieter they will be. However, it is important that they are not frightened in any way, as a bad experience can make a horse forever wary.

provide him with a feed so that he equates the event with something pleasurable. A haynet suspended at a safe height will also provide a diversion allowing relaxation. Put some bedding inside the box to make it more appealing.

• Always have a helper with you if at all possible.
• Always wear a riding hat, gloves and sturdy boots when leading.
• Try to keep the horse straight and aim

him at the centre of the ramp. Reassure him and give him gentle encouragement.
• Make sure the breeching straps or partitions are in place before tying the horse up. This can be done by a helper.
• Make sure the horse is secured with a quick-release knot and that the partitions are correctly placed to prevent him from turning around in the box or trailer. However, the horse must be given adequate space so that he can adjust his legs to balance himself.
• Be wary of all ramps and doors. They are usually very heavy and standing beneath them should be avoided.
• Make sure all equipment is stowed well away before the journey begins and that all haynets are very well secured.

When leading a horse into the confined interior of a vehicle, aim for the centre of the ramp. Walk with the horse alongside. Do not attempt to drag him up the ramp. If he hangs back, give him a little time and remain with him. Give him gentle reassurance, then ask him to walk forward again. Provided you remain confident and are patient, this will be transmitted to the horse and he will allow himself to be loaded without problem.

There are several reasons why a horse may refuse to enter a vehicle. It may be that he has previously been frightened, he may be generally lacking in confidence, or he may merely be stubborn.

There are many ways to encourage a

reluctant horse to load, but it is up to the handler to decide which method is the most suitable.

1. Horses are herd animals, so by putting a seasoned traveller in the box first, the reluctant animal will be more likely to follow.

2. If there is a front or a side ramp, it may be a help to lower it, as daylight shining through will make the horse feel less claustrophobic; this should also make him feel happier about walking forward and up the ramp.

3. Try lowering the angle of the ramp by backing the vehicle up a slope.

4. Ask a helper to stand behind the horse with a whip, making sure they are at a safe distance to avoid being kicked. A sharp tap can work wonders.

5. Try fitting a rope to each side of the ramp. You will need two extra handlers and each one will need to hold a rope each. As the horse is led forward the handlers with the ropes must exchange places which will have the effect of driving the horse up the ramp. The ropes must be kept taut and, if necessary, pressure can be applied around the lower hindquarters of the horse.

6. Always be patient and allow plenty of time. If you appear at all anxious, the horse will surely know and as a consequence will become anxious himself.

7. If you find that your horse is strong to lead in a headcollar, lead him from a snaffle bridle placed over the headcollar. Once loaded and safely tied up, the bridle can be removed to allow the horse to travel in comfort.

When travelling, horses are happiest when they can feed from a securely tied haynet. Make sure that the vehicle is driven slowly and steadily; great care must be taken when accelerating, slowing down, and negotiating corners and uneven surfaces.

Unloading
Make sure all partitions are well secured and out of the way before even attempting to lead a horse down a ramp. Lead the horse steadily down the centre, allowing him time to judge his step. If you have a trailer, untie the horse or horses first before lifting the front bars.

General Maintenance of Trailer or Horsebox
• After each journey, all bedding should be removed and the box thoroughly mucked out; the floorboards should be allowed to completely dry out.

• Regularly check fuel and water.
• If towing, check towing-hitch for safety and that it is at the correct height.
• Check brakes, lights, indicators, and

tyres for wear and correct pressure.

• Check that the vehicle is generally roadworthy.

• Occasionally check floor of horsebox and fixtures and fittings for soundness.

Air Travel
This used to be a rarity. However, it has become increasingly common for horses to be transported by air. Most adapt easily, the same as they get used to travelling by road. Provided that the compartment on the aircraft is wide enough and that there is supervision by a competent handler, the journey should proceed without incident.

Before departure, contact a professional company to advise you on cost, protection while travelling, feeding and health requirements.

PREPARATION FOR SHOWING

Getting horse and rider ready for a show is hard work and requires organization and skill. With practice, anyone can plait manes and tails and groom a horse to a high standard; moreover, the whole procedure can be most enjoyable.

It is assumed that you have already worked hard on your jumping, dressage or whatever equestrian discipline you have chosen before thinking of competing. Now that the eve of the great day has arrived, it is time for meticulous preparation.

Preparing the horse

Plaiting the Mane This dramatically improves a horse's appearance, accentuating the head and neck and adding elegance and refinement. Always plait on the morning of the show; doing it the night before is unsatisfactory as the horse will probably disturb the plaits and they will get covered in dust.

Tools required are a mane comb, thread in the same colour as the horse's mane, a fairly large, blunt-ended needle, a water-brush and scissors.

1. Make sure the mane has been thoroughly brushed and all knots removed. Dampen it down and divide it into an even number of equal sections along the neck and including the

1

4

2

3

2. Start behind the ears, leaving the forelock until last. Take the first section and plait/braid it right to the very end. Using the needle and plaiting thread, sew the end securely.

3. Turn the end of the plait under and sew it in to neaten the edges.

4. Roll the plait under until it forms a small, neat bobble. Make sure that it is nice and tight. Sew it all together, trying not to let too much thread show. Finally, carefully trim away the excess thread.

forelock. These can be temporarily secured with elastic bands.

OPPOSITE
Preparing a horse or pony for a show takes time and patience, but the final result is always pleasing.

LEFT
Plaiting a mane.

RIGHT
Plaiting a tail.

OPPOSITE
A pulled or clipped tail will
achieve a similar effect to
plaiting it; however, the latter is
rather more attractive and the
tail retains its natural fullness.

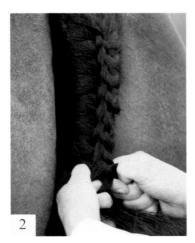

Plaiting the Tail This is a way of displaying the horse's hindquarters as well as giving the tail an attractive appearance. Like the mane, do not attempt this the day before as your work will probably not last the night and be spoiled.

1. After thoroughly brushing and combing the tail, incorporate small sections of tail hair from either side, starting at the top next to the dock to form a central plait. Continue down the tail, making sure the plait is neat and even.

2. When you reach the end of the dock, carry on plaiting the top section only until you reach the end. Turn the plait under and sew it in to hide the end. To keep the plait in place and to protect the tail when travelling, apply a tail bandage; when removing it, take care not to destroy the plait in the process.

A horse will require a thorough grooming before a show, which includes washing the mane and tail (see page 324 et seq.). Afterwards, put a day rug on or, if the weather is hot, use a summer sheet to keep the horse clean.

RIGHT
For a Riding Horse class, both horse and rider can be rather more colourful.

BELOW
Horse and rider are equipped for a Working Hunter class. For this, the rider should wear natural colours, and the horse plain leather tack.

The Horse and Rider

Before the show, make sure you have all the clothing and equipment necessary for your chosen event. Everything should be spotlessly clean and in good order.

For Showing
The Rider

Hard hat, jacket, gloves, long boots, cane, shirt and tie, jodhpurs, hairnet, if needed

The Horse
The Appropriate Saddle

Dressage/showing saddle for Non-Jumping classes or Jumping; general-purpose saddle for Working Hunter class. Double bridle, where appropriate.

For Showjumping

The Rider
Hard hat, jacket, back protector, gloves, long boots, whip, shirt and tie or stock, jodhpurs, hairnet, if needed

The Horse
Snaffle bridle or any other suitable bridle for jumping. Jumping/GP saddle, martingale, with or without breastplate, protective leg wear, brushing or tendon boots and overreach boots.

LEFT
Horse and rider are competing in a local show, and both are looking very much the part.

BELOW:
The horse has been provided with suitable tack and protective gear for a showjumping competition. The rider is also correctly dressed.

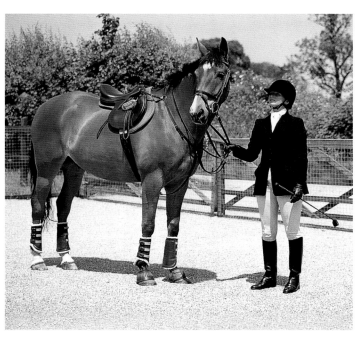

RIGHT
This shot shows horse and rider
in action and protected by the
correct gear.

BELOW
Horse and rider are correctly
attired for a cross-country event.
Note that the rider is wearing a
body protector over her shirt.

For Cross-Country
The Rider
Skull cap, body protector, coloured cross-country shirt, gloves, long boots
whip, jodhpurs, hairnet, if needed

The Horse
Snaffle or more severe bridle. Jumping/GP saddle with overgirth. Martingale with breastplate, overgirth and protective leg wear, brushing, tendon boots or exercise bandages and overreach boots.

For Dressage

The Rider

Hard hat, shirt and tie or stock, jacket gloves, long boots, dressage whip, jodhpurs, hairnet, if needed

The Horse

Preferably a dressage saddle, but a GP will do, with snaffle bridle for lower level, double for higher. No protective boots allowed.

Tack and Equipment

Make sure all tack, boots and other equipment is clean and ready. Remember that different disciplines require different gear, so be prepared. Take water buckets and a container of water with you, an anti-sweat rug, a day rug, and some concentrated feed and hay if you are to be out all day. Don't forget first-aid kits for both horse and rider. Relevant telephone numbers and a mobile telephone are also useful in case of emergency. The more preparation you do in advance, the more successful the actual day will be.

Confirm details of your show entry times and that you have the necessary dressage test sheets, if required.

BELOW LEFT
Correct attire for a dressage competition.

BELOW
For dressage, horse and rider should be elegance and harmony personified.

RIDING & TRAINING

Practising dressage movements in the manège improves the horse's balance and fitness.

Schooling/training in the manège or on a flat, soft area of ground does much to improve a horse's balance, strength, fitness and obedience and make him a pleasure to ride.

A horse that is an experienced schoolmaster will probably help his rider through the various points of dressage, along with an instructor to assist. For those with a less experienced or young horse, it is the rider's task to train the horse. All riders contemplating dressage or flat work must engage a good instructor, as bad habits easily develop without regular tuition. Choose an instructor suitable to your requirements. For instance, if you are very inexperienced and need to work on the basics, it is a waste of money to pay for a expensive and fashionable trainer who competes in Grand Prix dressage. When selecting an instructor, a good guideline is to check out their qualifications and general reputation; finally it is important that you get on well together, as a clash of personalities is the last thing you need.

It is important that you try to understand your horse. Be aware that he is a sensitive and generous animal, qualities which must never be abused. When an aspect of riding is difficult to achieve, don't blame the horse, first look to yourself and try not to let your own mood swings upset him. A heavy-handed, angry approach always fails.

Nearly all horses are capable of working well on the flat. This is because all the dressage movements are ones that horses perform every day while playing and relaxing in the paddock. It is such a pleasure to see a horse performing *passages* in front of his companions

when at play; all that is happening in the manège is that you are asking him to perform those movements on command.

Much can be done to improve your overall performance when you are not riding. Reading, attending lectures, demonstrations and competitions will all improve your riding skills, as well as helping you to identify your goals and aims.

The Position of the Rider

It is most important that you sit correctly, as a balanced rider seated in the proper position is a positive help to a horse when executing his movements.

Aim to sit tall in the deepest part of the saddle, legs stretched loosely downwards, and the heels pressed down. The upper arms should be relaxed with the elbows gently flexed and the wrists softly rounded. Fingers should be closed with thumbs on top. The elbows and wrists should trace a straight, imaginary line to the bit.

Achieving a good position takes time and practice, but there are some excellent ways to help you do this. Stretching, as a warm-up exercise is one of these.

Riding without stirrups helps to improve the seat and balance. This should be done regularly for short periods. Lunge lessons without stirrups are also beneficial, enabling you to concentrate on your position without having to worry about controlling the horse.

A rider seated in the correct position.

417

Training in the open is most beneficial as the rider has to work harder to keep the horse between leg and hand.

The Natural Aids

These are signals given to the horse to ask him to go forward, sideways, stop, turn, etc. Our own natural aids are our legs, seat, weight, hands and voice.

The legs should hang loosely but remain very close to the horse's side. The aid or leg signal should be given as lightly as possible. Refrain from continuous kicking which will eventually deaden the horse's reaction, ending in a vicious circle of disobedience.

The seat and weight has a great influence on the horse's way of going. The rider should sit as deeply as possible and go with the horse's every movement. Good control of the seat will enable the rider to slow the horse down or shorten or lengthen his steps. Remember your posture at all times; do not allow yourself to lean too far forward or back.

The rein aids need to be applied as lightly as possible, as any rough or clumsy movement will cause pain to the horse. While the hands should be kept as still as possible, they must still maintain an elastic contact with the horse's mouth.

The voice is a useful aid to reassure a horse or reward him. Horses have very good hearing so there is no need to shout. In a dressage test, however, use of the voice is not permitted. If the judge hears you talking to your horse you will be penalized.

Artificial Aids

The whip should only be used to

reinforce the leg aid, not to punish. Once you realize your horse has decided to ignore your light leg aid, one quick tap of a schooling whip should wake him up. Should he surge forward as a result of the tap, you must be very careful not to catch him in the mouth.

Spurs should only be used by experienced riders who can fully control their leg position. They are used to refine and aid movement rather than punish. Spurs should always be blunt and angled straight or downwards.

The Correct Way of Going

A horse going correctly is a pleasure to watch, with every movement appearing fluid and effortless. The horse should be completely relaxed but still feel powerful. His outline will become more rounded and his jaw and poll relaxed. Ideally, he will carry his head just in front of the vertical. Power will originate in the hindquarters which will be carried through the back to the bit. The way of going is known as 'on the bit'.

When a horse is on the bit it is very vulnerable; it is vitally important, therefore, that your hands move in harmony with the horse's mouth. The weight in your hands should be as even as possible and should be maintained through all the paces. This feeling is known as 'the contact'.

The Paces

The Walk A correct walk should be relaxed, rhythmic, energetic but unhurried. It should have four clear beats. The sequence of steps is near-fore, off-hind, off-fore, near-hind.

A free walk gives the horse a welcome opportunity to stretch and relax. He should be allowed to take the rein forward and down.

In a medium walk, he should be on the bit, moving with medium-length elastic steps and should over-track.

When making a transition from free to medium walk, or vice -versa, be sure the aids are given smoothly, thus maintaining rhythm and straightness.

The walk is a four-time pace. A good walk should have rhythm and balance and care should be taken that the rider does not push the horse forward out of its stride.

This elegant horse is performing a good working trot in a dressage competition.

The Trot This is a two-time pace. It should be rhythmical and active. Most riders find the rising trot more comfortable than the sitting trot, where the rider has to absorb all the movement. However, with practice, the rider will become accustomed to both. Do not attempt prolonged periods of sitting trot on young or inexperienced horses, as this could be injurious.

Once the working trot has been mastered, the rider can begin to ask for some lengthened strides in trot. The horse must be asked to cover more ground without quickening the pace. First establish a good steady trot, then use a slightly stronger leg aid to encourage the horse to step further

LEFT
During lengthened strides, the horse must cover more ground, but without quickening the trot.

BELOW
Practise canter initially along straight lines and enlarged circles. As the canter improves, more difficult movements can be attempted.

that the horse will strike off on the correct lead. Keep a steady contact on the outside rein with a more passive inside rein to maintain the bend. Place the inside leg on the girth, then nudge the horse, the outside leg slightly further back behind the girth. The horse should then strike off correctly. Once cantering, go with the horse's movement and be careful to retain your balance. Do not be tempted to look down.

forward so that he can lengthen his body. With practice, the horse will enthusiastically respond as you release the contained energy you have created.

The Canter This pace has three beats. It should be flowing and springy and have a clear moment of suspension. When riding in canter, the horse will seem light on his feet if he is going correctly.

Canter is a faster pace than trot and consequently requires more balance; before asking for canter, therefore, make sure you have the best possible quality of trot. Ask for canter in a corner or on a large circle. In this way you can be sure

The Schooling Session

It is a good idea to time this so that you can gradually build up the length of time spent in the school. When a horse is unfit, it may be that around 20 minutes will suffice, but in time the session can be built up to from about ¾ of a hour to one hour.

If the horse is going exceptionally well, you may wish to cut the session

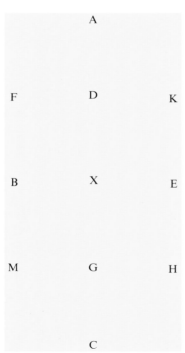

	A	
F	D	K
B	X	E
M	G	H
	C	

BELOW

A horse should stand perfectly still when halted. Make sure you practise this regularly.

OPPOSITE
LEFT
Grids help to promote athleticism.

ABOVE RIGHT
The correct jumping position.

BELOW RIGHT
Work over trotting poles improves balance.

short in order to end on a good note.

Make sure that you give the horse frequent breaks in walk throughout the session.

Always begin the schooling session with about 10 minutes in walk, walking the horse on a fairly loose rein. This allows both of you to loosen and warm up.

Begin the trot also on a loose rein so that the horse can stretch and establish his own balance. Once he is warm you can start to shorten the reins gradually and ask the horse to work on the bit. Large circles, turns and serpentines help to engage the hindquarters and improve balance. Make sure that you ride evenly on both reins and that you concentrate

on delivering the lightest possible aids; throughout this, sit up straight and concentrate on the job in hand. Practise upward and downward transitions between walk and trot so that you do not stay in the same pace for too long. Try to get the transitions as smooth as possible and concentrate on accurate circles and other movements.

Towards the end of the session, you can introduce canter on either rein. As canter is a strenuous activity for a horse, make sure it is not overdone.

The more experienced rider can now begin to introduce some lateral work. This will increase the horse's manoeuvrability and loosen his movements. Leg-yielding, turn-on-the-forehand and shoulder-in are all movements which can be learned fairly easily.

Finish up the session with some work on a longer rein to allow the horse to stretch; finally, walk for a few minutes on a loose rein, allowing the horse to cool down before putting him away.

Jumping

Jumping should be fun for horse and rider and is most rewarding when everything goes according to plan.

When schooling a young horse over jumps, start with a height that suits you both.

The rider's position and balance is most important: there must be a secure lower leg and the ability to 'fold' over the fence. The rider's stirrup length should be

a least two holes shorter than for everyday riding. Between fences, the body should be inclined slightly forward with the thighs and hips resting lightly in the saddle. The heels should be pressed downwards.

When approaching a jump, the rider must maintain the horse's rhythm, balance and impulsion. A light consistent contact on the reins and a steady lower leg resting on the horse's sides will instil confidence. Always approach the jump from the straightest angle possible. Just before the moment of take-off, the horse will lower his head; he will take a good look at the fence and measure the height. On take-off, the well-positioned rider should 'fold'

BELOW
Schooling a horse at home will pay off in the showjumping arena.

OPPOSITE
A clever, agile horse usually manages to get itself out of trouble.

naturally and hands, while maintaining a light contact, must allow forwards to give the horse full freedom of his head and neck. Occasionally the rider gets 'left behind' (this happens to the best riders). When this happens, the rider must learn from the experience and be prepared to 'slip the reins' through his fingers,

allowing the horse freedom.

For novice riders and for horses just learning to jump, it is a good idea to fit the horse with a neck strap. This way, if you feel in danger of getting left behind on the approach, you can hold onto it with a couple of fingers, which will help to avoid pulling the horse

unnecessarily in the mouth.

Be careful not to do too much in one session: jumping is strenuous for the horse and once tired he will begin to lose enthusiasm. Remember to finish on a good note and when you both still have plenty of energy left.

RIDING OUT

BELOW LEFT and RIGHT
When riding out, follow
approved trails and tracks; only
ride on private land with the
permission of the owner.

Riding in the open countryside is a wonderful experience and both horse and rider should enjoy the experience equally. Most horses are more enthusiastic when away from the manège as it gives them a chance to unwind from the rigours of training. Hacking out is great for improving fitness.

It is important that you are properly dressed. Make sure you wear a hard hat, secured with a chin strap, sensible boots, adequately warm clothing and, if you ride on the road, a fluorescent tabard. In fact, it cannot be overstressed how essential it is to make yourself as conspicuous as

Riding in Australia.

Only ride on the road or venture farther afield when you are confident that your horse will behave well in traffic. Make sure that you are both as conspicuous as possible.

possible to other road users. Unfortunately, there are too many accidents involving horses on our roads today, so the best advice is to avoid them if at all possible. If you have to ride on the road it is safest to ride in single file, but occasionally two abreast is the safest option, e.g. when a young, or nervous horse requires shielding from the traffic, or a novice rider needs a barrier between himself and a busy road.

When riding out, it is best as part of a group, when if anything untoward occurs, there is another person to turn to. Whether in company or not, you should always acquaint someone with the route you are intending to take.

After giving the horse a warm-up in walk for about 10 minutes, the paces can be varied throughout the ride, the terrain usually indicating the pace.

Where the ground is waterlogged, rutted or stony, it is best to walk. However, where the ground is good and the surroundings suitable, a trot and canter may be appropriate. Whatever pace you choose, make sure you maintain control over the horse and try to keep him working forward and in good rhythm throughout the ride.

Action The way in which a horse moves.

Aids Recognized signals used by the rider to pass instructions to a horse. *Natural aids* are conveyed through the legs, hands, body and voice and *artificial aids* include whips, spurs and other items such as martingales.

At Grass A horse which either lives in a field all year round or which is turned out from time to time.

Bad Doer (Unthrifty Horse) A horse that fails to thrive, even when fed the requisite amounts of food.

Bit The mouthpiece fitted to a bridle used to aid the rider's control of the horse. There are many different kinds such as the snaffle.

'Bone' A term referring to the circumference below the knee. If generous the horse is described as having 'plenty of bone', if not, it is said to be 'short of bone'.

Box, to To lead a horse up a ramp and into a horsebox, van or trailer.

Brushing (Interfering) When the inside of the horse's hind or foreleg is struck by the opposite leg. Brushing boots are a protection against this.

Cavesson Either a simple noseband or a lunging cavesson used for breaking and schooling horses on a lunge-rein.

Chaff Finely chopped hay used to bulk out feed or to prevent a horse from bolting its food.

Cold Hosing Using cold water to reduce inflammation.

Concussion The jarring caused to the feet and legs of a horse by hard ground.

Double Bridle This is where the rider, by using a bridle with two bits, the snaffle and the curb, can exercise a greater degree of control over his mount than he would if he used an ordinary bridle.

Dressage The training of the horse to perform in a classical tradition. The aim is to achieve obedience, control and suppleness.

Eventing A competition involving the three disciplines of dressage, cross-country and showjumping.

Frog The V-shaped part of the horse's foot which acts as a shock absorber.

Gamgee Gauze-covered cotton-wool used with bandages or leg wraps, or to give extra support or protection to a horse's legs.

Going, the (Footing) The condition of the ground.

Good Doer (Easy Keeper) A horse which remains in good condition, even where the circumstances in which it is kept are less than ideal.

Hack A term used for going out for a ride. Also a type of horse.

Hand A unit of 4 inches (10cm) used to measure the height of a horse.

Hunter A type of horse of any breed suitable for the hunting field.

Leading-Rein (Lead Shank) A long rope attached to the bit by which the horse can be led.

Lunge, to Training a horse on a long rein attached to a cavesson, and when the trainer uses a lunge whip to encourage the horse.

Manège An arena or school which has been marked out in the traditional manner. Used for schooling horses and for teaching people to ride.

Martingale An item of tack used to give the rider a greater degree of control over a horse.

Nearside The left-hand side of a horse.
Offside The right-hand side of a horse.
Points of the Horse Terms and names given to the various parts of the horse's exterior anatomy.

Pull, to The process of tidying or thinning the mane and tail.

Quartering A quick grooming before exercise.

School An area marked out in a traditional way where horses are trained and exercised.

Side-reins Used to steady the horse and improve his outline. One end of the rein is fixed to the bit and the other to either the front of the saddle or a roller.

Snaffle Bit A type of simple mouthpiece of which there are many different kinds.

Spurs An artificial aid or device fitted to the rider's boot to encourage the horse forward.

Strike-off The first step of the canter.

Surcingle or Overgirth A strap, usually of webbing, which passes over the horse's back and under his belly and is used to secure a rug or saddle.

Tack A collective term used for describing items of saddlery.

Thoroughbred Dating from the 17th century, this is probably one of the most famous breeds of horse.

Trailer A form of transportation for horses which is towed behind another vehicle.

Turn-Out To put a horse out in a field.

Twitch A device used to restrain a nervous or impetuous horse. It should only be used by an expert.

Vice Any bad habit a horse may develop and which may render it unsound.

Wind A horse's respiration when working.